The Sqinks Journal

Rudy Rucker

Transreal Books

The Sqinks Journal

Copyright © Rudy Rucker 2025
First Edition. Updated October 6, 2025

Hardback ISBN: 978-1-940948-64-5
Paperback ISBN: 978-1-940948-61-4
Ebook ISBN: 978-1-940948-63-8

The cover art is *Cyberpunk Forever*, © Rudy Rucker 2025
The author photo is © Bart Nagel 2025

Transreal Books
Los Gatos, California
www.rudyrucker.com/sqinks

Contents

THE JOURNAL
November 1-3, 2023. Accessing My Childhood. — 8
November 12, 2023. What Next? — 9
November 15, 2023. Pollock's "Lucifer." — 10
November 17, 2023. Rhythm. — 15
November 18, 2023. "Mistport" Opener, Take 1. — 17
November 20-21, 2023. "Mistport" Opener, Take 2. — 19
November 30, 2023. Reset. — 21
December 4, 2023. Xmas Tree. — 21
December 5, 2023. "Happy Christmas!" — 23
December 6, 2023. Down the Rabbit Hole. — 24
December 17, 2023. Mister Tidy, Grief, Sqinks. — 26
December 19, 2023, Everything Notes. — 31
December 26, 2023. Good Christmas. — 31
December 29-30, 2023. False Start. YA? Ugh. — 34
December 31, 2023. New Year's Eve. — 36
January 10, 2024. Story is Stuck. — 37
January 17, 2024. I Start the Novel." — 38
January 21-23, 2024. Library. Chap Two. — 43
January 24, 2024. Letter to Marc. Who Is Carol? — 46
January 27, 2024. Need Next Scene. — 48
January 28, 2024. The New Warhol Paintings. — 53
January 30-31, 2024. Gas. — 56
February 4, 2024. What Are the Sqinks? — 58
Feb 4, 2024. With Sylvia in Hilbert Space. — 61
February 5, 2024. Still Stuck. — 63
February 6, 2024. The Muse Came! — 65
February 12, 2024. Finished Chap 3. — 67
February 14, 2024. Synchronicity. — 69

February 15, 2024. Schemes. 73
February 16, 2024. After They Wake. 74
February 17, 2024. What Winston Trotter Wants. 76
February 18, 2024. Clean up. 77
February 20, 2024. Halting Briefcase Dynamics. 78
February 22, 2024. Finishing Part One. 82
February 23, 2024. Don't Know. 84
February 24, 2024. Dragons. 85
February 26, 2024. Frantic. 86
February 27, 2024. Chapter Lengths. 89
February 28, 2024. Stuck Again. Barb Ash. 90
March 1, 2024. Eden. 93
March 5, 2024. Expunging Dark Matter. 94
March 6, 2024. Enter Sqinkland. 96
March 10, 2024. Missing Moon? 97
March 11, 2024. The Sqink Quest. 97
March 12, 2024. Indie Sqinks. 101
March 17, 2024. Up in SF. 103
March 21, 2024. Pacific Grove. 104
March 23, 2024. Birthday. 105
April 1, 2024. At Isabel's. 107
April 2, 2024. Wolfram Says. 108
April 4, 2024. Mulling Over Wolfram's Words. 109
April 5, 2024. More Barb. Sqink Tourism. 110
April 9, 2024. Four and a Half Hours. 112
April 15, 2024. In SF. 113
April 15-17, 2024. Your Grandpa is Wild. 115
April 23, 2024. Cool Scene at Paul's. 117
April 28-29, 2024. Braincozies. 118
April 30 - May 3, 2024. Tunnel Timing Outline. 120
May 6, 2024. Match Humans with the Sqinks. 121
May 7, 2024. Wolfram at Synbiobeta. 122
May 9, 2024. Galactic Minds. 126
May 12, 2024. The "Oh Oh" Chapter. 129
May 12, 20204. Flying to London with Barb. 130
May 21, 2024. Barb's Ending. 131
May 25, 2024. Barb's Photography. 132
June 2, 2024. Back to Sqinks. 133
June 6, 2024. Pacific-Union Club. 133

June 19, 2024. Endsville. 134
June 28, 2024. Picaresque. 135
June 30, 2024. Where Is Stok-stok? 136
July 7, 2024. Too Misty. 138
July 15-17, 2024. Finishing Stok-stok Chapter. 138
July 22, 2024. Once More: Where is Stok-stok? 140
July 23, 2024. Doing Revisions. 141
July 24, 2024. Which Body Has the Soul? 142
July 27, 2024. Moving the Brain. 144
July 29, 2024. Fast and Slow Mail. 145
July 30, 2024. Irene? 146
July31, 2024. Oliver, Carol, Skeeze, Irene. 147
August 4, 2024. Outline. 149
August 5, 2024. Reviewing. 149
August 7, 2024. Barb is Jealous. 153
August 8, 2024. Sending Brains to Tiny Town. 155
August 9, 2024. No Floonberry. 156
August 11-12, 2024. Teleport, Biz, Parasites. 157
August 14, 2024. Mumper, Moo, Terras. 158
August 23, 2024. What Next? 163
August 27, 2024. Hacking. 165
August 31-Sept 2, 2024. Big Revisions. 166
September 4-7, 2024. Approximate Outline. 167
October 7, 2024. After the Lowlands. 169
October 8, 2024. More Outline. 171
October 13-14, 2024. New Lappy. The War. 174
October 15, 2024. Kill Mumper. 176
October 17, 2024. Life With Sqinks. 176
October 19-20, 2024. Huh Fads. 177
October 25, 2024. Sqinks, 8½, and Gemini. 179
October 28, 2024. After "Last Chapter." 181
October 30, 2024. Necking Down. 182
October 31, 2024. The Two Invasions. 184
November 3, 2024. Invade Earth vs. Invade Stok-stok. 184
November 4, 2024. Looking at the Outline. 186
November 5, 2024. More Earth vs. Stok-stok. 187
November 6, 2024. Principle of Plenitude. 188
November 12, 2024. Sqink Uptightness. 189
November 15-16, 2024. What Moo Do? 190

November 19, 2025. Triple.	191
November 20, 2024. Billion Sqink Mound. Math Alert.	194
November 21, 2024. Filling the Bowl.	195
December 11, 2024. On Mu9.	197
December 16, 2024. Need Mu9er Twist.	199
December 17, 2024. Muse Helps Me on My9 Scene.	199
December 19, 2024. Second Thoughts on Me-ware.	200
December 20, 2024. A New Me-Ware Move.	203
December 22, 2024. Sick.	205
December 29, 2024. Kutner.	207
January 4, 2025. The Yump Mine of the Mu9ers.	208
January 6, 2025. Sylvia's Death Date.	210
January 7, 2025. Grave.	212
January 9, 2025. Getting Huffed is Good.	213
January 15, 2025. Oliver Gets Huffed.	215
February 1, 2025. Back from Mexico.	216
February 6, 2025. Finished.	217
February 16, 2025. Revising. Story.	219
February 18, 2025. Me-Ware.	220
February 28, 2025. Corrections Done.	221
May 4, 2025. Big Fix #2. Kickstarter?	222
June 12, 2025. Trip to New York.	224
July 11, 2025. No Hope. Self-Pub Again.	226
July 26, 2025. Draft for the Pitch.	227
EXTRA NOTES	
Timeline.	229
List of Sqinks.	233
Outline.	234
Unused Bits.	239
Sqinks Novel Contents.	259
October 1. 2025. Farewell!	259

THE JOURNAL

November 1-3, 2023. Accessing My Childhood.

I feel like I've never *fully* dug into my earlier childhood for use as transreal inspiration for my science fiction. Somehow I've been—there's that dreaded word—blocked from fictionalizing that period of my life.

Well, that's not entirely true. *The Secret of Life* uses a few scenes from my childhood. Also I wrote a lot about my young years in my autobio, *Nested Scrolls*, which rolls along quite smoothly. I wrote these scenes like stained glass windows in a chapel.

Maybe a mean big brother in the story. The Cain and Abel theme. Abel is a stamp collector. Big brother Cain has snuck in and fiddled with his stamps. Abel notices a new stamp, a puce and magenta obtuse isosceles triangle containing an image of a tiny duck. An intense duck. The triangle everts, and the duck charges across the page of Abel's stamp album and comes to rest in Abel's lap. And then it Sounds an odd, reverberant quack. This summons the saucer?

I want to include the aquarium I had in my room when I was a kid. Loved that thing. Shopping for new fish in the Saint Matthews pet store.

Neon tetras in there, and swordfish, and guppies. Snails on the glass. The hum of the aeration pump. The mello yello light in a metal shade on the top that warms the water. Perhaps for purposes of the story, the aquarium only appears after the duck's quack.

No, the aquarium was there, and with, let's say an octopus in it, but at the sound the quack, the glass tank's joints bend at unnatural Lovecraftian angles. And for a moment it's a 3D screen of a holoscanner. The saucerians watch from within, noticing Willy. Just the lad they're looking for.

Possibly the octopus is what they keyed on. Maybe the duck quack is a signal to some demonic thing that Cain is friends with. An enemy of humans and saucerians. The thing that made Willy's mother disappear.

November 12, 2023. What Next?

On to fiction therapy. I've got three stubs, in order conceived:. "Starship and Vaalfisk." "I'd Pay a Fortune." "Cain and Abel." Phil Dick once remarked that it's a good idea to merge two stories into one, and that makes the result more interesting. Or maybe take pieces from all three.

Point of view is a young boy, maybe eight and in third grade. Too young to be an interesting character? Maybe ten and in fourth grade. That was the year I started in at Louisville Country Day. I was pretty much like my grown self by then.

The woman who died is his mother, she's the one he'd "Pay a Fortune" to get back. He's Abel, at the mercy of his mean big brother Cain.

Also I want to use that vision I used to have, the one of the endless shaft leading down through the floor of my room, like Alice's tunnel, but vertical, also like the Hollow Earth hole, with pleasant zephyrs and beings in little caves on the sides, little animals, women with big breasts, wind-up toys. I've written about it somewhere—*Nested Scrolls*?

I think I can use this for describing how the hyperjump feels. The tunnel is … the Road. Don't rush through it, spend a certain amount of time there, including perhaps a chase or a hunt. Maybe the vaalfisk live there.

And he's got an octopus in that aquarium by the wall.

Perhaps Cain and Abel aren't really brothers, but rather beings of different species. Cain being like an alien cuckoo who pushes into a birds nest and kills the deserving true nestlings.

The starship people extract the Caine-implanted *Alien*-type critter from Abel's belly. The catfish/mermaid flopping down metal stairs to the engine room.

But I don't want to write a frikkin novel, and I know that's unlikely. My last effort became that short-short, "Who Do You Love."

I went back and reread that story, and a note about it in my journals. I say I read the story to Sylvia, and she liked it, but also it made her cry. *Such* a sad story, and we two were living it in real time.

My poor lost darling.

November 15, 2023. Pollock's "Lucifer."

More and more I'm feeling like I'm going crazy. In the house all day, with my little chores, and many more of them hovering overhead, like the spiders Sylvia was seeing on the ceiling the week she died.

The friends I used to take walks with aren't around anymore. One moved to Colorado, one to San Rafael, one seems to have slipped into severe depression, and another has entered, rather abruptly, a state of being truly old.

Needing a break, I drove up to visit the Anderson Collection at Stanford today. It's one of my favorite museums, quite small, but with some wonderful works. Pollock's "Lucifer," de Kooning's "Gansevoort Street", Joan Mitchell's "Before IV," Lobdell's "January, 1971.

Had lunch in the cafeteria in the neighboring Cantor Museum of Stanford, then came back to the Anderson to lurk in their "Resources" room, an empty libraryesque space with good chairs, and the books all locked in glass cases. And I'm writing this note in here.

Disconcertingly they have a large TV that's on auto; it was playing educational things, but now it's playing prolonged Indian songs, the singers homing in on gnarly wavering vocalizations and then prolonging them ad infinitum. I just now unplugged the TV. Will "they" notice? Evict me?

Well for now I'm here, out of the house, writing notes.

Waking up alone yet again today, I thought to myself, "You really *are* through writing. It's over." I miss the writing, as it gave me something to do. The painting is good for the daytime, but in the evenings ... just TV, or reading my Kindle.

I'm reading Kafka's *Die Verwandlung* (*The Metamorphosis*) in German and in English at the same time, going back and forth, a chunk at a time. I used to like to say that the first few scenes are funny—things often seem funny to me in German, with those long wriggly words.

But by the end, it's unspeakably sad, hitting me with a double knife in the hears. First of all, the lonely and all-but-abandoned Gregor Samsa is like me these days: restlessly crawling around my quarters, over and over, with nothing much to do. Secondly, when he dies, he's like Sylvia was, truly ready to go, utterly discouraged, beaten down, yet filled with a glow of love for his family as he fades away, lying motionless on the floor, wishing the best for his dear ones.

Kindle is the only way I can read a book anymore. My eyes seem to get worse every week. Continually juggling my three pairs of glasses. That's a chore I keep stalling on: to go and order a progressive lens that does it all.

***

Let's pretend I might write a story.

Start with Cain tormenting Abel. To cover his ass, Cain preemptively tells the father that Abel is a liar. Abel is scared of Cain. Mom isn't here to protect him anymore.

Switch to Abel having those lovely "falling down the tunnel" visions that I used to have. Pleasant, not falling fast, drifting down.

Cain is menacing the prize octopus that Abel has in the little tank on his wall. Cain takes the octopus, named Miss Flipsy, into his room to do something nasty, but Flipsy bites him with her beak. Ridged circular outlines of sucker suction marks on Cain's face.

[Realtime! Approaching footsteps. The janitors will notice the cessation of the Indian chant and will take me to task. Call me on the carpet. Chew me out. Tell me what's what. Give me a piece of their mind. *Silence.* Back to plotting a tale.]

The starship lifeboat appears. A wind blows up through the tunnel and lifts Abel high into the air. Through the ceiling and the roof. No, no, it's too discontinuous to fly up. Stay with the vision of the downward tunnel, the shaft to the hollow earth.

He sees the lifeboat ship in the tunnel. This is like a subdimensional elevator. He sinks into the happy dream, but then he jolts, like when you're falling asleep and feel like you've fallen off a three-inch ledge. Jolt awake. Bite the inside of your cheek, with your molars. He is awake.

This is real. He's really sitting in a little flying dinghy with two new friends.

Excerpts of
The Owl and the Pussy-Cat
by Edward Lear.

The Owl and the Pussy-Cat went to sea
In a beautiful pea-green boat,
O let us be married! Too long we have
   tarried:
"But what shall we do for a ring?"
They sailed to the land where the Bong-
   Tree grows
And there in a wood a Piggy-wig stood
With a ring at the end of his nose
So they took the ring, and were married
   next day
By the Turkey who lives on the hill.;
And hand in hand, on the edge of the sand,
They danced by the light of the moon,
The moon, the moon,
They danced by the light of the moon.

I don't want to use that stuff at all. I just copied it out because it's cute.

I recently watched, for the third time, *My Octopus Teacher*, showed it to Marc Laidlaw. Owls are fine, I saw interesting photos of owls two days in a row, first a big one, then a tiny one, an owlet, these images are offerings to me from the Muse. So okay an owl. And the piggy-wig stands for Miss Flipsy.

Abel likes his new friends in the boat, but wants to go back for Miss Flipsy. So a smaller boat tweaks off the lifeboat. Like the big and small owls. Abel has to hurry to get out before Cain stops them. And he wants to save Miss Flipsy. Cain sees them escaping but they're free of him for now.

Let's be sure to kill Cain before Abel takes off. Cain't going to ruin things, so we hit him with a really large zig-zag lightning bolt. Perhaps he reveals his true form as he dies. He never really was Abel's brother. Never was truly human. *Zap!* Sweet relief.

Then Willy and Miss Flipsy are out in the big boat and they travel down the Road to Alpha Centauri or wherever it is.

Act 2. They go to Mistport. Go whaling in ... the Road. The hidden sea that laps the shores of all lands.

Act 3 Abel comes back and resurrects Mom. It's a Joseph Campbell heroic journey routine, like *Frek and the Elixir*, but it's going to be at most a novella or, if I'm not careful, another thousand-word short-short.

It was the Cain-thing who made Mom disappear. Like in a fairy tale. The connection is something that Abel learned about while at Mistport. A glowing red jelly-egg or something. Mom comes back to life, and Dad the woodcutter is happy again

Abel, the glowing shaft Road, the menace of the now-slain Cain. Abel's prior dreams of the Road are like a radar beacon on which the good ship homes in. Ship name something joyful. *Angel*, just go for it.

Okay, feeling better. Wrote all this in the Resources room at the Anderson Collection museum. Go upstairs and take another look at the Pollock and go.

***

Writing more when I got home.

I looked at Jackson Pollock's *Lucifer* for half an hour. It was like the surface opened and I slipped inside the painting. Like a cube of Jello. Lovely in there. Swapping my glasses around, the three pairs, savoring the fractality.

At home I looked up the value of the painting and it's estimated at $500 million. That's half a billion. Might well be the most valuable painting in the Bay Area.

"Once more / I'd pay a fortune / If I could see you / Once more."

That's some heavy *mana*, in the sense of "power," the half-billion-dollars connected to the painting hanging there, about 3 ½ by 9 feet. not all *that* large by Pollock standards. And hardly on the tourism radar at all. Only saw about five other people in the galleries.

I can go there, and hang out with it, and absorb *mana*, and then go into that comfortable Resources room and write notes about it. I'm going to do that again. Maybe not *tomorrow*, but again. Will the guards get suspicious of me if I come there over and over? Well, not if I can bring myself to act normal and talk to them like fellow human beings. I am, in a sense, an author writing about Pollock's *Lucifer*.

The painting can definitely have a part in the story. Maybe that's where the aliens and the octopus take Abel. To the space inside the painting. Remember that cosmology thing about the universe being encoded as a hologram on a cosmic surface?

November 17, 2023. Rhythm.

Cain can only be in the story if I kill him fairly quickly.

Did I already say that the boy is Willy and not Abel? Was that the name of the boy in *Frek*? Or no, wait, I had Villy in *Million Mile Road* Trip. The pet is an octopus and he can talk to it.

For sure use a version of that original Norway start, Better if the aliens are humans, so it's not a big complicated deal to talk to them. They can be Earthlings who live in the Mistport colony. What were the saucer aliens like in *Frek*? Can't remember.

Groping, but finding stuff. This story ... I have a sense of the mindscape, and I'm trying to carve out a seemly chunk of it, with all the threads dangling, massaging it, trimming it.

I'm sitting and writing in the Roaster coffee shop two days running. Like I'm coming back to life. Printing out the notes, marking them up with a pen, then typing the changes on my laptop in the Roaster. Returning to my rhythm.

So good to be surrounded by human voices. Not being Gregor Samsa alone in my empty house, running across the walls and ceiling using the *Klebstoff* on my feet.

I managed to buy painting hooks so I can hang a lot more of paintings. Want to put *all* of the new ones up, despite the fact that I'm a cockroach running around on those walls, and the ceilings.

I ordered the new glasses!

Synchronicity: the first 45 record I ever bought in my original Louisville aquarium-containing room was "You Send Me" by Sam Cooke, 1957. And, wow, here it is on the speaker in the Roaster. "At first I thought it was infatuation, but oh I've waited so long." When I got the record I was eleven, and I thought Sam Cooke was white, and I thought he was saying "Cindy" instead of "Send Me."

At that time I knew a girl called Cindy who I thought was cute. I danced with this Cindy once at a square dance at our church. The first time I ever danced with a girl. We liked each other, for the half hour that it lasted. Don't think I ever saw her again. But I loved her. I seem to remember that her father was a scary Paul Bunyan type guy. Ray Rouser?

I kind of want to mix this Cindy with a Julie who had a ponytail and lived in a "modern" house with a flat roof and was loud. Only saw her a couple of times, and I don't remember the connection. Art classes?

Julie lived near my friend Rick, who had very blonde hair, a bit geeky, and a serious magician. He had a trunk that said "Rick the Mystic" on it. He brought the trunk when he was at church camp with me, and one of the more sophisticated boys mocked Rick for that inscription, though I thought it was cool. Rick did shows for children's birthday parties. Once in high-school I saw him at the burger drive-in, leaning out of a car's back window, unbelievably drunk. The drunkest person I'd ever seen. "There's Rudy! Hey *Ruuudy!*"

Somehow fits with a future as a stage magician … if that's where he ended up. Me, I ended up as a *writer*, just as risky.

November 18, 2023. "Mistport" Opener, Take 1.

Seems like I ought to be able to write the new story pretty soon. Call it "Mistport". Let's work on an outline.

===

Willy is an eleven-year-old boy in a bud city near Louisville, Kentucky. (Cities are living organisms by now, and when F start getting to large, they bud off sub cities.) Spring of his sixth grade of schooling. Let's say it's 2157. (Two hundred years later than the childhood events in St. Matthews, Kentucky, that inspires the tale.)

Willy's father Hank runs a furniture farm, growing seeds and seedlings that will grow into furniture or buildings that people want. Surprisingly low tech. Most of it involves Hank talking to the plants, discussing options with them, making promises of good treatment. He has a young woman assistant Perky that seems bent on seducing Dad, the little whore. Mom used to help with the plants too. But Mom's been gone for ten months. Nobody seems to know what happened to her.

Willy misses her terribly, Hank is in a daze of grief, and Willy's five-years-older brother Kork is callous about Mom. Says she was a bitch, always hassling him about his hunting. Kork likes killing small animals. He hints around Mom that might not be dead. "Maybe she's just taking a nap."

Willy demands if Kork actually knows something, but he just sneers, bully that he is.

People can in fact hibernate these days. Turn into a glowing red gummi, soft and rubbery, waiting for better days, just add energy and they pop back. The original cosmonauts traveled to Alpha Centauri as gummies. It's only 6 light years away.

One used to think that with human-bearable accelerations and tech-feasible rocket powers the trip might take thousands of years. But gummies can go fast; they're light and tough and don't need life support. They can ride on a laser or microwave push like in Stross's *Accelerando*. See post about it with the following quote from Stross. The post also contains some cautions about how hard it would be to have enough energy to push that light-sail, but we'll assume that's taken care of by some stronger energy source in two hundred years.

The destination lies nearly three light-years from Earth, and even with high acceleration and relativistic cruise speeds, the one-kilogram starwisp and its hundred-kilogram light sail will take the best part of seven years to get there. Sending a human-sized probe is beyond even the vast energy budget of the new orbital states in

Jupiter system – near-lightspeed travel is horrifically expensive.

Rather than a big, self-propelled ship with canned primates for passengers, as previous generations had envisaged, the starship is a Coke-can-sized slab of nanocomputers, running a neural simulation of the uploaded brain states of some tens of humans at merely normal speed.

We'll send gummies instead of lifebox code. And once they're on Alpha Centauri planet they discover the *Road*. And soon they connect the Road to Earth.

The Road a is subquantum spine or pathway or tunnel network that underlies reality. The way it feels will be taken from young Rudy's visions of that endless shaft I've been mentioning.

November 20-21, 2023. "Mistport" Opener, Take 2.

Setup.

Willy is an eleven-year-old boy in a bud city near Louisville, Kentucky. 2157, spring of his sixth grade of schooling

His father Hank runs a furniture farm, growing seeds and seedlings that will grow into furniture or buildings that people want. Surprisingly low tech. Most of it involves Hank talking to the plants, discussing options with them, making promises of good treatment. He has a young woman assistant Perky3, a clone like the 3Jane in *Neuromancer*. Perky3 seems bent on seducing Dad, the little whore, and Dad is leeringly going along with it

Mom used to help with the plants too. She raised talking flowers like the ones in *Through the Looking Glass*. [Cryptomnesia alert: Have I written about these flowers before? In *The Big Aha?*] Mom had a big fight with Dad and she's been gone for a month.

Willy misses her terribly, Hank doesn't want to talk about it, he feels guilty. Willy's sixteen-year-older brother Kork is callous about Mom. Says she was a bitch, always hassling him about his hunting. Says he and Dad needed a break from her. Kork likes killing small animals and intelligent plants. Willy asks if Kork actually knows something, but Kork just sneers, bully that he is.

A divorce was impending and Mom owned the farm.

It's possible that Mom is hibernating in the form of a glowing red gummi, soft and rubbery. Kork might have the gummi in a lockbox in his room. Willy wants to know more about it, but Kork won't tell.

The gummi process is separate from space travel, although in the end the wonder egg that Will brings home will in fact merge with Mom's gummi. Maybe. Not really sure if I should do the gummi routine at all; it's just something that popped into my head.

The Road

The Road is subquantum spine or pathway or tunnel network that underlies reality. It's currently known to connect to Phampernel, somewhere far off in our galaxy or even in another galaxy, nobody knows the fuck where.

Theodore Wu discovered it while playing a VR video game.

The way the Road feels will be taken from my memories of visions of that endless shaft I've been mentioning.

There's the one particular world Mistport that we're connected with. The big activities there are hunting for vaalfisk and for wonder eggs.

Those are Mistport sailors who came to shanghai Willy. Or, better, to recruit him for his powers. (Vintage trope for an adventure tale for youths. The notion that "I am a hero just as I am," as Vonnegut put it.) How did they notice him. Perhaps because of Willys pet octopus Miss Flipsy. She's of their race.

On their way out of town they kill Kork. Maybe he attacks them. Is this too soon to kill Kork? Maybe Mom's gummi fits in here. But, no, save the show-down with Kork till the end.

This is a *Frek* style tale it's slipping into the Hero's Journey mode. I might take a look at that diagram once again …

Miss Flipsy is the Helper.

November 30, 2023. Reset.

So now I've completely forgotten about the story plan.

I was up at our daughter Isabel's near Mendocino for a big family Thanksgiving. Wonderful trip.

December 4, 2023. Xmas Tree.

Rudy Jr and his family came down yesterday to cut a tree on the Summit. I had lox and bagel ready for them, and I set the dining table with an Advent wreath, and tulips on Mom's little antique table by the front door. Penny noticed. It's the first "dinner party" I've had since Sylvia died. Felt comfy and normal and we didn't even talk about S all that much, although of course after I said grace I mentioned her lovingly and we had a moment of silence.

But it felt like a new stage of recovery, very uplifting. Had a great time getting the tree … Calder didn't have a tantrum as he did on the other tree hunts … the girls and I had been telling him not to, and he didn't. I congratulated him for acting like a grown-up, and he looked pleased with himself. He's starting to mature. I keep thinking maybe I was a little like him.

Rudy sawed off the tip of his very large tree and gave it to me to have for my own tree. Need to mount it somehow today, about three feet long. I couldn't face buying a whole tree. I got one last year, and Sylvia was happy to look at the lights from her bed in the livingroom. Maybe I already said this. We'd leave the lights on all night, she thought they were cozy

I'm going up to Rudy's on Tuesday to help them trim their tree, lovely.

Stil painting a lot, I have a new one underway. Day before yesterday I bought a big bunch of art supplies, almost a thousand dollars' worth. I sold eighteen paintings in the first half of 2023, but haven't sold one since July, don't know what the problem is. I alternately raise and lower the prices, put posters on my socials, I don't know. Marc Laidlaw said he thought my landsdcape paintings might sell better than the abstracts and space paintings and illustrations-of-my-novels … but I don't think that's really true.

I keep losing the thread of the Mistport story, I'll take a look at my recent journal entries. I was briefly obsessed with childhood resentments towards my older brother, but now, having talked about it so much to my grief therapist, the idea has faded. Might not even put him in the story. Yeah, just leave it out, it doesn't really matter. Liberate myself, as the therapist said.

And forget the gummies. Just have the sailors getting Willy. And his pet/helper Miss Flipsy is from the other world, Mistport, don't bother with the other name Phampernel. Strip it down. Or keep it; it's a nice word.

The travel on the Road? 'd like not to have an airship like in the original Norwegian idea. *Some* kind of vehicle. Not a fish. A gummie made of brainwave vibes. Node in a graph. A barrel. A shoe. A rowboat. A walnut shell. An eggshell. A flying carpet. A jellyfish. A balloon. A Flat Cow. Has to be something alive. Made of dark matter.

Maybe you just drift along in your own body; that's the best. Keep it simple.

What about Miss Flipsy? She's the guide.

December 5, 2023. "Happy Christmas!"

The tip of a tree.

I have the sawed-off tree tip from Rudy's too-big tree in a steel mixing bowl with water. Went down and looked at our ornaments in the box in the basement this morning, and selected Squawky Bird, a little bird with a bendable neck, dating perhaps from 1949. He's been around for my whole life. I love him.

And in the ornaments box I found a folded note from Sylvia, I think she must have hid it there last year after I decorated our tree in the living-room. I don't think she helped with the decorating at all, she was too weak, watching from her hospital bed in the living room, it was about two weeks before her death. Two and a half weeks. But she must have had the idea of leaving that note herself. So touching. She was still walking around a little bit.

Sylvia's mother Pauline liked to slip "suitcase letters" into packed bags for family members to find when they got to their destinations. My note from Sylvia was a kind of suitcase letter sent from last year to this year, Sylvia knowing she was about to die.

And the note simply says "Happy Christmas!" With a heart drawn underneath.

And it's not meant ironically, she's wholeheartedly wanting me and the family to have a happy Christmas this year, even without her, she's reaching out to us, loving us, wistful of course, but giving us all her love one more time, and kind of slyly amused to be surprising us, she liked to play a friendly trick. Dear Sylvia.

What makes it even more heartbreaking is that her handwriting isn't quite as crisp as it normally was. Not messy, but a tiny bit less perfect than usual. She was fading, not in good shape, but making this final effort. Probably it's the last thing she ever wrote.

Happy Christmas!

I put the unfolded note and Squawky Bird on my tree tip, and on the floor next to it I set a small ancient carton of tiny reflective-ball ornaments that Mom would put on the little peat-moss and privet-twig-tree that she'd make for herself when she was alone in the later years. Too much for me to take out the balls and hang them—enough to just have them there in the box.

I had a little tiny branch I'd broken off my tree tip, and I took it to Sylvia's grave, kind of sobbing, overwhelmed by it all. Rudy's tree, my tip, Sylvia's twig.

And then I drove up to Rudy's, and as I got out of the car, I heard "Hi, Grandpa," and it was sixteen-year-old Jasper coming home from school. A treat to be with Rudy's family so soon again. We got some lights up on his big tree, and tomorrow we'll put some ornaments on it.

December 6, 2023. Down the Rabbit Hole.

Still at Rudy's house. Walked up and had lunch at an Asian dumpling place in their Bernal Hill neighborhood with daughter-in-law Penny. She asked about the next story I wanted to write, and I started telling her about the Mistport tale.

The part she liked the best was my childhood image of falling down a seemingly endless shaft, buoyed up by drafts of warm air, not plummeting, more a matter of drifting than falling, with time to look at the little people, elves, cartoon critters living in the cracks and hollows of the walls, like denizens of a coral reef or an undersea cliff, waving to me or busy with their own activities, some of them singing in sweet high voices, the air filled with warm mild light.

It now occurs to me that the vision is like Alice's rabbit hole, and the Disney cartoon image of it. Not that I thought of it that way as a boy, nor had I seen the cartoon yet, but it matches, and I did like *Alice in Wonderland* and *Through the Looking Glass* a lot.

And now I'm a seventy-seven year old man, writing these notes in the Bernal public library, sitting on a comfortable leather armchair, light glowing from the gray sky above this old building's high, mullioned windows. Lewis and me, we go way back.

The first psychedelic lightshow I ever saw was in 1966, at Swarthmore College, a show brought to town by the then-obscure *Jefferson Airplane*. They'd made a loop out of the Disney rabbit clip. It impressed me immensely, also the jiggling images of colored oils in glass dishes with a curved disk of glass that chemists call a watch glass. I'd never seen anything like the blobby images before, and I adored them.

But now back to the purity and joy of those drifting down the tunnel dreams. Don't like to use the word "shaft," so sexual. This said, could I be having early intimations of the warm vaginas I'd slip into in later life?

So how do I bring the tunnel into my "Mistport" story?

Suppose I start with the thing itself, young Willy, aged eleven, envisioning this scene as he likes to do. And then there's a sensation of slipping off his bed. Dropping away from his room and fully into the tunnel. He twitches and makes an effort to "awake," but he can't. He's in the tunnel, drifting down, how pleasant it is.

And his pet mollusk Miss Flipsy is with him, impudently perched on the crown of his head, with a couple of wriggling tentacles visible from the corners of his eyes, the tentacles draped down over his forehead. This isn't so unusual, it's a game Miss Flipsy likes to play.

Miss Flipsy is small, no bigger than a girl's hand. Willy found her in an aquarium at the pet shop. The salt water specialties tank. The owner hadn't know quite what species Miss Flipsy was. She resembled a cephalopod, that is, an octopus, squid, or cuttlefish. She'd been curled inside a piece of live coral that he bought. He wasn't even sure if it was legal to import her, so he's been glad to sell her off. Willy has a good friendship with Miss Flipsy; my model here is the critter in *My Octopus Teacher*.

And I think we can assume that Miss Flipsy is from Mistport, she was sent here as a recruiter. Needing a sensitive, perceptive young human to help a vaalfisk find a kraken egg on the distant planet Phampernel, where Mistport is.

Willy has imagined Miss Flipsy's voice in his head before, but now, in the tunnel, the voice is much clearer. She talks like an *Alice in Wonderland* character.

"Much nicer in here. Back inside the Road."

By *Road*, as I may have mentioned, I mean a branching network of hyperdimensional tunnels or channels, like a circulatory system beneath the hypersurface of conventional space and time. Alternate names? Maze, tree, burrow …

December 17, 2023. Mister Tidy, Grief, Sqinks.

I'm at Rudy Jr's for two nights again. Yesterday we went to the Nutcracker at the Opera House … we'd gone there two or maybe three times before with Sylvia and Rudy's family. It would always be Sylvia's idea, a big splurge, about a thousand dollars for the tickets, crazy, but somehow worth doing. A landmark event. And this year it struck me that I should arrange it another time, why not, and I did, kind of late in the game in terms of ticket availability, but I got us six seats together in Row W of the Orchestra section, a little far, but very nice.

Almost like going to church, a solemn festive ritual. I was of course sweating about getting there in time, and finding a way to lunch on the way, but Rudy and his wife Penny knew a nice counter-service place on Hayes street a couple of blocks from the Opera, "The Bird,' with good broiled or fried chicken sandwiches. My ticket codes worked at the Opera entrance, and we were in with time to spare, ah.

The production has this scenery move of pulling up the tree to an immense height, and trundling out an enormous perspective-slanted fireplace, so that, in effect, the little girl is now the size of the nutcracker toy, and the size of a rat, and there's quite a few rats.

The almost boneless and jointless motions of the ballerinas' arms and hands, as the dancers stutter across the stage on tiptoe. The men leaping shoulder-high. The corps waving their arms in unison, like the leaves in a kelp forest near the shore. The beautiful passionate music, especially the descending, sobbing motif in something like the third movement from the end. Afterwards Penny said that part is the most beautiful piece of music in the world.

Sylvia inside me, looking out, smiling, deeply content, nay, brimming with joy. I've been on a serious jag of missing her over the last week, but today it's less, hardly present, nine-thirty in the morning, Rudy out getting pastry, Penny walking the dog, Calder and his pal Nate playing a new video game, Lego Fortnight, in the front living room, me in the rear living room, on a long couch, typing on my laptop.

Twenty days till the first anniversary of Sylvia's death date, which was Jan 6, 2023.

The tree that we cut together is here, and tonight friends are coming over to sing carols. I'm staying for that; I tend to stay two nights when I come these days. Such a relief from the emptiness of my house.

I'm not even trying to write a new story anymore, not even thinking about it. Somehow that's okay. At least this is what I tell people.

Very uneasy about switching from my corps of physicians to a new set of doctors at Kaiser HMO starting on Jan 1. My reasoning is that my regular years-long doctor isn't very helpful, and that now he's part of an HMO and wants to send me to substandard members of his group, and I feel I should get lined up with a good heart doctor. I'm taking an anti-seizure drug that I like, lacosamide, and I'm worried the Kaiser docs might want steer me away from it. I'm worried I have a cancer tumor in the skin behind my right ear, and my dermatologist won't see me for months. I'm always sore in my upper shoulders, and can't get reasonable advice.

Yadda, yadda.

Just walked up on Bernal Hill with son Rudy. Fabulous panoramic view of SF. I walked on that same path with Rudy, Izzy, and Georgia a few days after Sylvia's death, and I'm sure Rudy remembered that, but we didn't talk about it out loud.

Rudy always looks very touching to me. So good, and so eager. The other day I was thinking about a black and white photo of him that Sylvia had made around 1974, maybe for a passport, he would have been two. He's so utterly clean and tidy and personable in the photo, his hair smoothed by a soft hairbrush, his skin utterly clean, eyes bright, his knit clothing utterly spotless, plump cheek. Sylvia said he looked like Clark Gable, and that he was Mister Tidy, later shortened to Mister T. She had a copy of the photo underneath the heavy sheet of glass on the top of her dresser, and she'd lovingly look at it whenever she went by. "Mister Tidy!"

I told Rudy about this today, he was mildly pleased and interested. You know how it is with parents' fond memories.

With Rudy I try not to harp too much on the death of Sylvia, he doesn't seem to welcome it, and might not even respond. Even though he's thinking about it too. I think by now maybe he's tired of hearing me talk about it, and he'd like to move on and get well, and he doesn't like to see me unhappily wallow in it, . The daughters, who I don't talk to quite so often—they're more open to discussing Sylvia's death, as they don't have so much of an opportunity to talk about Sylvia, while Rudy sees me every week or two. And I do know that it's no use to talk about it all the time.

The view from that path. Small dwellings on all the hills, like a coral reef, and big warehouses in the flats down by the bay. SF thought: a future city where an alien species lives in the warehouses. Critters like the short chains of purple/violet spheres in my latest painting, "Riding the Flat Cows."

What would you talk to them about, what type of trade might you engage in?

Could "Riding the Flat Cows" be an illo for my as-yet-unwritten story? The image *is* in that Netherlandish illustration of a now-forgotten-proverb zone. A forgotten or *as yet untold* parable.

What would be the name of those purple critters? *Sqinks*. With no *u*, just a *q* by itself, which make for an *sk* sound. *Sk*-sound things are usually nasty: scuzzy, skeevy, skeezy, scummy, skanky. There *is* a category of lizards called sqinks, but they're fairly boring, in my opinion, and I am *not* talking about them. I reclaim the name with my *sq*.

Those lizard skinks have no neck, small legs, and a long tail which can be shed. Years ago we took Sylvia's French-speaking nieces Stella and Dini on a walk with our kids in the redwoods, and we saw a skink, and one of us grabbed the skink by the tail, and the tail indeed came off, and it was twitching, and Stella cried, "*Il y'a une queue qui bouge encore.*"

For *my* purposes a sqink alien's tail could grow to an alien *whole*.

I see those buildings as market stalls. Or trading offices. Suppose the sqinks are a hundred feet long, but as thin as a person. They like our food. They might send it to Sqinkland through the Road. They pay us with … what? Brainzap sexual pleasure and access to the Road. You get high and you're on the road.

Those negatively curved doors in my painting are sqink holes. Leading down to the Road. Like manholes that access the tunnels and sewers of a big city.

Try for a connection to young Rudy's Alice-in-Wonderland-Disney-Jefferson-Airplane-Lightshow drifting down the shaft? Maybe my Willy is using Dad's sqinkhole. Like a movie rental, a sqinkhole must be used within thirty days, and stays active for only 48 hours. If you don't come out before then, you're wherever you end up. And maybe you can find some way to get home from there, and maybe you can't, and maybe you don't care. Maybe you don't want to come back home.

Dad might come looking for Willy, but Willy hides, and Dad goes back home, and Willy finds his way to Mistport.

December 19, 2023, Everything Notes.

Last night I went over my hundred-thousand-word *Everything Notes* consisting of story notes and journal entries, organizing it a little bit. And in the process, getting a clearer idea of where the last couple of years went.

- In 2019 and 2020 I was working on the story "Everything is Everything."
- In 2021 I had my 75th birthday, Sylvia got cancer and I hardly wrote any fiction at all, although I did write a story "Tooniverse Telemarketer," which includes a man dying of cancer, but I don't think I made any notes about the process.
- The first half of 2022 I worked on an expanded version of "Everything is Everything," which I called "The Sea Pig and the Sun."
- The second half of 2022 I wrote a short short story about Sylvia dying, "Who Do You Love."
- Sylvia died at the start of 2023, and most of the *Everything Notes* are about that. In the summer of 2023, I wrote a story called "Big Germs" about eliminating guns.

December 26, 2023. Good Christmas.

I had a good Christmas at daughter Georgia's with her family, plus daughter Isabel and her husband Gus. This was in Madison, Wisconsin. Somehow I wasn't greiving nearly as much.

The girls wore some of Sylvia's clothes and jewelry when we went out for a fancy dinner on Christmas Eve Eve, and when Georgia and husband Courtney put on a big family dinner on Christmas.

Isabel was sporting the favorite necklace and earrings that I'd given Sylvia: a gold chain with semi-precious stones that I found in Bloomingdale's for a thousand dollars one Christmas, and a matching set of earrings that Sylvia and I found in a shop on a bridge in Florence on our last trip to Italy. And Georgia wore Sylvia's holiday blouse black with white stars, and her black velvet pants.

At dinners or in company I'd occasionally see a Sylvia-expression on the girls' faces, when in conversation. So touching. I referred to each of them as *"kis Sylvia,"* Hungarian for little Sylvia, and they liked that a lot. They loved and admired her so much. The love of my life. One of a kind.

But somehow I wasn't depressively wallowing in the grief. I've started telling people that I've crossed a three-year hole in my life. And that feels about right. I'm on the other side now. The two years of caregiving, and the year of heavy grief. Like a cigarette hole burned into a shirt. Not that I'm at all done with missing Sylvia.

Her death anniversary comes on January 6, about a week and a half from today. I feel like I'm ready for it. And Izzy's gonna be here.

I'd expected Christmas to be much harder than it actually was. But she's really gone, and for most people she's fading. Maybe even for me ... to some extent.

No idea what I'm going to be doing back in Los Gatos now. I'm eager to get a blog post out of that long interview/essay on higher dimensions that I started just before leaving for this trip, and kept working on during the plane trip, and during spare time in my motel. What can I say, I like to write.

But I told the guy I'd hold back on blog-posting it until he gets around to posting it on his site, which won't be till mid-February. So maybe I'll write a post about something else, if I think of something.

For months, this Christmas trip has been the main thing on my horizon. Also I'm dreading the switch to the Kaiser health plan on Jan 1. And uneasy about the business of repairing the wall on our driveway. Flummoxed by intractable mission of finding a woman. Drawing a blank on starting a new SF story. Galled by my lack of friends.

I've still got painting, yoga, journaling, and AA. I really need to try some painting "meet up" sessions … I've been talking about his for quite a while.

And at least I'm not drinking and smoking pot.

All through the trip I have been praying to the One for kindness, acceptance, and love—and it seems to work. I'm motivated by what I keep hearing at AA, that is, after twenty-seven years, I'm finally taking a little more of it to heart. I have a new sense of how to pray: I reach forward towards a white glow that's at the level of my chest, and I say, "Help me." It calms me, and at times, the prayer seems to bring good luck, and to make things run more smoothly. Magical thinking, but if you can believe in the magic, why not.

Christmas isn't a purely religious holiday. It's a collection of rituals, practices, symbols, customs, songs, and foods. With family gatherings paramount. All of this nourishes my soul.

As I may have said, I'd truly been dreading Christmas and the concomitant rush of sad memories regarding Sylvia's last two weeks. But somehow it was fine. Somehow everything fit into its own time and place. That was then, and will forever be there, but this is now, and where else can we be? We live.

I just said goodbye to Izzy at the Phoenix airport. Now on the last leg, bound for San Ho.

Maybe I can start in on that sqink traders, Wonderland tunnel, and Mistport story when I get home. You might say I've been doing a bit of worldbuilding. And who knows, the tale might be a bit longer than the ones I've been crafting of late. I hope so; would be nice to get into one of my "better worlds" and stay there a while.

As we flew down into San Jose, I had this irrational conviction that Sylvia would be at the airport to meet me. And when I walked out of the secure area into the meet-up area, I was actually looking for her, even though I knew it was impossible. My fantasy: Sylvia runs up to me and hugs me tight. Smiling and with tears in her eyes. Kissing my face.

"Oh Roo, I've missed you much. You've been gone so long."

So what do I do with that? Play it over in my head, savoring the majesty of the pain. Imagining that in some way it's an actual contact with her soul.

And pondering the psychic judo of having *me* be the one who's been gone. But, yes, in Sylvia's afterworld it is indeed Rudy who's been missing. In my Sylvia-haunted house, it was me who wasn't around.

So, yes, she came and met me at the airport. Like in the old days.

December 29-30, 2023. False Start. YA? Ugh.

I wrote a starter page yesterday, about 500 words. I might have a toehold now.

Crosses my mind that I might try and pitch my novel for the niche called YA, that is, fiction aimed at young adults.

For now I'm calling the story "Mistport." But surely that will change. And the structure I'm using right now is a false start, and will prove unworkable. But at least I'm writing.

A boy down at the warehouses at the base of Bernal Heights by the Bay. Sqinks have trading posts in the warehouses, they want produce.

What do the sqinks pay the farmers with?

Allays need to pick a point of view, that is, a POV. In *Million Mile Road Trip*, I had Villy, Zoe, and Scud alternate POV, though I think Scud not as much. In *Juicy Ghosts* I had about ten characters and many had POV. Hard to remember all this. Not sure I'm competent to write a whole novel anymore. Soldier on, old top, soldier on.

I'm tempted to just have the one boy Jimmy or Chimmie in Chap One. But this is an instance of the "white room" pitfall. I'm alone and I can't imagine someone with me, so I write longer POV. Make up a friend. A girl. It could even be the girl's POV.

Zadie and Jim, Zadie taller and a year older. Like a sister and brother, but not actually related, although maybe I'm thinking of grandchildren Zimry and Jasper as models, at least for speech patterns. Jasper is of course a girl, but I'd rather have a boy in there.

I won't go for a romance between these two, they're pals, and perhaps down the road the kids might pick up on some romances, or maybe we don't do much romance ... could stay at a kinda YA level, but without the rumored vocab stranglehold.

I wrote for two or three more hours today. I'm really out of shape as a writer. and it's hard to do. Like not training much for two or three years, and losing your runner's conditioning, and then trying to run a three-miler.

To tell the truth, I'd kind of forgotten how much micro work there is to writing, all the tiny things. Empire State Building out of toothpix. Mona "Gwenda" Lisa outta pixels or gnat whiskers. (Gwenda a random name that's in my head this week, belongs to an intriguing YA writer in Lexington, Kentucky, Gwenda Bond.) Differentiating the characters, choosing their names, doing exposition on the sly: via talk and eyeball kicks. And now I need for something to happen, awready.

The chatty small mascot-type sqink they call Skeezee, with his goth color scheme, three feet long … he should do something. (Myth of the Hero trope: the Helper.) Maye another gawker tries to capture him, and Z&J save him, and then the gawker gets rough, he's like a game hunter, and maybe Skeezee's mother zaps the malefactor with an energy bolt.

And the kids fall into the sqinkhole. Yee *haw*!

Might as well get that over with, as it's inevitable, and right now that's as far as I can see, plot-wise. The next landmark in the woods. So don't hoard and stall, go ahead and do it.

December 31, 2023. New Year's Eve.

Went to church this morning, and met a nice old woman and chatted with her. She used to work at Apple. Has two canes, probably over 80. No sex thing there, just a pleasant person to talk to. I might even go to church again next week to see her again. Suzanne.

I went to see my dear SF-writer friend Terry Bisson yesterday afternoon. He has cancer, just like Sylvia had. He'll be dead in a couple of months.

January 10, 2024. Story is Stuck.

We made it past the one-year anniversary of Sylvia's death. January 6, 2024. Rudy and family came down. I made them a big lunch with a tablecloth and fine china. It was jolly, in a restrained way. We went and visited the grave for about half an hour or forty-five minutes; it started raining just as we left. Rudy wore sunglasses, and it took Isabel to privately explain to me that he was wearing them because he was crying. Just unbelievable, a whole year.

One of those landmark things. Again that sensation, as with granddaughter Althea's graduation, of having crossed the Great Plains and passed the Sierras. Isabel helped clear a ton of Sylvia's books out of our bedroom, kept some, and gave some to the Los Gatos Library, where Sylvia liked to do volunteer work. Isabel took the two little bookcases as well, also the big Eiffel Tower collection. I'm going to hang a few of my paintings on the now-open wall space.

Moving away from having so many parts of the house be "shrines.".

I was going pretty well on the story I'm calling Mistport, but then I put in a violent scene of a sqink biting off a bulldog's head, and I felt that steered the book in the wrong direction, so I took that out, only now I need some *other* kind of action or event to kick in on page three.

I think the characters are Zimry and Calder. Calder's been begging me to put him in a book. In a way the little brother Scud in *Million Mile Road Trip* was like Calder, also the boy in *Frek and the Elixir*, I might try and get him to read *Frek*.

Sorry to leave out Jasper, perhaps I can fold aspects of her into the Z character. And what about Georgia's kids. I really can't be thinking too much that way.

I need something to happen right now and I don't know what.

I had about five pages done, and I felt like was getting somewhere but, now, looking it over, those pages are mostly just story-exposition done via dialog. I need some small event. What if the kids are taking down something to give to the sqinks in exchange for "good luck." Could they have grown a bunch of squash? Or … what *could* they have grown in January? Maybe I don't insist on it being January.

Or, how about this, I have Zimry and Calder make off with the box of fresh veggies that their parents get delivered. That's not much of an offering. Gourmet mushrooms? Cabbages. Do they steal some? Will the truck farmers be mad? Do lots of people bring veggies? Lilies?

I need a villain.

Could be useful to build up the idea that lots of people don't even believe in the sqinks. Maybe you don't see them unless you believe in them. Like elves. Maybe the book is like *ack* a fantasy.

January 17, 2024. I Start the Novel."

I have about 1,500 words done on a start to the story I have been calling Mistport. I'm might change the title to Farmers Market, and leave out the Mistport part. I feel so old and distracted that I can't visualize doing a novel or even a novelette. Just want a short story.

It's not going to work for me to do that girl and boy character structure, it feels too hard. I'm not writing for fun, or to express myself, I'm writing for imagined standard of a YA book that might please my grandchildren, but come on. They don't even read my other YA type books. Write for *yourself*, Rudy.

Also, what do I know about kids anymore?

I'm just going to do an old-school first person transreal Rudy story. So I'll have to throw out a lot of what I have.

Stick with my POV, as I say, but possibly could be looking at some kids later in the story, but maybe not.

Main thing is that I need to start the story a month or two earlier in the timeline. I like my new character Carol Cee. Narrator is old-age Rudy and Carol Cee is his gal. Now you're talking. Not YA but OA. As in Old Adult. I know Bruce did a novel like that and that guy in San Diego, the nice guy who did something first, CS teacher as well, Vernor Vinge, two years older than me. The first to talk about the Singularity, of course, also a lot of augmented reality. The novel with old people is *Rainbow's End*. I'll see if I can read that.

YA is square, boring work. I want to write hip and wild the way I like to do. Like I did in *Juicy Ghosts*. Free, loose, crazy ... amusing myself.

Have my story start with a chapter about the transition into the alien traders situation, and not about falling into the holes yet. That can be the travel part.

I quite recently did a drop into a tunnel story with that disorganized story "Tooniverse Telemarketer"; used the old fairy tale trope about the girl who falls into a well and finds another world. I read this story when I was visiting Grandma in Germany when I was just 13; it made an impression on me. I almost feel like Grandma told it to me? Or maybe we went through it as a German lesson for me? And of course I have the falling into the tunnel thing in *Hollow Earth*.

And, yet again, as I noted earlier in this set of notes, I had that fantasy about falling down the hole as a boy, so, yes, I probably will find a way to use that anyway.

But the way I was writing and rewriting my draft for the last couple of weeks, my characters were falling into the hole almost right away—thus leaving behind the new part that I might really want to write about.

I could of course have Sylvia's dead soul in the sqinkhole. And she tells the hero or the kids something crucial for saving the Earth from the aliens. Kind of obvious and heavy-handed, that. But it could obliquely and perhaps inform what I do. I mean there could be a *smart ant* down there, and *I* know that a smart ant means Sylvia, but the readers don't have to know.

By the way, better to have cuttles than the dick-like wedges in my painting.

Something that's been hanging me up is this: why isn't there a huge furor around the Bernal Heights sqinkhole, with unheard-of aliens making trades?

Well, we have to start with that sqinkhole being found by my hero ... what's his name? Ken? Kenneth Turan, retired film critic for the LA Times? No, no, it should be me. Writer or professor? Grieving widower ... no, too obvious, and I've written a little about that already.

A guy who is in some way on the skids, like the "old writer" who lives by the river in that late Burroughs novel whose title I, being an old writer, forget.

Found it on my blog. *The Western Lands*. I blogged a long blog post about *The Western Lands* in 2011.

So yes, I can use that *Western Lands* character. The old writer this, the old writer that. Obviously plagiarizing Burroughs or, rather, I might claim, having an episode of cryptomnesia, like, I didn't *realize* I was copying Burroughs. Oh, hell, it's just literary influence, Rudy. A gesture or respect. Burroughs is my lifelong hero. Up there with Pynchon and Borges.

Here's the key quote. And the first time I read it, I knew I wanted to use it. Wanted to be this man.

But I wasn't yet alone. And now I am.

> The old writer lived in a boxcar by the river. … Often in the morning he would lie in bed and watch grids of typewritten words in front of his eyes that moved and shifted as he tried to read the words, but he never could. He thought if he could just copy these words down, which were not his own words, he might be able to put together another book and then … yes, and then what?

So okay, great, I've found my character. I *am* that old writer, and I'll use first person POV rather than B's close-in third. "I was living in a container by the Bay."

I'm thinking of that art group the Box Shop, who have a combine of shipping containers they live in. Daughter Isabel painted a huge squid mural for them, once, it was kind of party or festival. She knew most of them.

My kids have long been one of my connections to the scene.

Shit, I'm gonna reread B's book on Kindle. Get some cryptomnesia. Cook it up and shoot it, kid. Oops, it's not on Kindle. Well, I have a copy in the house, just saw it today, as a matter of fact. Where? Cryptomnesia. Maybe I saw it three months ago. Synchronicity.

Anyhoo, I'll say that my character, Bill, he sees a single sqink worming out of the brittle dirt near the bay.

Just one of them. The sqink has telepathy, and it talks to Bill. It noses at the blasted dead vegetation. And Bill has a tangerine in his pocket, and he sets it down on the ground and the sqink, her name is Loulou, she noses into the soft tangerine with her snout and shudders in ecstasy and teeps to Bill, "I will give you luck." Like the fairy tale about the Magic Fish, you wave.

If I call the character Bill then "they" might think I mean Gibson. Call him Bill B? My character in *Million Mile Road* Trip was Villy, I think. Could just call him Rudy, or Roo.

Heard the word "roo" on a radio station in the northernmost Wester spike of Australia last night: "I'll have two, said the kangaroo." Rusty world-sized armature of synchronicity creaks into visibility as I begin.

Do the sqinks have eyes or not? I keep wanting them not to have eyes, and to just use teep, and I painted them this way, but if you get on a sqink's wavelength, it can see phantom eyes on the sides of its head. Virtual eyes. Like flickering spherical mirrors with images inside, but gauzy.

And do they have voices? I think that might be more fun than teep. A papery husky Burroughsian whisper. "If I had veins like that, kid, I'd have myself a time."

With teep you can't really write good dialog, and its dull and otiose if you're all the time doing "seemed to hear a voice I in his head that said blah blah." Just hear the frikkin voice from the sqink's snout okay? Wheezy. Piping. Thin squeal.

So at first there's just the one sqink, and we see Roo's first stroke of luck.

This morning I was thinking about Sylvia calling me "Darling Roo," and how I told that to Greg Gibson, and then of course he wanted to tease me by calling me

Darling Roo in the third person, but I could tell that deep down he envied me for being Sylvia's Darling Roo.

Call my character Oliver and Oll—not Rudy and Roo. Sylvia can be Sybil, I called her that in *The Sex Sphere*. The Cumaean Sybil.

Connections. It's coming together, synch by synch. The Muse/Cosmos is ready to dance with me. As long as I'm ready to loosen up and do some real writing.

January 21-23, 2024. Library. Chap Two.

I wrote for the last six days in a row, Thursday-Sunday, writing in the Los Gatos Pubic Lie-brary, and I might keep doing it. A nice tall-backed chair on the second floor by a window looking out on some green, and a building that used to be the cop shop, but is now admin offices. Electrical outlet in the floor by the chair, and they have wireless in the air.

Got in nearly 4 hours of writing in the library every day, well, sometimes just two. Not even thinking, just sat down and wrote flat out. Haven't done that in quite a while. Did write two or three short stories while S was sick for two years and when I was in heavy grief for a year … kind of forcing those stories out.

But now it feels like old times. Making stuff up on the fly, surprising myself, chuckling. Like narrating a dream that I'm having, feels so good.

Rockin' it.

Saturday, I wrapped up the first chunk into 3,000 words which in fact comprise a nicely rounded story. Chapter One, I'd like to say. And Sunday I polished that.

By the way, in the *Sqinks Journal* I repeatedly refer to chapters by their numbers. But the *Sqinks* novel itself doesn't have printed numbers on the chapters, an aesthetic decision of mine which is perhaps inconvenient.

But if you flip to the back of the *Sqinks Journal* you'll find the final chapter numbers there.

The novel's narrator is an old man like me whose wife has died. He feels his life is over, but he's gonna write one more novel. It was raining hard outside the library window as I wrote … so the rain went right into the tale. Realtime transrealism.

Fantasy payoff for me: my narrator gets a new woman (who at this point is very much like Sylvia.)

Went in again on Sunday, today, after Sunday morning church, and, after, the actual farmers market in Los Gatos square. Realtime transreal.

And again on Monday and Tuesday, polishing that Chapter One into something like a solid story, waiting for momentum to get into Chapter Two. Help me, muse!

***

By end of Chapter One, they've fed a sqink, and asked for a gift, and sqink says, "I grant you good luck." It's raining and bare-headed Oliver finds a top hat and Carol Cee realizes that suddenly the lump in her breast is gone and she doesn't have cancer, more realtime transreal, or rather an echo of S's breast lump some years ago. Major good luck.

For Chapter Two. I could jump forward in time, and go to that setup I was using when the characters were those two kids … but that would be kind of a copout, as then I'd be summarizing the intervening events in a paragraph. I really *would* like to work out the events a step at a time. Like it's a novel.

So, okay, Oliver and Carol get back to the Box Farm complex, and Carol's daughter Loulou is awake now, and they tell Loulou what happened.

Loulou hasn't noticed that she's been getting good luck, but now she thinks about it.

Maybe Loulou's been talking to a different sqink than Cynthia, call that one Kanka—after those horrible gum-ulcer drops I happened to buy in Maine when we were newlyweds, and Sylvia snatched it away from me, and threw it into the ocean for being elderly and icky, laughing at me. Still reminiscing about Sylvia, at one time I was trying to wear bow ties, and over and over she would reach over and untie my bow tie with a swift tug, and laugh. So I gave up on bow ties.

By the way, in the final Sqinks I used the name "Doink," instead of "Kanka."

Anway, what kind of luck does Loulou get from the sqinks? Let's say that she's a painter and that suddenly her paintings are much better. She does random drip and flow and now everything is landing in the right place. Or, no, she's using Flybuzz, an art-generating app like Midcentury or ChatGPT, and by luck she's coming up with magically great prompts. *Relevance alert!*

We're going to have a couple more characters in from the Box Farm gang. Loulou has a loudmouth greedhead who studied, for a short time, at a business or law school. His name is Tobin. He wants to sell sqink access which is an overreach, and Loulou turns against him, and Loulou's luck is that Tobin goes broke or gets busted for fraud or somehow goes away. A sqink eats him. Or maybe not that bad a fate.

One person's luck is another person's disaster. "Luck Wars"? Sounds a little boring, that. Like an article in *The Journal of Philosophy of Science*. Bleen and grue. (Classic staple for a bunch of stupid papers.)

Need to have a lot more sqinks showing up pretty soon, or right away.

Oliver and Caol Cee go to SFMOMA and see something odd. Another sqink, in a corner. It eats an Andy

Warhol installation, this big grid of a hundred portraits that I like, the sqink starts in one corner, and gobble-munches all of them down, clearing the wall like a hungry rat, absorbing the synchronistic quantum vibe of the analog painted work.

Sqink turns into the urbane David Niven? No, no. But maybe. Dapper skin strolls out of the museum with them. Could be funny, to me at least. Some star younger than Niven.

Just the one sqink in the museum, or more. One of those 3D happy face heads also. An eater. All three kinds from my *Farmers Market* painting. Maybe don't have third ones look like flying dicks. Squid or cuttlefish.

And now with the many critters coming on the scene, this grows into a crisis. Alien invasion! Ollie and Carol have to solve it. So the story becomes a little like *Million Mile Roadtrip* where they're fighting off evil UFOs. Maybe find a fresh angle.

Moment of doubt thinking of *MMRT* or my more recent one, *Juicy Ghosts*. Can I really manage to write something that long again?

January 24, 2024. Letter to Marc. Who Is Carol?

[Begin letter to my writer pal, Marc Laidlaw.]

Very lonely this week, distracted. I miss Sylvia so much. Can't believe it's been a year. She's fading a bit, but then she comes back very strong. My poor dear lost darling. This morning I was apologizing out loud for all the bad things I did, large and small, and she was talking back, "Don't worry so much Roo. You took care of me. You were there to the end. I love you." Good to hear that. My Zoom therapist day before yesterday got into this thing about "what is eidetic" when you hear a ghost talking to you. Only one more session left.

As you know I think/hope I'm starting a novel, and Chap One is a nicely rounded story now, but now I can't figure out what goes in Chapter Two. Some kind of surprise is needed. Can't just have the characters' standing around and bickering. Or ... even worse, an SF trap ... have them discussing what might come next. Fuck that! Akin to the blank white room. Reification of the author's boring uncertainty. I mean, like, do I write about my computer setup too? Yes, Windows 10 ... .

I just have to hit the reader hard with a hardcore surprise now. Ruckerian. Wham. Rudy and Sylvia, that is. Oliver and Carol Cee, they go to the SFMOMA museum and one or more critters appears and eats a big Andy Warhol tableau of portraits. That would be good. I have a photo of me there with my painter friend Paul Mavrides, photo taken by Sylvia, us in Mick and Keith pose, maybe with Paul leaning his elbow on my shoulder.

I have a preliminary idea of what sqinks look like thanks to my Farmers Market painting. Maybe we have a whole LOT of sqinks come out at the museum, from an unnoticed dark, dusty corner of the room, overhead, unlit—like a swarm of bees. YES. Don't stall.

I've been writing in that soft chair with a high back in the LGPL Lost Gatos Pubic Lie-berry for five days in a row. Should shower and go down there now. Wind and rain, exciting, maybe I can walk.

Scene in four lines:

> *Zzzzzt!*
> Where'd that Andy Warhol assemblage go?
> Let's get some coffee and a pastry.
> But do you want to fuck?

There's your frikkin' outline, ye hawkers of a Master's Degree in Creative Writing, huh?

The female lead is, as I just said, Carol Cee, a person much like (in my mind right now) one S. Rucker. But a little different. Makes it fun to write about her. Screwball comedy dialog. Looking forward to when they/we fuck, but you can't throw that bone to the readers too soon. Give the slobbering, furiously masturbating audience something to live for.

[End letter.]

***

The Warhol-eating sqink turns into urbane David Niven? No, no. Dean Martin, but that's only relevant and funny if you've seen the wonderful movie Kiss Me Stupid. Or the sqink looks like Andy W. himself, yes, that's perfect. He's the artist in question, and he's in some ways a living (well, used to be living) cartoon. Banal, but perfect, and won't seem corny all that quickly.

Or a 3D happy face instead of a human. An eater, like in my *Farmers Market* painting.

And now with the many critters, this grows into a crisis. Oll and Carol have to solve it. So this is a story a little like *Million Mile Roadtrip*. Can I really make up something that long?

January 27, 2024. Need Next Scene.

I wrote the scene where the sqinks eat the Andy Warhol paintings at SFMOMA. Olivier and Carol escape the ensuing hubbub by flying away, riding on backs of two sqinks who make themselves like big rubbery caterpillars for this. Doink and … let's see I changed her name from Cynthia because it felt confusing … I picked Better, don't really like that, I think Belle would be better. Or Lilac.

Anyway, right now I guess they're going back to Box Farm, flying low, hoping to escape detection and pursuit.

Don't know if we can get back to that peaceful farmers market scenario that I wrote before, with the kids on bikes and lots of people bringing food in. Eating those paintings was kind of harsh and terroristic.

My idea, if I have an idea, was that the sqinks like to eat anything that some human has a strong attachment to. Like to see how it tastes if we like it so much. Or to analyze the structure ... like my ancient *Software* deal about eating someone's brain.

Should build up Loulou's attachment to the vegetables that she gave Doink, let them be nice winter cabbages and melons that she grew. Maybe she even fed Doink one of her print/paintings of Doink, which would incline him toward eating art.

But now what? People offering the sqinks beloved mementoes or artworks or art projects. Baseball glove, surfboard, bicycle, Oliver's car. Offering these things in exchange for good luck

This is somehow a symbol for computer modeling and virtualization devouring our most beloved possessions.

Where does it lead? Do they go to Sqinkland? Might be like world they go to in my story with Terry Bisson, "Where the Lost Things Are." Piles of "collected" items.

I'm not seeing enough through-story for a novel at all. It's feeling more like a novelette. But it's often that way. I'm still in the foothills.

Was it horrible mistake to have that scene of eating Andy's paintings?

I need a better description of the paintings in there, really thick and visual.

Enjoying so much the snappy dialog between Oliver and Carol. I don't want that to stop. Their conversation is the core of the story, the living thread. So the question is how to keep the conversation going. If its "The Adventures of Oliver and Carol," then the details of the sqinks don't matter so much. I could go episodic, with other aliens showing up as well. What's the word for that kind of novel other than episodic … yesterday I couldn't remember and then I did, and then I forgot it again. Picaresque.

I feel Oliver is being too sexist and slobbering by repeatedly asking the newly-met Carol to fuck him. So I'll dial that down and in fact have Carol and her daughter Loulou mocking him for it.

If Carol was a real actual woman, and not a lonely old man's fantasy, then she for sure wouldn't like the requests, as I learned earlier this year when I was trying once again to date women, and I kept single-mindedly asking for sex, and thus repelling them. Need to be smooth.

***

Down in Satna Cruz, I had a long talk about ChatGPT with my computer science professor friend Jon Pearce. We were wondering how well it would work with fiction writing. Joh and I both taught CS for decades at San Jose State University. Much of the time he was my office-mate.

I was thinking that in a sense I do ChatGPT internally, in that as a highly educated and well-read person I have something like an internal large language model, that is, a very wide range of possible "next phrases." My so-called "temperature" is set to a high level … which means that I very often will chose a somehat unlikely version of the next phrase. I tend more towards surrealism than toward legal boilerplate.

After talking to Jon, I wrote for an hour or two in the Verve coffee shop on Pacific Ave, and got another five hundred words done. Going good.

***

Back in Los Gatos, I finally went online and gave ChaGPT 4.0 a try. I went ahead and fed it the newly written section of my novel to see what the AI would spit back. It was the section where Oliver and Carol are flying away from SFMOMA after the sqinks eat some of his paintings. Flying on the big sqink Moo's back, I think.

Frankly I'd been thinking the hype over ChatGPT is a bunch of bullshit. But after this test, I'm staggered and flabbergasted by how well ChatGPT works. As my other CS prof friend Michael Beeson put it, the method of "choose the next word based on the odds" seems, on the face of it, like a pedestrian and uninteresting approach. But now—presumably thanks to the size of the vast neural net large language model that is in use—it's undergone a phase transition.

By large language model, or LLM, I mean an immense simulated neural net that was evolved by Earth's mightiest computers. The net consists of a zillion nodes with numerical weights along the lines connecting the nodes. Nobody understands, or can understand, the meaning of the individual weights. As Kurt Gödel proved back around 1930, understanding these weights is, even in principle, impossible. Our AI techs calculated the weights for a human-emulating neural net by a somewhat opaque process of simulated evolution. And, as I say, they can't understand the neural net. It's an interesting a paradoxical answer to the old question of whether AIs can circumvent Gödel's limitation. Gödel himself knew this would happen, and he once remarked that we'd be able to bring into existence human-mind-equivalent devices.

But, once again, without understanding them. That's what machine-learning does for you.

As a proud writer, I assumed ChatGPT could never write anything colorful or interesting. That it could only churn out bland pap akin to political speeches. But I wanted to try. You can feed ChatGPT a text file as input, so I fed it a five-hundred chunk of my novel. This was as long a prompt as the ChatGPT would currently accept.

I was very, very surprised how good the output was. The writing isn't bad, and it's got originality, and a bit of verve. I'd asked for "in the style of Rudy Rucker," and there's more than enough work of mine online for ChatGPT's vast neural net to know what that means. The AI app used some pet phrases or scenes of mine. And even introduced a new character or two, as well as fresh wrinkles in the plot. Kind of unbelievable. The only real criticism I might make is that the extinction didn't seem to have much humor. Or any heavy meta-level subtext.

But the really crushing thing was that, when I went ahead and ran ChatGPT twice in a row, feeding it the same segment of my novel each time … it wrote two utterly distinct continuations. It could go on writing new continuations all day long.

Somehow this is very deflating. It makes the ground shift beneath my feet.

And, no, I didn't put any of that frikkin ChatGPT writing into my novel. And I'm not going to be steadily asking it for possible extensions. Like for inspiration. That would be too much like having a know-it-all, full-of-ideas roommate who won't shut up.

I'll return to scorning ChatGPT from afar. And you'll find me alone with my word processor in the coffee shop, or in my home office, or on my living room couch, or in the town library, same as usual.

By the way, I'm not yet sure what the title of my novel will be, The working title used to be "Mistport," and then it was "Farmer's Market," neither of which is, by now, reallly relevant. At the end of my experiment with ChatGPT today, I asked it what the title should be, and based on the passages the app had seen, it made a few suggestions, including: "Sqinkland Odyssey," "Warhol's Whimsy," "Sqinks in the Canvas," "Pop Realms," "Artmover's Dilemma," and "Surreal Serendipity."

Not bad, although none of them is perfect, and again as the novel grows, I'll need a broader title.

When I tried feeding all six thousand words of my manuscript to ChatGPT, the app crashed, but it did display a pretty cool phrase as a label for our conversation, or maybe as a message, nor sure, but the phrase was "Sqinks in Rubber Flight." Now *that's* a good title, and it's cool that it comes from an AI crash, which gives it a meta and transreal significance.

January 28, 2024. The New Warhol Paintings.

So, coming back from ChatGPT land, is my novel still alive, or did I totally kill it by consorting with the Devil? For starters I'll reread and revise the last part of the latest chap, which is called "Warhol." The part I actually wrote!

I left it where the sqinks ate the Warhols, and Oliver is flying through the rain with Carol, and she's just had the idea of having the sqinks somehow replace the Warhols that they ate.

Now with the SFMOMA staff all riled up over the vandalism, I don't exactly see how my couple could go back in and do the fix. Seems like they'd have to sneak in at night.

Or I could keep on escalating the plot, like rocketing upward, and have them go back and boldly carry out a televised replacement process which, one might suppose, Andy might not mind. Weird publicity! They talk to the museum director.

"Please let us make it right," charming Carol tells her.

Initially the director doesn't want to let these insane vandals and their fat alien critters back in. But my heroes and sqinks persuade the director. They pipe a hypnotic flute song, lay down a bullshit rap, or have a sqink hatch a sample replacement of one of the Andys, and make the point that this will be an amazing news story … as long as, at the end of the story, there's Warhol art for people to admire and buy. And if the replacements are made, the museum might not be viewed as having lost money.

And the sqinks have to promise not to make more dupes, so these can be unique. Even though the sqinks don't quite get the NFT notion of a painting as a unique object because, for a sqink, any object is "fungible," that is "subject to eidetic reproduction."

They all troop back and, in effect, 3D-print the paintings and put them back in place. It's a higher-level 3D print which has molecular integrity. Squirted by a sqink as a blob on a canvas that forms into shape as its own. Like that Daivd Povilaitis illo in my Fourth Dimension book, of God throwing a bucket of paint onto a barn wall to create a synchronistic spacetime cosmos all at once.

Okay, so if SFMOMA is happy, there's no more conflict, and we're back where we started, and we haven't advanced the plot. So something new has to go wrong. A tycoon hires the sqinks? People worship them? A lot more sqinks show up, and here we might visit the Farmer's Market scene that I painted before I started the novel.

Sure, a sqink only wants to eat *one sample* of a given kind of fruit but what if lots of *different* sqinks are coming to the market. Like people attending a movie theater, only visiting once or rather only returning when the movie changes. So we'll have the seasonal attractions at the farmers market, and of course, even though it's a limited palette of produce types, younger or less centrally located sqinks will show up. Like people going to Vegas to see the various Circus shows.

Could get a whole carnival thing going around that. The Human Lima Bean tosses fitfully in the straw.

I did get other ideas about the new sqink-made paintings, rather unwillingly, from a list that frikkin ChatGPT presented me with because I input the Prompt: *What do you think should happen next?*

Really asking for trouble doing this, because I hate when outsiders offer (usually) idiotic ideas about what should happen in my books. And I didn't in fact read ChatGPT's suggestions very closely. Also there were some further suggestions about the paintings that were built into my test ChatGPT's extensions of my chapter as well.

The ideas had to do with the notion that the sqink-created paintings might in some important ways differ from ordinary human-made paintings. They could be iridescent at the very least.

But more than that, they might flow out of their frames onto the floor and slime around. Or move as if animated. Or be actual windows into alternate realities such as, perhaps, Sqinkland. Or be doors you a pass through.

So that's food for thought. But I'm not gonna go there. Too *slobbering*, as Bruce Sterling would say about overly fannish SF tropes.

January 30-31, 2024. Gas.

Wrote 1,500 words yesterday. I set up the scene where the sqinks reconstitute the eaten paintings. And then a cop kills Doink with a stun gun; turns out this is (conveniently) the one thing that can kill a sqink.

And then I hurriedly wrote a closing scene where everything gets smoothed out. Some off-stage character comes in with a hefty donation to the museum. They'll drop charges, let Oliver and Carol and Lilac go home to the Box Farm, keep the videos secret, and keep the paintings, temporarily storing them in a locker to see if they're stable.

But this kills the action. And I worried all night and all morning about "What Next!"

There have to be some loose ends. The video gets out, for instance.

And why would the authorities release Oliver, Carol, and Lilac so easily.

How about this! Lilac hypnotizes them with *sqink gas*. Now you're talking. They release our three, also they release the videos.

Lilac wants the videos out because she's mad at the cop shot her and killed Doink. Also Lilac wants to have a brisk flea market business. And with everything out in the public, they can't really come down on our little crew. The sqinks have outed the baddies via mass media. This in fact a standard SF move: go public with the disturbing secrets, and then the pig can't harsh you in a hidden dungeon.

Thinking of crazy media breaks, I go off on a research foray:

Sunday, Sunday, at the Atco V-va-va-VOOM Dragway! Radio Ad I heard in late sixties at Swarthmore College. Speaking of drag racing, I always wondered what are "funny cars," well, these are nitromethane dragsters with engine in front of driver and a plastic shell lightweight mockup of a street car covering up. I look like a Honda say ... I'M A FUNNY CAR ... going 300mph a block past the light ... burning fifteen gallons of fuel in a thousand feet of driving ... with thirty-foot-long flames streaming back from my front wheel wells.

I return from my research foray, a better person for it.

So now, Chapter Three *might* lead to a scene like the discarded startup I wrote with the kids on bikes at the farmers market. Problem here, in that the Oliver parts are 1st person and the kids are 3rd person ... I mean I *could* do that, in experimental literature mode, not unheard of.

Well, wait, I could stay in first person and, logically enough, the kids could be Oliver's grandchildren. Which, transreally, they actually are.

I was leading up to the kids jumping or falling or being dragged into the big hole, the Road to Sqinkland. But I'm also thinking of Carol and Oliver going in there.

Regarding the second option, there's the Myth of the Hero or, more accurately, the Orpheus and Eurydice option: Carol is kidnapped by the sqinks, and Oliver goes to save her. Or I flip it, with Carol saving Oliver.

I like that.

I feel like I've written an Orpheus and Eurydice novel before, but I can't remember if I did. A variant is daughter Persephone and mother Demeter as Loulou and Carol. Carol goes to Hades to save Loulou, and then Oliver goes to save the two of them. That would be good. I could set that up right now.

Either way, it's Carol and Oliver down there. Extra twist: the annoying Tobin is with Loulou and in fact it's *his fault* they got taken, and he'll make a lot more trouble for everyone down in Hades, that is, in Sqinkland.

Summary for Chap 3.

- Videos get loose.
- Goobs stream to Box Shop.
- Tobin organizes a trading post. Like my original farmer's market scene.
- Lilac is the sqink boss of the trading post.
- Tobin and Loulou are taken by the sqinks. Tobin's fault.
- Carol goes after Loulou.
- Oliver goes after Carol and catches up with her after a chapter of looking.

February 4, 2024. What Are the Sqinks?

I'm halfway through Chapter Three, and the Trading Post thing is about to kick in. Six sqinks are in the big room of the Box Farm, talking to the gang. Tobin is haranguing the box farmers with plans for how to run the Trading Post.

I've been stalling about the question of what the sqinks are doing here. Because I don't know. Tap dancing around it. But I really have to come up with the answer right now. Take the story to the next level.

It is possible that the sqinks' initial answer will be a lie, or a half-truth, and that later we'll have a reveal about the real reason they're here. But we need to have at least a watered down reason now.

So far, I've been thinking of the aliens as being like naturalists, anthropologists, zoologists, sociologists, or psychologists. Simply investigating us. Beings with an intelligence on a par with ours, or perhaps a bit higher But of course they want something more.

- Making us Slaves seems pointless.
- Making us into Puppets. Making us into actors for a show to watch. Like watching a tribe of imprisoned monkeys for entertainment. Or like a very large reality TV show. And their "luck" incitements are graduated in order to steer our doings in directions they consider dramatic, funny, or otherwise interesting. Forcing us into, for instance, romances, wars, or crime shows. Variation could be to use as remotes, or juicy ghosts, but I think I did that in *Frek*.
- Using us as Guinea pigs. Maybe their doses of "luck" are the same as doses of "sqink gas," and the sqinks want to know the long term effects. Would be a nice reveal when they learn the two are the same. And this can shade into a quantum field thing. Life is a long, wonderful dream. Luck is synchronicity. An alteration in your Hilbert space wave function that is your life. Careful here not to slip through the trapdoor to *ugh* a many worlds novel.

Let's change the question.

Instead of asking *what the sqinks want* from us, let's ask *what they are*.

- Ghosts from the afterlife. Kind of obvious move, given that I'm in mourning for my wife, and so is my character Oliver. Not a good idea. Even a sympathetic reader would feel it was pathetic of me to be writing such a book, and they'd be right. Wish fulfilment. I mean that *is* something I might want to write, but it can't be so obvious. I'm already doing it, in a lighter way. Oliver has a new girlfriend Carol, so just settle for that, and don't try to raise the dead. Carol's a human, not a sqink.

- Creatures from an alternate reality level. If I have the sqinks be from an alternate or subdimensional world, we don't have much of a Myth of the Hero setup. But they could be some other modality of the physical universe. Something not quite so slippery and woo-woo as ghosts. Like the 4D beings of *Spaceland*. And I've written about subdimensional realities before. Not a multiverse, mind you, just a single parallel sheet for one alternate world.

- *Sqinks* are denizens of Hilbert space. Go up to infinite dimensionality. I don't think I've done much with infinite dimensional critters before although, again, there were some things in *Juicy Ghosts* a bit like that. I forget their names. I think I used Islamic or Kabbalistic angel names? Azaroth? And one or two of the human chracters in Juicy Ghosts had been reconstructed as lifebox software pattern, and these patterns transmogrified into patterns in Hilbert space or in, I'll be saying, in the Ruliad.

Also keep in mind my recent story, "Who Do You Love," written shortly before Sylvia died last year. The story had a female Hilbert space character, as I recall.

To make it fresh, and to "wiseacre for the swing of thought" (as the sage G. I. Gurdjieff put it) I'll start thinking of Hilbert space as akin to Wolfram's Ruliad, and I might as well use that nomenclature. The reader may be intrigued when you give some old trope a fresh name.

So yeah, we'll go with that. The sqinks are patterns in the Ruliad. It's a worthy goal. This could be my last mountaineering expedition, so I'll pick a high peak.

Feb 4, 2024. With Sylvia in Hilbert Space.

Day before yesterday I was walking around the St. Joesph's Hill area above our house. By the end, a fine, but non-negligible, rain was falling. The grass so wonderfully, intensely green. I felt very happy. And, as ever, those all-but-last words of Sylvia were prominent in my thoughts.

The world is beautiful. The world is so beautiful.

On the hill, I felt a deep, almost physical connection between my now-current world, and the world Sylvia was in when she said "The world is beautiful," to me, a bit more than a year ago.

As I like to do, I geometrized the situation, thinking of my mind and Sylvia's mind as patterns in Hilbert space, a.k.a. the Mindscape, a.k.a. the Ruliad, that is, the plenum of all possible sensations and thoughts and processes. A pattern in the Ruliad, or a multi-dimensional shading thereof.

I see the Ruliad as dark, and the mind pattern as a lighter-shaded brown glob, with tiny twinkling lights. Neurons. I reflexively want to see the pattern as moving. But if it is in spacetime, it doesn't have to "move," it just is, and the lights don't in fact twinkle on and off, they just glow.

Or they're spacetime trails, and the trails are striped, indicating flashing when played forward in time..

Sylvia's mind pattern of a year ago still exists in the Ruliad which, as I say, includes all space and time. Sylvia's pattern is generally adjacent to mine, or even merged with it, although I have a bump or slight plateau that's a bit higher than the terminus of Sylvia's zone, because I'm living longer.

I think of cut-out wooden maps of state that, as a child, I'd puzzle together to make a whole USA. Together, Sylvia and I are, say, a bit like Colorado and Kansas, that is, one extends a bit further north than the other.

But along our adjacent edges we're fully merged. As one. And saying this, I return once again to the very last time we two were in our king bed together, before her isolating hospital bed arrived. What a key interval it was, that last hour together, the lengths of our bodies pressed together, with perhaps my leg thrown over hers, or hers over mine, I later saw two thin, bark-peeled tree trunks washed up on a beach north of Mendocino, with the thick sticks slightly overlapping, and, seeing them, I thought *that's what we two were like*.

And during that last union, Sylvia said those words so precious to me now, "You're being so nice to me Rudy. Staying with me. I'm grateful. It's meant so much. I almost don't like to say this, but I forgive you for all the mean things you ever did. I do. I love you."

We two are merged forever, that is to say, timelessly. A pile of legs, like the washed-up trunks, one mind, one soul. That part of my life is in my past now. Down there, in the sense that the past is down, or south, or lower. I'm up here, still alive, with a narrow remaining edge still growing, or rather existing, but perceived as moving. My last upper edge, and currently alone.

And somehow this relates to *what the sqinks are*. They're conscious living processes or diagrams-of-processes or, hell, call them beautiful entities in the Ruliad

How do I convey this without tangling the readers in the weeds of higher math?

As I say, in *Juicy Ghosts* I had some characters in Hilbert space for a time. Infinite dimensional. And certainly there's still some oomph in that trope. There are some properties and characteristics and experiences and states of mind to be ferreted out.

So the sqinks are patterns from the Ruliad. And again, my task is to make this experiential and real.

It helps that, when physics is mathematically formulated, the world's entities or processes become quantum mechanical waves in Hilbert space, or in the Ruliad. Those are the "real" things. And our minds are Ruliadic flows as well.

Another phrase that was in my mind yesterday, in the lovely spring rain, on my steep hill, among the perfect day-old green grasses, with Sylvia clearly and sensibly present in my reality—as if one leg of my pants was soaking wet and clinging to me, the soul of Sylvia being that warmly wet pant leg, adhering to me, Sylvia's mind a bit "lower down" on my Hilbert space body, down there and fully adjacent to the part of me that's in the still-extant and never-to-be-destroyed past.

Life is a long and beautiful dream.

February 5, 2024. Still Stuck.

I cleaned up and revised the previous entry, and sent it to the kids. Was thinking of putting it online, but not right now.

Get back to the prob. Where are the sqinks from? What do they want? How do I keep the plot going?

This morning it crossed my mind that if worse came to worst, I could call the book Hollow Earth 3, and have the sqinks come from down there. Some mid conceptual continuity issues. HE and Return to HE don't mention anything like sqinks. But I could finesse that. Like it's a big world in there, right? Also Rudy Rucker himself is a character in Return to HE, but he could get a walk-on in HE III.

But this move wouldn't really do anything for explaining what the sqinks are up to. It would only make things worse. A lot worse.

Looking back at yesterday's rap, I was heading for making the sqinks be some kind of Hilbert space spirits. But why make it so hard. Can't they just be critters with strange powers?

The notion of them eating things people love, and memorizing them, and then maybe giving them back—that's a setup for a lampoon of the growing AI economy where the bots memorize what creators do, with an eye to emulating it.

The sqinks could be interstellar explorers with pungent (yes I know that's the wrong word, should be draconic, but I wanted to say pungent, as the word itself stinks, not sqinks) weight restrictions, which would be why they don't keep things, just the info thereof.

Shouldn't the sqinks eat Oliver's car? He goes outside, "Where's my car?" "Flubsy ate it."

They live in the ground. Did they land as spores? Migrate up from the depths? Sashay in slideways from Hilbert space?"

Do I really want to write a whole book where Oliver and Carol go to another world? Feels so been done for me. *Frek, White Light, Spaceland, Million Mile.* The amazing journey. Could I do it without a journey? Then I guess it's best if the sqinks are indeed like spirits. From Hilbert space. Somehow want a science explanation. The next round of radically new AI's.

Our quest would be to defeat—or learn to coexist with—the super AIs.

Again I ask, what do the sqinks want? They're offering good luck nearly free. Suppose it's a publicity campaign. All about brand building and market penetration.

I want to keep on writing the novel. And not get bogged down in bullshit plans. So let the sqinks run wild, and be nonsensical, and do crazy shit, and I can postpone figuring out the why.

But don't ruin it, e.g. don't have Ollie get a blowjob from the flying cuttlefish.

And have the sqinks look somewhat different from each other. The chains-of-balls sqinks are just one style. Which I happened to paint in Farmers Market.

Lilac, Doink, Flubsy, Skeeze, and Moo. I like these guys. "They're my imaginary friends."

Is it going to ruin readability if I introduce character after character, with a silly name for each one? Oh, why not. Have fun. "Haah gaahs. I'm Ned Cuttlefish."

February 6, 2024. The Muse Came!

(A long email to my writer friend Paul DiFilippo.)
***

Muse stopped by last night. The "aliens" aren't from hollow earth, subdimensions, our galaxy, the afterworld, the Hilbert space wave function that is All ... naw, man, they're from something like a biotech near future Google! A new level of web scraping!!! Done by kritters I call sqinks. You give a sqink an object you love, they eat it, deconstruct it, turn the matter into raw info, save that, and then maybe vomit the object up for you, perhaps as Burroughsian "UDT: undifferentiated tissue" that reassembles the object. Or maybe they don't bother making a copy, if the object isn't incredibly precious.

In return, said gunjy sqink gives you "luck" which somehow "rigs" (as evil Prez T would say) social events in your favor e.g. jobs, meetups, bets, and they can even, with sqink skill, cure cancer or other bodily ills.

The surprising and unheralded and surreptitious release of these alien seeming biotech kritters, that is, the sqinks, is meant as a publicity rollout, and for this, Meatiepie inflicts the first instantiations upon our characters, Oliver and Carol, who are living in repurposed shipping containers near SF Bay, the southern, unfash end of the bay, one understands, and Oliver is a 77 year old very-nearly-washed-up transreal cyberpunk SF writer, a widower, happy to have met Carol, his age, with Carol's daughter Loulou a part of the Box Farm container-inhabiting art/hacker posse. Meatiepie is warping the rollout's consequences for max publicity, with double-crossing and surreptitious bribes of the powers that be, like whenever our two are about to go into the klink, the head cop or museum director or psychoanalyst gets a secret huge bribe from Meatiepie, and the captors are like, Go thou and sin no more.

Of course there's going to be a looming Very Bad Outcome, so Oliver and Carol must, *ta da*, save the world.

I'll need to find ways to stretch it out … keeping in mind the game-designer Will Wright's dictum … whenever your characters need to get from A to B, a C intervenes. (One of my xitter followers quipped that thereby Zeno can never start a race, but obviously that's not a row for me to hoe.) And I'm hoping to find some meaningful plot arcs so I don't end up going full-on surreal picaresque as one is of course prone to doing, but whatever works. I'm enjoying the interplay of Oliver and Carol very much, and hoping not to let it become an old man's pathetic wish-fulfillment fantasy. Going for, I think, a screwball comedy tone, Carol wised-up and slightly mocking.

Yours, Lookin' Up The Muse's Skirt,
Rodolfo Pigmentato

February 12, 2024. Finished Chap 3.

I'm calling the book *Sqinks* now. I had a K, and a QU, but plain Q is best. And , as I think I've mentioned, this evades the annoying fact that "skink" actually means a certain lackluster lizard, which these guys are *not*.

Rocking the book. 15 K words in one month. Not to count chickens, but if I maintain this rate, I'll finish by September, 2024. Feels SO good to be hittin' it. In the libe today, I didn't even look up from the laptop for two or three hours. Somehow I have a sense of "hurry up, write faster before it stops coming".

Yes, somehow I bullshat (rare past tense) through 3 chaps already. Have kind of an idea for number 4. The setting is this nice isolated off-grid motel near the ocean where I stayed with Sylvia during the End Times. Seal Rock Inn, where the end of Geary St. hits the beach.

Being quite modernistic experimental in the book at times. Break the fourth wall. In this bit today, my chars are embroiled in this endless chunk of pompous dialog-bossed exposition, and I really question if I should be doing it. So then I did something to break it, and I laffed my ass off. But in reality I'll find a way to dial this down,

==============

[The sqink character Skeeze is holding forth]

" .... The universe is like a novel or a movie. With synchronicity. If you dance with world, the match-ups pop."

"This is boring as shit," I tell Skeeze. "Like an indoctrination session for a cult. I don't give a fuck about your woo woo jive. Isn't anything ever going to happen?"

"Well, Moo is going to kill me pretty soon," says Skeeze. "Will that make you happy?"

"Shut up," says Moo. "It's my turn to instruct. We're explaining luck ... "

[followed by more exposition from Moo and Skeeze, and then, a couple of pages later, Moo *does* savagely and unexpectedly kill Skeeze.]

==============

I'm realizing that if the sqinks do in fact have a shared hive mind, then no memories are lost if you kill one sqink body. Moreover, thanks to sqink compression, you might be able to chew up a sqink, and then restore said sqink to hale normality later. But restoring poor Skeeze does not in fact work. So the resurrection-move seems not to be fully debugged yet. Sorry about that Skeeze.

So far I've killed Doink, Skeeze, and Moo. But maybe I revive Skeeze after all. And maybe Moo isn't really dead. Good old Lilac is still around, and we just met Hummy, which is an unpleasant name, change it to Xavier.

I'd like Oliver and Carol to meet Winston Trotter at the motel. He's the top scientist at Floonberry, the company which is perhaps manufacturing sqinks.

***

I'm going apeshit. Forcing the miracles down to one single thing: the precise nature of sqinks. Are they biotech? Dark matter that (if necessary) isn't subject to quantum rules; it can be infinitely divisible if I need that. Sqink memory is enough to contain tiny copy of big object. Sqink luck is based on cross-temporal synchronicity that emerges from sideways threads.

Levitation is from sqinks ... somehow.

They say dark matter levitates with dark energy. Yes. I found "evidence" for this on the site Space.com.

> Dark energy is a hypothetical form of energy that is proposed by physicists to explain why the universe is not just expanding but is doing so at an accelerating rate. Think of dark energy as the "evil counterpart" to gravity–an "anti-gravity" force providing a negative pressure that fills the universe and stretches the very fabric of spacetime. As it does so dark energy drives cosmic objects apart at an increasingly rapid rate rather than drawing them together as gravity does.

February 14, 2024. Synchronicity.

I integrated most of the latest changes day-before-yesterday during a long session at the LG library, and last night during another long session on my couch at home.

Did rewrites, and we're fully out of the Box Farm luck market locale now, with Carol and Oliver getting a ride over to the Seal Rock Inn, to be dropped there by their friends Bety Byte and Smokestack.

Now what?

***

One minor thing. Going back to the name of Winston's tech company, that utterly random name I thought of is Floonberry. Or maybe not so random; I now recall a Thornberry's Toys in St. Matthews, a Louisville suburb near where I grew up. I loved Thornberry's. Maybe Winston Trotter has the design codes for sqinks, if they happen to be some kind of new tech.

***

I need for Moo to came back to life. She got a big jolt from a zapper as they were leaving the Box Farm to head to Seal Rock Inn. Could the little sqink Skeeze and big Moo have sex? Skeeze flustered and sweaty, handing a spermatophore to Moo. No gnarlier than other forms of San Francisco intersex. *So* nasty.

Winston Trotter is upset that Moo is gone. But she'll be back. She's important, kind of a prime node for the sqink hive mind. I was wondering if Bety and Smokestack might have brought Moo's body to the Seal Rock motel in the trunk, but I think it's better if she shows up on her own. Leave her totally out of the picture for now. We've got Carol and Oliver alone at the Seal Rock motel, in the same room that Sylvia and I had in, I guess, the summer of 2022.

I'd like to avoid endless dialog for a bit. Would like to see things happening. But I don't see quite how. Don't want a chase scene now, as we just did that, by fleeing Box Farm and, before that, fleeing SFMOMA.

Winston Trotter shows up at the motel for sure. Maybe he's already there in the room when they arrive. Possibly it was a setup with Bety and Smokestack.

First impulse is that Winston Trotter is evil, being my third fictional transreal version of the late John Walker (cf. *Hacker and the Ants* and, I believe, *Spaceland*). And Trotter's very creations (the sqinks) are rising up against his dastardly plans. Like a palace revolution. A mutiny against Captain Hook.

Or I could flip that, and Winston is good, and the uprising of the sqinks is evil, and to be suppressed, and we're into an archetypal "Crazed Junkies Fight Killer Robots to the Death" routine, as memorably drawn by S. Clay Wilson for *Zap* #7, 1974. What a perfect title. Not that my chracters *are* junkies, but the title taps into the beat William Burroughs thing, as Wilson in fact acknowledges in a dedication on the edge of the image itself.

My heroes are outsiders and artists, which is a variation on being junkies, or at least on a youth's ignorant and romantic and William-Buffoughs-style notion of them.

Speaking of characters to enlist, I might bring in clones of Zep and Del as Ocean Beach surfers from that last story I co-authored with Marc Laidlaw, "Surfers at the End of Time." Would be great to have them in the scene when some bithcin' extras are called for.

Maybe Zep and Del right there at the motel, and they take Carol and Oliver out surfing. Yeah. What time of day is it?

We can have surf gang versus the Floonberry company. Like that.

What exactly are the stakes they're fighting over?

By way of background on synchro, I have an image of a coarse trawler-style fishnet that's a grid of diamonds or squares or quadrilaterals. An orthogonal grid that appears skewed from some viewpoints, like special relativity's Minkowski spacetime.

There are two underlying axes: space and time. Time is causality and space is synchronicity. That is to say, matching or seemingly connected events can be connected by one of two ways, that is by causality or by synchronicity.

This is a viewpoint that I picked up by rereading C. G. Jung's little *Synchronicity* monograph. It's quite a simple book, and what I'm talking about here, about the two axes, is one of the few specific points that Jung makes, but he says it several times, and in different ways, and that was indeed what it took for me to really get it, or to internalize the idea of causality vs. synchronicity.

===

[Summarizing or quoting C. G. Jung]

Nothing startling about synchronicity, really. It's sort of obvious and natural. Why *wouldn't* there be synchronistic patterns! And do keep in mind that we may really want to be talking about meaningful coincidences, and *not* about patterns that are linked by a shared common cause in the past.

Okay, but this desideratum is not so easy to satisfy. Because as you look deeper and deeper into the past for shared causes, the emanating future light-cones from past eras become very broad relative to our present space-like cross-section of spacetime. All encompassing, really, if we're just looking at Earth. Something that happened ten minutes ago might, in principle have a causal connection to any point on Earth.

For instance think of news on the radio. I hear the same news as Makito hears in Tokyo. And nobody would call that synchronicity.

And if our universe is a hypersphere created by a single big bang, then indeed everything comes form that one single cause.

[End Jung rap.]

===

So that was a tangential divagation. I'm looking for a way that synchronicity can have some meaning as a space-like connection. We have to accept that in principle there *could* be a common time-like paths of causation. But it should be a case where positing such paths is unreasonable.

Exaplex: if daughter Isabel sees her first and middle names on a gravestone near mother Sylvia's grave, we don't say there is some paranoid-type plot that has arranged this. We just say it's a coincidence. And if it seems heavy and meaningful we call it synchronicity. And synchronistic events don't arise by time-like cause. They arise via space-like patterning. Artistic touches to the great "novel" that is our world. A quintessential masterpiece.

February 15, 2024. Schemes.

So how did Winston know to be in the motel room before they get there?

Bety, Smokestack, or a sqink told him. I see Bety and Smokestack as good and I don't want to corrupt them. They didn't say out loud where they were going, so the sqinks couldn't have eavesdropped.

Perhaps there was a sqink listener in the car. Maby Moo wasn't really dead, and she crawled over and affixed herself to the bottom of the car and listened to Bety and Smokestack talking. Snuck a spy tentacle up through a rusty hole in the bottom of the passenger's compartment. Alerted Winston and he went there.

Maybe Oliver even glimpses Moo scuttling across the parking lot like a rat.

And the clerk at the motel gives O & C a funny look. He already knows that Winston is up there.

Winston has been fired, or, no, he's resigned. Hostile takeover of Floonberry by Yeehaw, who want to use the sqinks for applications that Winston doesn't approve of.

Call his company Briefcase Dynamics instead of Yeehaw.

February 16, 2024. After They Wake.

So now they're settled into the Seal Point Inn. Oliver, Carol, Winston Trotter, and the sqink Xavier. I wonder if I could use that green one instead of Xavier, what was his name? Doink, but I think Doink got killed. Well, I'll have to give Xavier a personality, he's pretty much a zero right now. Moo the cuttlefish almost died, but she's alive, and she'll be back later on, but not yet. Save her.

Anyway they ordered some Grubhub type food and for the moment Oliver and Carol are taking a nap. Not certain how long the security will hold up, but for now it seems okay.

I'm only five pages into this Chap Four, and now I need twice as much more than what I have. I need to pose a challenge and find a fix.

The challenge ought to be some completely new and as yet unmentioned issue. Some side effect of the sqinks. Alien head poking out of the floor. Winston Trotter going on a really strange trip, like he becomes a coat of paint on the room's inner walls. "Don't bother me, I'm thinking."

That cosmology thing about a small area being a hologram of the entire universe. Not that I want to do that.

Really really strange shared dream by Oliver and Carol. But dreams are boring. Maybe I'll watch that bowling movie about the stoner. Can't remember the name of the actor or the name of the movie. By the Coen brothers. The Dude abides? The Big Lebowski. I think I own a CD of it.

***

I feel weird sometimes, like disconnected or unsure where I am. I particularly feel weird when I write a whole lot, which is something I'm doing almost every day this month. Really hitting it and having long writing sessions, and after a while, in my head the story scene merges with the physical scene that I'm sitting in. A little unsettling.

But I enjoy this state too. It's a kind of a high. But, as I say, a little disturbing. Even so I want to keep doing it; the word count is piling up. I'm almost at 17 K. Five times that would be 85 K, which is enough for a novel. Hell, I'd settle for 70 K, if I need slack. And I've put in about a month, and it's February now, so I could be done in September. Or November if I take time off for trips, although I might write while traveling. Counting my chickens before they hatch. It always takes longer than I expect, what with the dry spells and the rewrites.

***

Oh, I know, a good thing to have happening when Oliver and Carol wake up is a synchronicity session. I still haven't quite nailed down how that works with the sqinks. And the session needs to *not* be dialog-based exposition. It needs to be a miracle, a wonder scene, a Bosch postcard, a room-filling hologram, a visit from the spirits. No talking. *Doing. Seeing. Hearing. Tasting. Touching. Smelling.* Action and the five senses.

I like the idea of Winston being a coat of paint on the walls. And then have balls bounding around like in a game of 3D Pong. A full "unknown allegory," that is, something that looks like an illustration of a proverb, but nobody knows what the proverb was. Medieval surrealism, Boschian Bruegelian Ruckereque. I can almost see it, not quite yet, but it'll come.

At the very end of the chapter when things are looking to turn deadly, then *ta da* Moo shows up. I wonder if it would be in any way possible to have sex with her. "Pass me that tentacle."

Carol gets jealous and runs outside and gets kidnapped by Bety and Smokestack in their speeding beater. Two criminal surfers in the car as well. Zep and Del with different names and slightly worse character traits. Actual criminals.

Oliver is like, *sob* "All my fault."

Then we can have a *rescue Carol* in the next chapter. And perhaps Loulou and that annoying guy Tobin show up and get involved. Of course I want to be leery of adding too many characters.

February 17, 2024. What Winston Trotter Wants.

As I said before, when I get past the first third of the book, I need a global threat that they have to fix. Eighteen chapters could be enough. I have 3 chaps and I'm in 4. I'd need the crisis by end of chapter 6. End of the first third of the novel. So not time for the crisis yet.

After the rollout of the sqink product, there's a rich vein of sociological SF at hand. What happens if lots more people get their wishes. How does that play out?

Big sqink synchro is a matter of tuning reality to accord with people's desires. A quantum mechanical entanglement, as per usual trope, I guess. And of course a number of unspoken or subconscious wishes would come true, in harsh ways, in the style of "The Peasant and the Sausage." Didn't I already write about that fable once? But where? Feels very familiar. Perhaps not so interesting, kind of corny.

Big Sqink Synchro. Ponder the mantra. A tagline for thinking about the book.

I'll change it so that Trotter is *not* fired yet, but his job is in danger, and he needs to scuttle the deal with Briefcase Dynamics. He wants Oliver to help him, he will literally use Oliver's imagination. Mind coupling.

A power outage in China. A flood. A crocodile eats the CEO of Briefcase Dynamics. I Googled for crocodiles in China. Found a story on *Guangdong crocodile farms*. A monsoon brought floods, and seventy crocs got loose from farms growing crocs for their hide. So, yes, I can actualize a headline: Croc Kills China Exec.

February 18, 2024. Clean up.

Hardly know what I did today. Well, I went to church in the morning. Big hit of synchronicity there. Day before yesterday I was at the Anderson gallery in Stanford with this new woman friend of mine called Barb Ash, our first real date. I met her in the Los Gatos Roasting coffee shop about a week before.

Quite a nice person, seems like a bit of a worrier, but she's pretty and she laughs at my jokes ... anyway I was showing her my fave painting there, Jackson Pollock's Lucifer, really very spring-like to my eyes, and not devilish, has a pale blue sky with clouds in the background, and black wiggly lines, maybe like rain-wet fruit tree branches, and spots of color here and there. And at church today, after the service, a friend of mine gave a talk on art, and he showed a slide of Pollock's Lucifer.

I might mention in passing that, although I talk about going to church, St. Luke's Episcopal, I'm not super-religious, although certainly I'm into what you might call the hippie God. The One. These days, being a widower, I might go to church about once a month, for the exalted sense of meditation, and to see people. Sylvia liked to go maybe every two weeks. She was more sociable than me. My father was ordained as an Episcopal minister when he was forty. Me, when I was forty, I moved my family to California, and became a computer science professor. I let the chip into my heart.

Getting back to my date with Barb Ash, we went over to the main Stanford art museum as well, the Cantor, and I was sitting on a marble bench alone for a minute. Near a statue of a thousand-headed Buddha. Sitting there, I felt an emanation from the cool marble. Rising into me. As if telling me, "Get ready. This is the one." Yes.

Anyway, today the farmers market was closed by the time I got out of church. I went home and messed with social awhile. Organized my email and my photos, which took at least an hour. Watched half an episode of *The Throne*. Read a story by Alice Munro. Cleaned the kitchen. Had a grilled cheese sandwich. Talked to daughter Georgia on the phone, and then to Barb. Then finally started writing, maybe around four. And now it's almost five hours later, and I didn't really add many new words, but I did a lot of fixes.

Don't get all bent out of shape about "real science," just write down some bullshit pseudoscience.

The sqinks are coherent dark matter. Sqinks can emit dark energy, which (1) allows them to levitate, (2) networks their hive mind, and (3) mediates synchronicity, that is, is the "horizontal patterning" of spacetime.

[I should mention here that in the final version of Sqinks, I have no mentions of dark matter at all. It's just a red herring that I thought I was going to need, but then I didn't.]

February 20, 2024. Halting Briefcase Dynamics.

Briefcase Dynamics is dummy corporation formed to mediate the purchase of Floonberry and manage the sales of patents. A shell. I was thinking the crocs could devour or disable the CEO of Briefcase Dynamics.

It would be awkward and tedious to physically transport Oliver and Carol to a province in Southern China.

But possible they could get there via teleportation. Which can be "faked" via synchronicity. And I can do that thing I wanted of having Moo line the walls of the motel room with her body and make it into a virtual teleportation chamber. That would be cool. Doing, not talking.

Maybe the head of Briefcase Dynamics is a Scandinavian guy, and he's injured by the attack, and he'll come back again. A villain. Maybe he could be a tedious logician with a penchant for kayaking. And instead of China, how about Elkhorn Slough near Monterey. Shark, not crocodile?

Floonberry and especially Winston Trotter value Oliver because, as an off-beat SF writer, *he can invent scenarios*. They like the scenarios to be "sticky," that is, memorable events that people chatter about. Like the sqinks eating the Andy pictures, and the Box Farm Lucky Market riot. Oliver is a good publicist.

Jumbo "flying" Humboldt squid, about four feet long. *Diablo rojo*, meaning that they get red when aggressive. Typically 1000 feet down, but once in a while they surface in schools. Attracted by flashing lights or reflective metal.

Big one is 100 lb, six feet long. Aggressive. They like low-oxygen zones. Cannibalistic when in feeding frenzy. Found a video. Eight tentacles and two long arms. When attacking, they grab prey with long arms, pull in and hold with tentacles, eating it with the beak, "like an ear of corn."

Problem is that Humboldt squid are so similar to my star character, Moo the cuttlefish sqink. But I guess we could play on the similarity, the fellow feeling. Could be Moo's idea. We go after the logician Bengt Vatvedt. They leave him floating unconscious in Elkhorn Slough, but he will be back.

Looked some more, found a great white shark biting a paddleboarder's paddleboard off Lover's Point by Monterey. Perf.

I think I need to drop the idea of the sqinks being mindreaders. Otherwise there's no action having to do with the flow of information from us to them.

And maybe Oll is too recondite a nickname for Oliver? Just go with comfy Ollie? I mean, "Oll" is fun for me, just because it's so odd, but it makes unnecessary trouble for the reader, who wants their eyes to smoothly skid along.

I want to say I finished chapter 4, with Oliver scaring off Bengt Oberg, but the chapter is only 10 pages, and the other chaps so far are 15, 20, and 21. So I should write a little more on 4.

Well, we could set it up so that Winston buys out Floonberry himself. It's not even 6 pm yet. There could still be a deal, and a celebration, though the celebration comes tomorrow.

And I guess the next chapter is about what happens after pretty much everyone gets sqink luck, and spacetime is fully stitched and basted and appliqued and embroidered with sideway synchronicity connections.

And then what happens to the world?

Stehen Wolfram once said to me that the essence of really high intelligence is the ability to push a line of thought much further than anyone else would.

So okay, go ahead and finish Chapter Four. Bengt Oberg makes a deal with Winston Trotter. To some extent he's scared not to. The goal is for Trotter to take ownership of Floonberry, or, rather, to spin off his own company unit, carve it out of Floonberry. But Bengt has to lose the commitments he made to the money guys who were backing him. Chinese gangsters? Russians?

Trotter wants his own company, and it's not a corporation and he owns 51% and Bengt can own 49%.

Where does Trotter get money? Well, of course the sqinks can get any amount of pirated NixCoin, or they can print counterfeit money, or they can get bank transfers. Any kind of fraud.

We'll have some violent gangsters from Briefcase Dynamics fighting with them. Moo can kill them.

That takes up the rest of Chapter Four. So they reach a steady state by the end of the chapter. Good.

And then in Chapter Five we get into the explosion of the sqink population and the universal synchronicity issues. I keep thinking of a potholder with lots of sideways stitching.

And later on, who knows.

Looking ahead, I truly need to avoid going to the afterworld to look for Oliver's dead wife Sybil (Sylvia), and to hold back from resurrecting her. As I said early in this Sqinks Journal, it would be too sad and pathetic and even a little repellent if I wrote something like that. Transreal in a bad way.

Motivation. Winston Trotter isn't really after money. He's more messianic. He has some higher program for Sqink Sync. He worked for Floonberry simply because he needed the labs and support, but now he wants to disentangle from them and keep control of his patents.

Floonberry is not a corporation, it's privately held. There actually is a Mrs. Floonberry who runs it. And she can get the money for the sale, maybe. Or she can turn down the sale and make a deal with Winston. His company can be called Sqink Sync, why not.

Now what do the Briefcase Dynamics backers get? Well they're going to want billions for those patents. So Winston, Oliver, Carol and the sqinks will have to discourage them. Mafia style. Make them an offer they can't refuse.

And I think I can do all that in the remaining 6 pages of Chapter Four. Remember the structure I used for Juicy Ghosts: Each chapter is a complete, self-contained story.

February 22, 2024. Finishing Part One.

I had a disaster last night, I worked on Chapter Four for about three hours and the fucking updated version of my file disappeared. I haven't done this in years. Still don't understand how it happened, which is scary, as therefore it might happen again. Tried all the obvious recover moves. Will reinstate the Word autobackup routines that I usually turn off because they might slow down my word-processing.

I still had yesterday's version of the file, so I got over my loss and frikken rewrote the changes. No great harm in the end. It's not super hard to rewrite something I just wrote. My brain has its own kind of backup.

So now I guess I finished Chapter four, but I feel like I've ruined the story in two ways.

- What is that travel-via-inversion trick of Moo's? It's a cool headtrip that I used a long time ago in story whose title I can never remember. So look it up. "Guadalupe and Hieronymus Bosch." I got the idea for it when I was teaching Advanced Computer Graphics at SJSU. It has to do with the mathematical projective transformation matrix that is used to convert three-dimensional coordinates into locations upon a painter's canvas. You had to ask? My worry here is that it's a great power if a sqink has the ability to embody such a transformation. Nobody will understand this. Oh well. Maybe drop in some BS about the Absolute Continuum while I'm at it. I used that one in a story of mine, "Everything is Everything," in Ver 1 but not in Ver 2.

- Undercutting. Winston reveals that sqinks are self-reproducing. Meanwhile he's involved in a deal for Briefcase Dynamics to license the use of the sqink patents, supposedly to manufacture sqinks. Or perhaps the patent for Winston's device for attracting sqinks. But, confesses Winston, "The patents might not matter all that much. The sqinks are self-reproducing. And by now they know where we live."

Tweaked this back and forth in my head all day. I think I'll save the self-reproduction and sqink-summoning reveals for Chapter 5. I don't think they're in Chapter 4 right now.

I feel like I've finished Part I of the book and now comes Part II when everyone has sqink luck. I wonder how long you can stretch that out, though? I mean what are the conflicts then, what goals?

I need an idea for the, um, next 2/3 of the book.

The whole thing of everyone being lucky at once, maybe I can iron that out. Or our reality turns into a dead leaf that scutters off down the sidewalk tumbled by a chill wind.

I'm still sick with my cold/flu. Coughing horribly.

Had a second date with my new friend Barb Ash tonight that I couldn't stand to cancel, even though I'm sick. But it was hard to keep up a happy face. She said I looked "pensive" and that made me sorry for her, for having to date a dud.

But in the end it was a good date. She really liked the Bluegrass Jam at the Los Gatos Coffee Roasting

Company. And the dinner was very good too. She thanked me several times and said she had a wonderful time. I hugged her for a while, but didn't try to kiss her lips, as I'm hideously diseased.

Was thinking of driving out to Half Moon Bay with Barb tomorrow but to both of us that seemed like too much. I may go alone, but only if I'm well. Or could just spend the day in bed.

Saturday I'm supposed to go up to Rudy's with Isabel to watch the Chinese New Years Parade, featuring granddaughter Zimry as drum major for her high-school band. And I so much want to do that.

And again I worry that the flu I have is one of those six week things that I often get in the spring and that I'll be dizzy and in a bubble and slightly feverish and horribly coughing and post-viral-depressed until end of March. It happens almost every year.

This Barb is touching and sweet and kind. A good person with her own concerns. She's a great photographer, and for years she taught classes on Photoshop and other Adobe wares. We talked a lot about a color inkjet printer she's bought. I have one too. Very balky devices.

February 23, 2024. Don't Know.

Still don't see where to go with the story. Winston gets control of the sqinks and then what? Do they self-reproduce and everyone has one?

Can't fully visualize a situation where everyone has sqink luck. Describing and settling all the conflicts would be boring.

By the way, how do we visually *show* someone getting sqink luck. A glow or a token? Need to figure this out, and weave it back in. A halo?

And then we need to have a problem to solve. Totally stuck right now, no ideas.

It was fun having Oliver and Carol go around together and talking. But if the sqinks are everywhere, can they (we) still have fun?

February 24, 2024. Dragons.

I usually think of a novel as having three parts. Picked up this simple viewpoint in Hollywood, when they almost made Software into a movie, and I spent some time with the execs. Part one of Sqinks is done now.

The reveal at the end of part is that Winston did almost nothing to make the sqinks. They're aliens and not any kind of tech at all. An emanation of dark matter? Oh, fuck dark matter. What if we think of them as dragons in the Chinese sense? Elemental spirits.

I'm thinking this because I just went to the Chinese New Years parade with Rudy Jr, Penny, Calder, Izzy, Gus, and me. With granddaughter Zimry marching as drum majorette for the Burton High School band. Huge crowd.

We saw Zimry go by, doing a kind of robot-walk dance step, so graceful and syncopated. Occasional huge twirls of her mace (an extra-long baton).

Other marchers had hundred-foot-long dragons made of paper and cloth, the segments held up by the marchers, and huge toothy heads weaving out toward the crowd.

So now I'm stoked on dragons. Could be a nice bit for Part II.

I had a really happy ten minutes of mind at the parade. I was tired, so I sat down in a store's smooth doorway, out of the way of the foot traffic, like a homeless person, but I'm clean prof Ru, legs folded yoga style, looking up at the handsome old buildings with yellowish lights, hearing the steady tintinnation of gongs cymbals, snatches of song, hundreds of voices, occasional firecrackers, and bits of music. The feet and legs walking by, and a wonderful moving collage of leg shadows on the sidewalk, stripes parallelograms triangles and trapezoids, in multiple shades of light and dark, constantly shifting and sliding, unhurried and beautiful. My loved ones are twenty feet off, standing and watching the parade, aware of me taking my rest, unworried, leaving me to myself. I imagined all the brains in all the humans walking by, each brain with a world-image much like mine, with sights and sounds and a sense of a crowd, all of us with similar mind images, like a field of onions and us the bulbs, a field of wheat and us the heads of grain. Lightbulbs. Mirrorballs. Peaceful meat.

Such ease, sitting there.

But then someone said, "Let's go," and I did, and that was okay too, but not so peak as those five or ten minutes sitting there.

February 26, 2024. Frantic.

I've been uptight, feeling the book is dead. Battling to get out of the blind alley I blundered into, lashing out with my broadsword, cutting away all suffocating walls.

I'm adding a visual sign for being in a sqink-luck "state of grace." You glow, faintly or brightly. Like a full-body halo in religious art. Initially, before this phenomenon becomes well-known, those who are not in the know won't particularly notice that you are in fact literally glowing. They might just think that you look metaphorically radiant.

Later on of course the glow is what poker-players call a tell, but by then, I'm guessing, very many people will have sqink luck.

So today I'm plowing through the book and putting in the glows.

***

The sqinks have a sense that they created the space patterns around them. That they wrote this novel, that they dreamed up the patterns of the world. In each location they have the sense that they arranged what's next door, and their minds affect this. And time patterns, I suppose, feel arbitrary and unwilled relative to them. They're surprised that we can affect temporal flow via cause and effect. For a sqink, space synchs up smoothly at all times.

Time connection is cause and effect, which *we* understand but which is strange to sqinks.

Space connection is synchronicity, which is natural to the sqinks, but strange to us.

If we or the sqinks change worlds, that's smooth if we don't sweat that space is 3D … as the 3+1 spacetime transformed to 1+3 timespace feels awkward. But if we just think of it as 1+1 it's okay. As I just said, space connection is synchronicity, which they understand. Time connection is cause and effect, which we understand.

All very nice but it would be hella tough sledding to try and have the sqinks act this way … like they talk to one of them for a few minutes and then come back and they're like, "Oh wow, you still exist how is that even possible."

Could be done though, just during the initial "getting to know you" phases, and could be fun. And then they adapt and accept. In the same sense that we adapt and accept synchronicity.

A interesting challenge, and maybe I'll accept it. Will have to ruminate on it.

***

Here's a somewhat relevant passage from Jorge Luis Borges's amazing tale, "Tlön, Uqbar, Orbis Tertius." Tlön is a strange alternate world that the narrator learns of. In Tlön, they don't believe in the consistent existence of objects that you don't see. They deny, in a sense, our notion of cause and effect.

> Of all the doctrines of Tlön, none has caused more uproar than materialism. Some thinkers have formulated this philosophy (generally with less clarity than zeal) as though putting forth a paradox. In order to make this inconceivable thesis more easily understood, an eleventh-century heresiarch conceived the sophism of the nine copper coins, a paradox as scandalously famous on Tlön as the Eleatic *aporiae* to ourselves. There are many versions of that "specious argument," with varying numbers of coins and discoveries; the following is the most common:
>
> *On Tuesday, X is walking along a deserted road and loses nine copper coins. On Thursday, Y finds four coins in the road, their luster somewhat dimmed by Wednesday's rain. On Friday, Z discovers three coins in the road. Friday morning X finds two coins on the veranda of his house.*
>
> From this story the heresiarch wished to deduce the reality—i.e., the continuity in time of those nine recovered coins. "It is absurd," he said, "to imagine that four of the coins did not exist from Tuesday to

Thursday, three from Tuesday to Friday afternoon, two from Tuesday to Friday morning. It is logical to think that they in fact *did* exist (albeit in some secret way that we are forbidden to understand) at every moment of those three periods of time."

February 27, 2024. Chapter Lengths.

Made more progress on the novel, cleaning stuff out. The sqinks really are a type of alien now; it was unrealistic to suppose that a Valley hacker could design them.

Not aliens from another planet, aliens from the "timespace" that dark matter lives in. Still don't have the dynamics and epistemology of timespace straight.

Might as well assume that they're in some sense local, as opposed to being intergalactic.

Re-edited the chapter breaks so each is about 3K words. Tidy that way, easier for me to shape a chap if I have a target length. And can see when the escape hatch in sight. Up to 20K words. I really think I might make it. Shit, if I settle for 80K, I'm 25% done. Though I still need another big twist.

New chap, perhaps we'll go to the Floonberry labs and see some dark-matter-related processes. If they are in fact manufacturing sqinks. Which I'm starting to doubt.

Big question is: do they start selling or distributing sqinks? I'm leery of having a huge wave of them, as that kind of floods the story. They're dying out after a couple of days? And what about Moo; I see her as a somewhat different form of being. Is she perhaps an alien shepherd?

We need an enemy, and a threat or a goal. Or Carol is kidnapped and Oliver goes on a quest for her. That's an easy trad move. Maybe Carol and Diana get kidnapped, twins of Sylvia and Diana Vaughan. What did I call Diana in that story about Lynchburg? Luanne. "Monument to the Third International."

February 28, 2024. Stuck Again. Barb Ash.

What if we stayed in SF with the sqinks in the Box Farm field and the luck spreading, what if we just did that. More interesting. Don't flinch away from that. Stay there and see what happens. Go with the complicated synchronicity stuff.
***

Someone, I think Douglas Hofstadter, once wrote a little piece about what someone might do if they had a magic touch that could heal any disease, and how they could have a conveyor belt trucking millions and millions of the afflicted past the person with the healing touch. And this was boring to read about and to think about. Performative empathy. I don't want to get into the healing business here. "But how dare you not heal all mankind when you can? There can be no higher goal!" Oh god spare me that.
***

The stock exchanges, casinos, and lotteries close down almost right away as now they're all, in a sense, rigged. Winning prizes? There can no longer be prizes, I suppose.
***

Inventions! Lots of them. Lucking into things. Super high tech overnight. With pollution evasion. Lucky.

Is this supposed to lead up to a tut-tut moral like, "Beware of getting what you want."? All the luck and fulfilled wishes breed unhappiness? So boring.

What if the sqinks are using us to amplify science, making us lucky so we get further faster. Might they burn us out?

We San Francisco types are tasked with finding some lost Great Secret, which luck-driven beings have discovered before, always to end with annihilation. The Curse of the Big Aha. Judgement Day?
***

Love matches, well that's nice. A million weddings in a month.

Property disputes?

Huge starship like in District Nine, hovering over the city, the ship of the sqinks. But it's not a kit-bashed-model kind of a ship. Maybe it's a chunk of the landscape. Like that island in the sky called Laputa in *Gulliver's Travels*.
***

Carol is whisked down into a hole in the sea cave, and Oliver goes after her. Like I was saying when I first started working on this story and there was a hole in the ground.

Don't like the sea cave setup. Hole in the ground in the woods is better. Mound of sqinks like seething maggots.
***

Sitting at my desk, writing these scattered notes, waiting for Barb Ash to show up. That new woman I met. I think that in some sense she is my character Carol. My transreal life.

I'm going to show her how to use a color inkjet printer, go for a walk with her, and have pho together. Brave of her to come to my house alone. I won't try and put the make on her in the house. Wouldn't be fair.

Can hardly remember what Barb looks like or how she talks. All I know is that I've been missing her after our two first dates. Wanting to see her again. Because I'm lonely all the time.
***

I was listening to this song "The Tracks of my Tears" by Smoky Robinson and the Miracles. "Take a good look at my face, and see my smile's out of place, and if you look close see the tracks of my tears." I know so well that sense of my smile being out of place. Like talking to the SF in SF crowd about our newly dead friend Terry Bisson. And I'm smiling and making jokes, but my smile's out of place. The tracks of my tears.

***

Now it's night, nearly 10, and I had another date with Barb, quite nice. Out of habit I'm tempted to blurt out, "I love you." But I know not to do that.

I made her a really nice large-size color print of one of her photos, of some guavas, on that Hahnemühle Museum Etching paper, 13 x 19 inches. She was very happy with that.

***

I'm trying to avoid plot-death and keep my sqink story alive. Trying not to go picaresque and or to have huge random plot changes.

Gradual changes would be better. Is the book an allegory of AI? Could be. If, as I was suggesting earlier today, the sqinks were stimulators meant to make us get higher toward some transcendent revelation. Our race goes up in a little *pfft* of smoke and light. A cosmic meadow with little *pfft* flashes twinkling on it. Like lightning bugs.

***

I'm seeing space dilation within the Box Farm field. Like the size of Treasure Island. Lots of people can get in there now without rioting. Like what Moo did with her space inversion, but this is space dilation. Our space can be bent and stretched by the dark matter sqinks. Spanish moss, bayou, swampy areas, hills, redwoods, it's all in there. Claude Monet haystacks. No longer Lucky

Market, now it's Lucky Park. Oh, wait, I'm forgetting there's a big Lucky supermarket chain in SF. Just say Luck.

March 1, 2024. Eden.

So I eked out another thousand words today. Nipping and tucking. Adding maybe four pages as well. Chap 7: Eden is about half done. And I broke 20K words. Could get by with 28 Chapters. 21 more. That's a lot more plot that I need.

They're walking into the space-warp-enlarged Box Farm field, now fenced off, and there's old native trees in there and birds and lots of flying sqinks.

And now, by god, I need a big reveal. Writhing pit of sqinks. Vortex leading to picaresque adventures—no, Rudy. A Moo the size of the Graf Zeppelin Dirigible. Complete loss of time and immersion in synch, like a heavy acid trip, and I have three pages of surreal freaking, and then they stumble out. Wha hoppin?

Actually we might as well spend a (short) chapter on the surreal dark matter acid trip view, Carol and Oliver together. Need to pick off another chapter whenever possible.

He remembers some scraps of a big reveal, but he can't exactly remember what it was! (Mirroring my current state as a plot-groping author.) Oliver was fully into the sqink worldview. It granted him a view into some things to look out for. Doing this with synchronicity style remote sensing. Suddenly the world is like a snow globe landscape that Oliver can peer into. Or an aerial photo ... but it's a 3D photo like a 4D being would see. But when he comes down, a lot is gone.

And let's suppose that as they exit Eden here comes ... *the attack*! By whom I do not know.

Carol is whisked away. Again, I don't want to go too picaresque on the pursuit, maybe it could be something local. Like Carol is with the Daughters of the American Republic, the San Francisco version of that, I forget what it's called. Could be funny. Organizing a cotillion ball for the sqinks, and laying down some rules on how the sqinks appear and how they comport themselves.

Give the sqinks full shapeshifting powers? I'd rather not. But maybe that can go part way there, assuming they're still like garlands of balls.

I just about finished a painting of "Moo the Cuttle" that I've been working on. I learned that cuttles' eyes have pupils like hourglasses, I'd thought they were like the letter W.

March 5, 2024. *Expunging Dark Matter.*

So now I've got Oliver and Carol falling down a tunnel that leads to the homeland of the sqinks, where things are made of dark matter, at least according to what I've been saying. But I'm seeing a lot of problems with this set-up.

Do the humans' flesh and blood bodies really have to be converted to dark matter? Much easier if the answer is no.

Just did a little reading. Dark matter has no electromagnetic reactions at all. So its invisible and intangible. What if I just dropped all mentions of dark matter? Who fucking needs it.

Looking back, when the sqinks eat the Warhol paintings, they supposedly converted the paintings into a different substance so that they could shrink them. That was the only path I could see to make it work.

But what if they didn't convert them, but just "unmoor" the matter from Planck's constant. Tug that pesky survey-marker out of the ground. Less awkward than converting. And then you can shrink. Okay, but that's pretty hard to think about.

Alternately, and even easier, why not suppose that they simply expand the space within their bellies to hold the canvases. Like Moo did with her insides for that trip to Monterey, and like the sqinks did with the Box Farm field, and like a boa constrictor swallowing an elephant in Antoine de Saint-Exupéry, *Le Petit Prince*, where a shape that looks like a hat is alleged to be a side-view of a serpent who has swallowed an elephant.

Joke: the prince shows a drawing to the narrator, and says (bad French) "*N'ayez pas peur.*" [Don't be afraid.] And the narrator says, "*Pourquoi avez peur d'une chapeau?*" [Why be afraid of a hat?]

The sqinks come here from Sqinkland. We're not "manufacturing" them at all. They're not made of dark matter.

***

And by the way, how did Winston meet Moo? Moo appeared floating over Winston and Diana's bed. Scared Diana. Winston immediately got the legal property rights to Box Farm field. The sqinks installed themselves there.

How did Winston track what happened? What if Carol is Winston's agent. Yes. Winston set up the contact with Loulou. How? And then he decided it would be better to work through Oliver, who has some name recognition.

Winston started with Carol, who's a friend of Diana's. Was observing. Noticed that Loulou goes for a walk every day.

March 6, 2024. Enter Sqinkland.

So I got rid of dark matter, and cut it down to just one patent, and had Winston buy the Box Farm field a few days earlier, and added a subplot about Carol being an agent for Moo and Winston, and Oliver figures it out, and they quarrel and make up, and now she's fully on his side, and they're deeply in love, and they go to the grown-larger and walled-in-overnight Box Farm field, and in the middle of it they find a hole with light in the bottom, and they fall in, and I do a tap-dancing routine about how I don't know what to write next but I'll write it anyway.

And now I need some ideas for effects and action and a big character or two in Sqink land. And they have to assign a mission to Oliver and Carol.

A simple effect is to see spacetime trails over there, as Sqinkland is in some sense perpendicular to our time. And I can get a few things from the trails, but not all that much. I wrote about it already and that fills, like, half a page.

There might need to be both a good and an evil boss over there, or two of them competing like the noble and Death playing chess in Bergman's The Seventh Seal. Or maybe a wasp nest with a million sqinks hatching, or a homeostatic gustatorial omnisapient lollygagging flabbergasting view of Earth's future, its downfall, and how to save it.

And then and then and then. Jesus Christ, how am I going to fill 21 chapters. I'm working on chap 7, and I'm out of plot, and I have to write 14 chaps more. This is impossible.

But yet, when I'm actually writing, I'm so happy, and having so much fun. It's been wonderful the last few days.

Burn a candle to the muse. And maybe she'll make love to me again.

March 10, 2024. Missing Moon?

Haven't been doing much writing at the growing tip the last few days. Did a bunch of revising. Maybe I was in the back yard painting on a picture one day. Trying to imagine Sqinkland.

Went hiking with Jon Pearce at Rancho del Canada Oro one day. And went to the supermarket. And then and hung out Rudy Jr.

Had yet another date with Barb, and kissed her, so great.

Anyway, getting back into writing today, before the Oscars start at four, and I had this random absurd idea for the quest that I need for Oliver and Carol so they'll have something to do in Part II of the novel, now coming up.

The idea? Sqinkland lost their moon. A fairytale type problem. It seeped over to our side, to Earth. And you can notice this on our side as our moon now looks odd.

What phase is the moon? Well, that's the moon right now that I'm asking about. It's waxing gibbous, which means a bit larger than half. The March full moon is called the Worm Moon because that's when the earth thaws and the worms return from underground. Calling all sqinks.

Writing the lost moon quest request … it's ridiculous. A case of auto-ChatGPT, that is a case of me choosing the first random Rudy-style extension that comes to mind.

March 11, 2024. The Sqink Quest.

Think of something better than a lost Moon, Rude Dog! A jewel? Something more in the spirit of what comes before in the novel. Jokey old Hollywood screwball romance comedy. The style I'm having fun with. The Oliver & Carol routines.

The problem shouldn't be so huge and boring as a lost moon. I mean, give me a break. The prob needs to be, at least at the experiential level, human scale.

And maybe there can be some giant thing underlying the adventure, and that could be something huge like, e. g., a Sqinkland theft of our (oh no!) Moon. But anything huge would only appear in a reveal that's at least two-thirds of the way through the book.

For now we want a quite minor and tactical kind of mission. Organized along Raymond Chandler private detective lines. Clue, clue, clue … reveal. As in Chandler it doesn't have to be all about the final reveal. It's the colorful steps along the way that matter. Each chapter introduces a wacky new character.

I could do that, and I'd want to be mixing the synchronicity with the cause-effect. Seems possible, in principle, but would take some inspiration along the way.

I won't have to plan it, just go the "spontaneous bop prosody" route, a process of discovery, not trying to deduce it a priori.

Now, where does this picaresque private detective routine take place? My reflexive thought is to have it be a search across Sqinkland. As in *White Light* or as in *Spaceland* or Million Mile Road Trip.

But let's make it fun and easy. They visit Sqinkland, they come back, and then they bounce around San Francisco and the Bay Area. My transreal beat, with transreal characters, akin to *Hacker and the Ants* and *Juicy Ghosts*. Transreal cyberpunk Silicon Valley SF novels are one of specialties. And try to make it a love story as well. Gotta have love.

Possible twist. All these freaks who Oliver and Carol meet have had sqinks in their lives for several years. The infiltration began well before the action of the novel. Akin to the late 1960s introduction of LSD in the Bay Area, well before it hit the news.

The sqink presence is a distributed alternate reality that the public doesn't yet know about.

It's like, what if all that spirit power stuff is *actually true*. Ditto meditation, mind-improvement, higher reality, witchcraft, mind manifestation, alien contacts ... all of that woo woo stuff. It's all true. But true only because in each and every case some sqinks are involved.

Yes!

We'd want to have two rival groups of sqinks. One is for the low-level infiltration they've been doing all along. The low-level partnership that enriches the realities of both worlds. And the other group is for full-on invasion and domination—which is of course a standard SF trope, as in Heinlein's *The Puppet Masters* and in my take-off-version of Heinlein's book, *Master of Space and Time*.

For the twist, it might be that the first guy they meet on the bench in Sqinkland is bad. Sort of the queen of Sqinkland. She's for the big invasion. Or, keeping my options open, maybe you think she's bad, and then you realize she's good.

Now how about the indie sqink contacts. Let's call them the *seers*. Familiar, applicable word. How about the seers, what are they like?

***

I was discussing this with two outspoken women whom I happened to be sitting with at the coffee shop just now. Lauren and Robin. I brought it up to gain insight; I said something like, "What if freaks who think they have special powers really do have these powers, at least some of them do, thanks to the fact that a sqink lives with them, that is, the sqink is in their mind, or slimes around in their house, or haunts them like a ghost, and has done so for a number of years?"

I like the sqink that slimes around the house. Like a very nasty pet dog. Good visual way to write it. Could also look like a snake or a bird or even an ant. You might say these sqink-assisted people have weird pets. Scary centipedes. Cute mice. Each seer's pet sqink looks different. Like those little Native American carvings.

And Lauren and Robin started bringing up zillions of cases of mentally ill people whom they know, or have known, or have in their families, or have heard of: paranoids, schizophrenics, psychotics, burnt-out acidheads, and unhappy people with crippling delusions.

Lauren said, "When you're truly touched by a higher spirit, the spirit never tells you to something cruel, evil, or destructive." And that's a nice thought.

But then Robin and I bring up those who are criminally insane, or who imagine the devil or an evil spirit is telling them what to do, and they feel compelled to obey.

And then there's the religious egotists who imagine that God has chosen them to lead a cult. And the mental patients who think saucer people are talking in their heads. Or those with "ideas of reference," imagining that everything around them is a sign.

Unfortunately these psychotic-like episodes are very nearly the same as what I'm extolling as incidents of synchronicity. In other words the illusion of synchronicity can be a type of mental illness.

- Everyone on the bus is talking about me.
- People on TV are talking about me.

- The TV is in fact talking directly TO me.
- My thoughts cause events to occur.
- Headlines are messages to me.
- And so are the branches of the trees.

Like Oliver and Carol are with a completely screwy person.

Carol: "There's no sqink here. This guy is just plain nuts."

Oliver: "But maybe the idea that someone is 'crazy' is a regressive social construct?"

Carol: "Oh, wait, I found the sqink. See that mole on his cheek? It's crawling around."

The Seer: "Flubba goop!"

March 12, 2024. Indie Sqinks.

I like the idea of a distributed group of sqinks in the Valley. Maye just a few of them. Five or ten. Each of them is paired up with some person.

Have the indie sqinks been here for a long time? Nah, for the sake of simplifying the novel, it's better to suppose that all of the visiting sqinks arrived recently, along with Moo, who made a tunnel to get there.

Oliver and Carol are going to visit a series of them. Like a treasure-hunt party game, going from lead to lead. Or like, again, a Raymond Chandler novel.

Missing piece: what are they looking for? What do they *think* they're looking for? What's at stake? Still don't know.

Meanwhile I'm thinking of some colorful personages who might serve as the partners of the sqinks? Some contemporary, some remembered.

Interesting people I've met: John Walker, Roxie, Paul Mavrides, Faustin Bray, Carol Mellberg, Gunnar Vatvedt,

Bart Nagel. Katie Rubio, Allison Kennedy, Ken Goffman, Marc Powell, Kathleen Hall, Jon Pearce, Ronna Schulkin, Jericho, Linda, Gary Singh, Marc Laidlaw, Richard Kadrey, Eileen Gunn, Susan Protter, Paul DiFilippo ¼ and now Barb Ash.

And I can invent characters from whole cloth. Like Riscky Pharbeque in *Hacker and the Ants*, he was a good one.

As for the sqinks, we've got Moo, the indie sqinks and the big sqink, Mumper who is the mean one on the bench in Sqinkland. A tendril runs out from one foot, branching across the city.

So, again, what is the quest?

Mumper, the big sqink in the green shirt, she wants them to seek out the Earth indie sqinks and kill these sqinks with powerful electric shocks? Moo nixes that, and suggests that they cajole the sqinks and their users into joining Mumper's cause.

Mumper, again, wants to flood Earth with sqink reality. Engulf it. Of course, this is a trad SF invader's goal. And is an objection correlative for our culture being eaten by LLM, genetic algorithms, ChatGPT and the AI still to come.

And how would Oliver and Carol be expected to help Mumper? Mumper wants them to ferret out and kill or convert the indie sqinks.

Carol and Oliver of course are on the indie sqinks side, and their goal becomes the closure of the Box Farm portal, and the banishment of Mumper.

Where does Moo stand in this? She's seemingly Mumper's acolyte, but she's secretly on the side of the indy sqinks, or, more accurately, she's out for herself. She wants to replace Mumper as Queen of the sqinks. The indie sqink users or seers are zonked out of their gourds on sqink vibes. That's kinda why they haven't been in touch. Their minds have been overly amplified by the rebel sqinks. Whoops! Psychedelics creeping into the picture again.

March 17, 2024. Up in SF.

Spending a couple of nights at Rudy & Penny's. Sticking around so I can go to a memorial event for my uber-hacker friend and mentor, John Walker, who fell down a damn flight of stone stairs, alone in his house in Switzerland. Event in Mill Valley. My friends and loved ones are dropping like flies.

And Tuesday morning I head down to Pacific Grove with Barb for two nights. I was surprised how readily she agreed. She wants to get out, wants to have fun. Separate rooms at this point. Very excited about the trip.

It's so crazy to sit on Barb's couch with her, cuddling. So high-school. And at our age? After fifty years of marriage each? Utterly insane. It's the only game in town

My friend Jon Pearce says women think through the meanings of affairs much more deeply than we men do.

Whatever. I'm glad I have *something* going on. Barb and I had a very nice date the other day, doing things around San Jose and then sitting on that couch. Feels so good to hold a woman close and to chat with her and stare into her eyes and murmur sweet words. Like rain on a desert. It's been over a year for me. I like Barb's voice. And she says I'm handsome.

***

As usual I'm struggling for the next scene of my novel. I added a bit in an all-but-endless taqueria. I might flesh this out so that something about it relates to the plot. With a dizzying montage of quicker and quicker kaleidoscopic *clicks*. I don't always worry about the details.

Go full surreal on the task and fill in whatever hits me. Later I'll find ways to make it fit. A dwindling perspective with yin-yang black-white light at the end.

And now, *pouf*, they're back in the Eden-like forest on Earth, by the sqink portal tunnel that Moo dug.

***

Later in the day. Had a great, jolly dinner in Vega, a Bernal Heights restaurant that our family loves. Just me and the three local grandkids: the twin girls and young Calder. Missed Sylvia terribly in this group, but it was fun, in a different way, to have the kids to myself. Raucous and cheerful. We ordered four tiramisus for desert and our heads practically exploded. So much sugar at once!

The novel's moving along well today. I wrote a few more scenes in Sqinkland, setting it up for visit to Paul Mavrides and to a version of Faustin Bray. They already had roles in, respectively, *Freeware*, and in *Hacker and the Ants*. Great characters. I think of Fellini and Bergman, using the same colorful actor-friends again and again.

March 21, 2024. Pacific Grove.

Great view out the morning window in my loft attic room at Centrella Hotel in Pacific Grove. I'm here with Barb. The windows don't have sash weights, so I have to prop them open with wooden hangers from the large wardrobe. Wonderful lighting effect of the rising sun's sideways beams on the pale tan hanger. Roofs, and the blue sea to the misty horizon. Blue dome overhead, shading from gray to magnesium. Contrails. Two sparse monkeypod pines.

Oliver and Carol take flight through this window.

Today is exactly 60 years to the day since I met Sylvia on the charter bus from Swarthmore to DC.

March 23, 2024. Birthday.

Rudy Jr and his family came down yesterday, it was wonderful. My 78th birthday. I made a chicken stew that they all liked and we played a few silly games that Penny brought. Cozy and loving. I'm so lucky to have my family.

Such a difference from birthday #77, two or three months after Sylvia's death. I got up, came upstairs, and broke down in tears at the dining table, even though dear Isabel was here with a few treats for me.

I didn't go into the heavy grief on this year. Cheered by the grandkids and by thoughts of Barb.

***

How do Carol (now being played by Barb) and Oliver (still me) end up in Pacific Grove so they can fly out the window like I visualized the other day? Maybe something to do with that guy who wanted to buy the company, and what were all the made-up names involved? Bengt Oberg, Floonberry, Briefcase Dynamics, Winston Trotter.

Do Carol and Oliver have sqinks to ride after the Eden scene? Or a sqink to do the space inversion shrink method of travel? I think stick to flying, that's visually much more interesting. Like flying with the cone shells in *Mathematicians in Love*.

I ought to keep Moo around for the trip. Moo will be the Helper figure in the Campbellian "Myth of the Hero" monomyth. We can nail down the fact that Moo is very definitely against Mumper. And we are (mistakenly) sure that we can trust Moo absolutely, with no fear of a double-cross.

Moo floats off with Skeeze right after the return from Sqinkland but fairly soon she'll come back. Bringing big trouble.

What's waiting for Carol and Oliver outside the fence? Lots of press, and people yearning for sqink luck. We might run part of a chapter on the chaos when they come back. But I already did that. And I don't want to jump right into a new chase scene.

Let's say that they step through the vanishing point of a wall mural painting. Carol makes the mural. Or they use Carol's camera, and they see the perspective point on the LED on the back of the camera.

Maybe they get to Paul Mavrides's studio that way. Oh, hell, just drive there in Oliver's car. And meet Paul's sqink friend.

***

I've lost track of the book's plot, to tell the truth. I've been so distracted by Barb that I'm hardly thinking about it. Barb is coming to spend the day with me on Tuesday. I can hardly wait. We can hold hands and take a long walk and maybe watch a movie and cuddle. Paradise.

The last two weeks I was pounding on the novel almost every day. Right now I don't feel like diving back into that. Shoulder to the wheel, nose to the grindstone. I'm taking a birthday vacation, at least for today.

It rained a lot last night, but maybe I can go in the back yard to paint for a while. Or paint in the basement with my canvas on the workbench. Or just putter around gardening. To start with, I might as well take a shower.

***

I really do need a fresh plot twist. I was thinking of having Carol be kidnapped and Oliver has to fetch her. But I enjoy Carol's presence so much that I don't want to do that. I want to keep writing conversations between her and me.

***

Right now the best thing is to print out what I have and read it, and hope I see some hints about what could happen. Build up momentum for another jump forward.

Tomorrow is Palm Sunday, I'll go to church.

April 1, 2024. At Isabel's.

I was up in San Francisco for a memorial event for my SF writer friend Terry Bisson. Organized by a local group called SF in SF.

My eulogy went really well. It's been so long since I was in a group of my peers, that is, other SF writers. Some of them may think they're more important than me, but they're not. I'm the Shadow Captain.

I noticed something different about myself at the SF event, and again when talking to Izzy and her husband Gus at dinner when I got up here to where they live, which is Fort Bragg CA, near Mendocino.

I'm chattier and friendlier and warmer than I've been in a year or two. You might say I'd forgotten how to be happy. And it's changing all at once—thanks to Barb. I feel like we two are helping each other escape the quicksand of sorrow. And having a great time doing it.

I emailed this thought to Barb, and she wrote back: "What a lovely and touching message. We *are* helping each other. Our relationship is going to make both of us happier and younger."

I'm on the inside track.
***

As I said before, the *Sqinks* novel still needs to be three times as long as what I've got—and I need some drastic addition to the plot.

The raw alien invasion for the sake of power or exploitation is stale. Maybe they're not all coming over here.

Just sending a few for a certain purpose. Key question: what do they want from us? What are they using us for?

What *are* the sqinks, transreally speaking? What do they stand for? AI sims of our world?

Side angle: A common move is to have two or more groups of invading aliens.

Would be fun to have the first happy days of sqinkdom with, as I said, everyone being lucky. I felt that way on Friday when I went up for Terry's memorial, my mood so elated by my assignation with Barb. Everything clicking.

Maybe they have probs, and if they can make our world better, then their world gets better. And if we make their world better, our world gets better. Reciprocal performative altruism for the sake of personal gain.

Restating this, if something bad is happening in Sqinkland, the only way they can change their world is to improve *our* world. Entangled worlds.

April 2, 2024. *Wolfram Says.*

What do the invading aliens want from us?
I asked my genius friend Stephen Wolfram. His answer.

> Anthropology? Understand an alien mind to understand yours better? [And leverage someone else's irreducible computation.]
> At least, that's what I would want.

A cryptic and gnomic response. Let me break it down.

If we regard minds as computations, these are "irreducible" computations, that is, processes whose outcomes cannot be readily predicted. The only way to predict the outcome of a thought process is simply to emulate it all the way through. This restriction applies to everyone, even to aliens.

So how would looking at human thought processes give an alien some "leverage" on predicting their own thought processes?

> If I'm so curious about how a whale thinks about the world, and believe I might "expand myself in rulial space" / "expand my paradigms" by knowing ... perhaps the aliens will be curious too
>
> I don't think it's so much leveraging a single human mind as the whole consistent(?) structure of knowledge/language/culture that we've built up.
>
> Though of course I'm projecting.

April 4, 2024. Mulling Over Wolfram's Words.

So, okay, Wolfram's not talking about the irreducible nature of the evolution of an individual mind, but about the evolution of a social group. And that goes back to "anthropology."

And I've been suggesting that it might be *entangled* anthropology. That is, the evolution of the one society might mirror and model and influence the evolution of the other. That's gonna work in somehow, later on.

There was my earlier thing about Sqinkland being patterned by synchronicity, and ours by cause and effect. It would be great if I can tie this into mutual mirroring. Each of us filling in a lack for the other.

They don't know "What's next?" and we don't know, "What's over there?"

Sqinks walking directly into walls, due to lack of cause-effect reasoning?

Perhaps there's a pattern of a synch society teaming up with a causal society. Each is so-to-say leveraging its powers on the powers of the other.

Perhaps you'd get some really extreme mental power by combining cause-and-effect linear computation with all-at-once parallel computation. Not unlike my beloved continuous-valued cellular automata. That could be a late development in the novel.

To start with, get rid of the plan for a volcanic sqink invasion. Do *not* want invasion. Let's work on that error first. [In the end, I do go for an invasion, a big one, with a billion sqinks.]

April 5, 2024. More Barb. Sqink Tourism.

Barb came over for the afternoon again. . Wonderful, wonderful day. I'm truly falling in love with her. My face gets tired from smiling, like the way it does when I'm with the kids. I'm happier than I've been in a couple of years. A miracle.

***

Another fix for *Sqinks*. I might say that each sqink is here to partner up with an individual human to get to know their mind and mode of thought. Like people buying dogs … or dogs seeking masters … or kinky lovers seeking alien mates.

Or like an overseas exchange student lodging with a family. Let's go with that. A sqink lodges with a human family. And then the human host lodges with a sqink family!

Let's dig into the foreign exchange student trope. Oliver's and Carol's first trip to Sqinkland (which I'm just now writing) is chaotic, surreal. And I'm going to rush off on a picaresque journey in there. I'm going to bring

Oliver and Carol back on Earth to see the sqinks settling in. But then, later, have them go back to Sqinkland (transreal mirror of my planned trip to London with Barb) and give them a guest house AirBnb exchange-student type experience.

Perfect! Multichapter scenario! Oliver and Carol lodging with the sqinks. Almost breaks up their relationship—but love conquers all.

Also note that if the sqinks *are* telepathic, the partnership doesn't absolutely have to involve "moving in together," although for clarity it should. Maybe once in a while they *don't* move in immediately, but they find you. The back-alley hooker comes to your house. Like, they're waitin' for you at home.

"Eek, sqink!" "Don't worry, I'm your new assistant."

This is a nice gloss on acquiring a (possibly uninvited) AI assistant. Like the "pilot" that shows up on my Windows toolbar now. Perfect. The pilot is mining my data, but helping be with its hive-mind record of its compatriots mining lots of the other humans.

That's the transreal hook I was looking for, yes. The sqinks "are" AI assistants. How would it feel to be a lodger in the cyberspace land of AIs?.

Keeping it butt-simple, if a sqink lives with you, they're certainly going to give you good (probably good, unless sqink has nasty ulterior motives, and eventually they will) advice about what to do. Just like how the pilot or google-assistant knows shit from the web.

Do I *really* need for the sqinks to be telepathic?

Always best to whittle down the number of wonders being invoked. At what key points in the book are they actually using telepathy? To some extent telepathy drags the story down, as then characters can't sneak and surprise each other.

[In the end, I do have something like telepathy based on, wait for it, twirlware.]

I need to clarify the role of Mumper if she's not the Supreme General of an invasion army. She's more like a chief scientist? Or, no, the Queen. And she's only letting a certain number of sqinks go over to start with, but may send more? What's the story with too many sqinks or too few, why does this matter to the characters?.

I'm starting to say that Moo is a tour guide, and the visiting sqinks are the tourists she leads. Mumper could be, you might say, the head of a travel agency, and Moo works for her.

Mumper's true appearance should be quite multifarious. Like a P. K. Dick scramble suit. A crystal. A multidimensional polytope. Mumper is in fact managing many travel groups at once. No just to Earth, but to Galaxy Z, and Zoombar, and Level #669, etc.

Transreal move: mirror my growing romance with Barb as the growing love affair between Oliver and Carol. Put it right in there. Carol's been Barb for a while now. The other day I told Barb she's in my novel, and she seemed to like that.

I didn't realize how deeply Oliver would fall in love with Carol. And that's what happening in the "real world." So write about it!

April 9, 2024. *Four and a Half Hours.*

Today's Tuesday. I'm planning a two-week trip to London with Barb, finding Airbnb room, planes, etc. Sunday she came over and it was like a beautiful dream. Wonderful woman. This is the best thing that's happened to me since Sylvia died. If I lean close enough to Barb to smell her natural fragrance, it's a sensual thrill.

"Why did you choose this woman?"

"I liked the way she smelled."

It was the same way with Sylvia. The pleasure of the scent announces a pheromonal fit. Not exactly *scent*. Something subtler than that, not obvious to the conscious mind. A feeling of ease and comfort.

My heart pounds, thinking of Barb. When I talked to her on the phone today, she was giggling like a schoolgirl. Smitten. Same as me.

"I can't believe you're real," she says, very satisfied with how I'm turning out. "Are you real?"

"I'm real," I assure her. "You'll see when you visit."

On Sunday, Barb's birthday, we're going up to SF to spend two nights in an inexpensive hotel on Union Square. I got two separate rooms as she still prefers. She thinks it'll be exciting. And it will be.

Kind of reckless that we're doing that trip to London so soon. "What if we find out we don't like each other," Barb worries.

"We'll just have to suffer through a luxurious vacation with good food and sights and romance," I say. "Tough it out."

It's like someone threw the two of us out of an airplane and we're in free fall. And who knows where we'll land.

She still forbids me to say, "I love you."

April 15, 2024. In SF.

I brought Barb up to SF yesterday for her birthday. We saw a great acrobatics show at the old Club Fugazi in North Beach. It was Chinese Youth Day, so lots of Chinatown kids in the audience.

The young woman ringmaster asked if anyone in the audience had been here in the Sumer of Love and I held up my hand. The only one. Sylvia and I were here for a math conference at Berkeley, and came over to Golden

Gate Park to check things out. Maybe it was a year or two later than 1967, but close enough.

Later Barb and I were leaning against a wall on Stockton Street, hugging for a long time, and some of the Chinese kids from the Fugazi Club show walked by and recognized me from my big shock of white hair and they called out, "Summer of Love," not exactly jeering, more like cheering that here we were, still doing it, embracing on the street. I felt proud.

Stopped in at this ancient Grant Street bar, the Li Po, with huge paper lanterns inside, the bartender almost threw me out for asking for non-alcoholic drinks, but he relented. We needed a place to sit for a while. A lot of hoofing. It was cozy in there, and I noticed they had a back room. Good setting for a scene of my novel: the back room at the Li Po.

What is it with this woman? I'm so infatuated with her. Like I said, it's like rain on my desert. And I'm rain on a desert for her.

I'm freely telling her I love her now, and she likes that. And saying it makes it somehow more true. She's surprisingly innocent and unexperienced, doesn't know her way around San Francisco at all. Even though she grew up in the Bay Area, and has lived near San Jose for fifty years.

She appreciates having me as her guide. "Man about town," she calls me. I love the gratitude and praise. She's my special friend.

After dinner, we lay on my bed in the dark, propped up on pillows, not making out, just being cozy there, talking and talking. About our relationship, like the (short) history of how we met, and what we've done, and how we feel about each other—I remember this phase with my college and high-school girlfriends so many years go.

Bonding. And listening to her personal history, and to her thoughts about things. I'm keeping in mind my grief therapist's dictum: "Women want to be *heard*."

April 15-17, 2024. *Your Grandpa is Wild.*

Today Barb and I went for a huge breakfast at David's Delicatessen, then killed time in the room, then went to SFMOMA and looked at photos and at a Yayoi Kusama mirror house, had a snack, walked back to the hotel. Bewildering and delightful.

Went to the SF Botanical Garden, and I shook lots of blooming-tree blossom-petals down onto Barb and she, wonderful woman that he is, loved it. It's the old spring courting rite that I developed with Sylvia in 1967, and here I am, reflexively doing it again, like some kind of bower-bird. And perhaps Barb might deduce this, but she didn't ask, she stayed in the present, enjoying our moment together.

Went over to Rudy Jr.'s house at 6 pm for Calder's birthday dinner with Rudy's little family, casual and cheerful, eating homemade pizzas and a tiramisu made by Penny herself.

Barb bravely stood up to the family scrutiny, looked good, spoke well, and I think made a good impression, She liked the family and their free-flowing relationships. She found it amusing and strange to have the kids calling me "grandpa," which is not at all how she thinks of me!

Barb especially liked Penny; perhaps the two of them have an immediate bond because they're both beautiful women. Beautiful outside and beautiful inside, as Barb put it, talking about Penny, and a phrase that I'd apply to Barb as well. Oh, and Barb and Penny are both non-Ruckers.

Back at my house Barb stared into my face, and asked, "Do you *like* me?"

A tough question. I romantically love Barb. But she was asking if I like her as a pal, as a companion. Trust a woman to put her finger on any weakness in a relationship.

And of course it's hard for Barb to match my friendship with Sylvia, who was, after all, my twin of fifty-five years, completely on my wavelength. But would I find another exact Sylvia in my dating pool? Don't go there! Every woman is different.

And, yes, I like Barb, even love her, and date by date I'm more of a pal with her. We're talking in increasingly relaxed ways, and Barb, initially somewhat reticent, is opening up and telling me more about herself, and expressing her deeper feelings. Keep in mind also that, as time goes on, our relationship grows, and we're more and more at ease with each other.

I'm making a conscious effort not to be bossy, or contradicting, or judgmental, and to let her freely talk. And we're repeatedly discussing these desirable points of conversational etiquette, and laughing at each other, and the issues of who's bossy and who isn't, and when they are, and how we can relax and adjust and let things glide.

I tell her I'm learning to say, "Yes, Barb." And to think she's perfect. And, why not? You don't go into a relationship at our age and expect to change your partner. Accept, accept, accept. Let it ride. And, says she, don't say she's perfect.

And vice-versa of course, though Barb is now telling me what to do more than she did before, as a woman will do when you're intimate with her, and, again, it's up to me to accept this, and even to be grateful if what she says is right, and if it's not right, then I need to let it slide, and don't be resentful, or act like I'm fighting for my life, let her talk, and in the end that's all I want, for Barb to be talking to me, no matter what she says. I want to hear her wonderful voice.

We're feeling more like twins all the time. Slowly getting there.

When I hug Barb, I feel a wonderful flow of energy entering my chest. Several minutes may pass. And when we move apart, our arms trail along each other and we end up holding hands.

Barb's never in a rush to terminate a connection, and I love that. We have time. Time for love. If we're sitting on a bench, flirting, petting, canoodling—before you know it, an hour has passed.

Love it, love it, love it. There's an old slang word that describes me these days: a *mooncalf*. A person so dizzy with love and besotted by pheromones that they have no idea what they're doing. Huh?

I didn't think I'd ever be this happy again.

April 23, 2024. Cool Scene at Paul's.

I'm once more trying to roll the novel forward. It's a big stone that's somehow gotten a corner stuck in a dip. Won't roll further.

I polished the Sqinkland chapter, making it clear that the bossy Queen there, Mumper, she wants Carol and Oliver to let a big wave of sqinks into Earth. Supposedly the Hundred, that is, the sqinks who got in, supposedly they're somehow blocking Gunnar from sending in a stream of a thousand sqinks.

Why does Mumper want to send more sqinks? For money? To have the sqinks fetch something that she wants. Human brains? Good classic move, goes right back to my third novel Software. Actual brains would be more fun. The old ways are the best ways.

To soften this, the sqinks give a stolen brain some type of body over there in Sqinkland. Call it a braincozy. And, get this, they install a sqink inside the donor's skull! A squatter. A parasite. A tourist.

The braincozies are better than having the Sqinkland human brains being brains in jars. Oliver and Carol will have noticed some of those braincozies on their first visit to Sqinkland. I was thinking of having the braincozies be large cockroaches, with a bunch of them in a building like an old schoolhouse or orphanage, scuttling around, and being interviewed by sqinks seekers, or being assigned gig work. But, nah, we want fleshy blobs.

April 28-29, 2024. Braincozies.

Let's say we have Twelve sqinks on Earth, plus Moo. Moo brought them through a big tunnel, the same one that Moo, Skeeze, Oliver, and Carol fall through.

When Moo brought the Twelve through in the first place, the tunnel widened to its present size, about ten feet across. I have this notion that there might be some kind of thread connecting the visitor sqinks back to Skinkland. The threads comprising what mathematicians call a fiber bundle.

How did Moo's Twelve sqinks end up all over the Box Farm field? Well, once they're here, the can relocate.

A sqink on Earth maintains a fiber connection to Sqinkland. That thread that goes through the tunnel. They might own a braincozy on Sqinkland. And when they cut out a human brain, the brain travels along the thread and settles inside the braincozy, like I said.

What does the braincozy look like? As I mentioned, I was thinking a cockroach, but maybe a hovering crystal ball. Give the ball has a number of floating eyes, maybe five of them. And the ball has to have room for a human brain.

Stay-at-home sqinks like to look at the braincozies; a type of entertainment. And if a human brain is inside the ball, it's more interesting to look at. The braincozies like goldfish bowls and maybe the human brain is scaled down in size to be a like a goldfish, and it swims up to the edge of bowl, and presses against the glass, staring out. The brain didn't bring eyes along, although maybe it should, or maybe the braincozy can spare an eye that connects to the visiting brain.

Can the brain move the braincozy around and have a kind of life down there? Well, sure, why not. They fly. The braincozies aren't like glass; they're rubbery and they bounce off each other. Like a 3D game of billiards. And on Earth, the sqink in your skull can walk its commandeered human body around. It's symmetric this way, and symmetry is good.

Need more about the place where the human-brain-hosting braincozies live. I don't think the 19th Century Sutro Baths natatorium is a good choice. Something more like Hans Castorp's TB resort in *The Magic Mountain*? No, no. Make it simpler. How about Esalen with the hot springs and the bluffs— yes. Braincozy body balls bopping around Esalen with human-brains inside. Little ecospheres. Each with a shred of seaweed, and a few tiny shrimp.

Another issue.

How might the Twelve sqinks cut off Sqinkland invaders' access to Moo's tunnel?

Paul's sqink Doob suggests: "All we have to do is to stop thinking about Mumper. Stop thinking about Sqinkland. Stop reinforcing our fond memories. Abandon our nostalgia for the homeland. Let that shrivel up. Go fully ex-pat. And the tunnel shrinks down to a subdimensional fiber bundle, and no way that stupid pig Mumper is ever gonna find it.

Let's have a visual scene of the tunnel shrinking.

But if at even *one* of the Earthside sqinks Twelve misses Sqinkland enough, that leaves the tunnel wide enough that Mumper and his customers can find the hole and can wriggle through.

A traitor in the crowd. That's a scene. Developing that one. There just happen to be Twelve sqinks, as it's a traditional number, and one of them's a rat..

The rat sqink might in fact living in a the skull of human body and is, oddly, in love with the human brain he displaced, and wants to let the brain come back.

So the rat betrays the Twelve and goes over to Moo and Mumper, and the rat's force keeps the tunnel open just far enough that a sqink-settler tidal-wave can bust through.

To be clear, Moo is fully on Mumper's side from the beginning of the book—until later on Moo "sees the light" and goes over to the good side, and closes the tunnel.

But for now, Moo *is* trying to be pleasant, and she's not being too heavy about her and Mumper's plan, and she's using double-talk, but she *is* for the bad guys.

Or something like that.

April 30 - May 3, 2024. Tunnel Timing Outline.

Re. the tunnel, let's lay out the timing. As written in the current draft, when Carol and Oliver go through the tunnel to Sqinkland, the tunnel is wide open, so why wouldn't Mumper be sending emigres already?

Note that I *do* want the tunnel open at first, as it's a good narrative and visual effect.

Let's say that Mumper and Moo are holding back, and not rushing through the invasion because they think they have plenty of time, and they don't realize the Twelve will rebel and pinch the tunnel closed.

Might as well have a visual of a big crowd of Mumper's customers, ready to go. These might be the sqinks in that Sqinkland taqueria.

Complication is that Mumper might pressure the Twelve by threatening to harm their base bodies.

***

Might Oliver and Carol actually *see* Doob swapping out Paul's brain. Like, go ahead and do this and, as I like to pronounce. "Don't hoard the reveal."

This prompts a new issue: if you're a sponsor of one of the Twelve sqinks, and if you swap out your sponsor's brain, might you still oppose the open tunnel and the invasion? Well, maybe. It could still be a matter of that first-arrivals-only.

And it would be maybe a little two-faced of Doob in Paul's head be running this rap. But it might be funny. Maybe Paul *likes* it. He probably would.

May 6, 2024. Match Humans with the Sqinks.

It might not actually be Twelve. Only as many as the plot needs.

I'm tracking this in a table that's in the "Writing Tools" section at the end of this volume.

***

The *Sqinks* (plus one)

Moo, Lilac, Doink, Xavier, Flubsy, Skeeze, Doob, Do-Re-Mi,

Doink got killed by the police.

Moo killed Skeeze, then revived Skeeze.

I lost track of Lilac, what is she doing now? Let's match her with a human sponsor. Ditto for Xavier and Flubsy
***

Scenes in the novel. I visited Paul the painter, now with Iris the choreographer, who next? Maybe a mathematician, that would be good, maybe Gosper or Hellerstein. And Wolfram too.

As it happens, I'm having breakfast with Wolfram Tuesday morning at 8 am. Yes, I'll definitely use that meeting. Meanwhile how about Terry Bisson as a mechanic, like Oily Al from *Spacetime Donuts*. Linda as a costume maker. Ronna as a painter, but I already have Paul as a painter, could Ronna be a potter? And Carol Mellberg. Judy Bisson / Sylvia and their quilts. Loulou is a VR designer / AI artist.

More sponsors. Are Oliver and Carol specifically sponsors? They really ought to have personal sqinks of their own. Well, Lilac was Carol's … but I lost track of her. Need to bring her back in. How about Loulou? Her sqink was Doink, she died, but she came back.

Diana and Winston? Yes, go visit them too.

Doing this, with the idea of all these creatives having pet sqinks, it dramatizes the idea of the new AI, that every kind of knowledge worker can have a pet AI to help them. So this becomes a "topical meaning" of *Sqinks*. And I kind of half-suspected that, but now it's more clear. And to get sales and reviews I can pound on that a bit more, but not, I hope to the point of being corny and obvious. (I think Sylvia liked that phrase, "corny and obvious." Something she was *not*.)

May 7, 2024. Wolfram at Synbiobeta.

Met up with Stephen Wolfram at this conference in San Jose, "synbiobeta," intended to bring together developers of new bio-tech apps and big investors. A pass costs $3K, but Stephen got me a free one. In the huge San Jose conference center; haven't gone into the trade fair hall yet.

Had breakfast with Stephen. As usual, he immediately starts blasting a firehose stream of ideas at me, and as usual, I interrupt him after a while and tell him some of my ideas. Immensely rewarding.

For me, Wolfram is up there with Kurt Gödel, John Walker, and William Gibson. The conversation is rapid-fire, almost like telepathy.

We share so many of our ideas and worldviews, that we use very condensed references to certain large ideas. Infinite divisibility, incompressible computations, nature-based minds, hydrodynamics, and so on.

We share the key dictum: "determinism + unpredictability = illusion of free will". We call a computation incompressible if there is, even in principle, no way to speed it up. Nearly all naturally occurring and interesting processes behave like incompressible computations, and are, for us, unpredictable. You can't think faster than you can think. You imagine you have free will but you don't. And it doesn't matter.

He thinks the new AI is being overhyped: "Extrapolated from a single data point," that is the great leap forward of ChatGPT 3.

He liked my *Juicy Ghosts* idea of having "gossip molecules" that communicate and instantiate your neurochemical state, via pheromones, hormones, etc.

He's always open to new ideas, and was intrigued by my belief in the absolute continuum, as opposed to his ruliad-based notion of quantized space and time.

He thinks "dark matter" is akin to "heat," in being a property of the spacetime quanta, as opposed to being a substance, cf. phlogiston.

I raised the issue that surely a galaxy has a mind and is conscious, but I don't have a sense that the galaxy has "effectors" in the way that we have muscles and limbs which create physical consequences of our thoughts.

Stephen pointed out that the motions of our limbs are manifestations of physical and chemical processes within our bodies (including the brain), but we find it useful to view the body's motions as being caused by our thoughts, via the self-image that we maintain in brain.

He also remarked that if physics truly is deterministic, then the body/brain ensemble is deterministic, and it's not as if the mind stands back from the body and issues orders.

Here I'm reminded of the fact that most of an octopus's "brain" lives in its tentacles.

If a galaxy were to be like us, it might view the intricate dances of its stars and swirls as being caused by higher-level summary-type patterns that are its "thoughts," nested in its self-image. One question would remain: *does* a galaxy maintain a self-image pattern, as we do?

Well perhaps the central black hole maintains a self-image, maybe the central black hole is a galaxy's brain. Attractive thought. And there could be some type of mirroring effect, with the gravitational fields of the galaxy's stars forming ripples on the surface of the black hole.

Alternatively we might compare the galaxy to an octopus, the (slow) swooping and sweeping of the arms is, for the galaxy, a dance. I don't think an octopus would have the kind of self-image that we do, that is, nothing like a homunculus in the central knob.

We do at times forget our homunculus as well—for instance when dancing, or prancing, or having sex.
***

Wolfram remarks that it's easier to talk to philosophers than physicists, as the philosophers are more open to radical changes of paradigms.

He noted that if your mind ran a million times as fast, then you would notice the light-speed lag between near and far events in your Earthly environment, and you wouldn't automatically have the simple notion of "space" as "everything I see right now."

He raised the point that, due to Gödel's Incompleteness Theorem, you'd expect to see numerous undecidable problems in math. And the fact mathematicians see very few of them might have to do with the kinds of math that we choose to do. Orderly math?

He likes to try and imagine utterly alien kinds of "intelligences" existing in his "ruliad" model of reality. The ruliad which is based, I think, on some version of the set of all possible computations. He speculated that some "beings" in the ruliad dispense with reality-as-a-three-dimensional-space, or even that they may not have at all the same notion of math itself.
***

In our discussion of imagining the inner lives of different sorts of being, he mentioned he'd once written a piece on "What it's like to be a computer." (This might be a 2003 video relating to neural nets.) He pointed out their version of birth and death: being turned on, and crashing. He also mentioned the necessity of some kind of framework for communication. Unless the computers happen to be utterly identical, it won't do to simply copy a swatch of binary code from one to the other … as inevitably it won't end up in the precisely right place to be readable. And something like this is true for humans. You don't try to exchange neural patterns and biochemicals. You work at a higher, more abstract level.

Regarding my old notion of the lifebox, he hadn't known that Microsoft went so far as to patent my idea for themselves.

Some of Stephen's followers have put together a Stephen lifebox.

Speaking of lifebox, he himself has, incredibly, made about 250 live-stream videos, roughly one a week for the last four years, "Ask Me Anything About Science and Technology," ostensibly for kids, but fine for adults, and each video is an hour and a half long.

I wished I was taping our talk in the breakfast room for a podcast, but I didn't think of that in time. And there would have been a lot of background noise, also it was nice simply to enjoy "this rare experience in life's long journey of conversing with a truly intelligent man," as I've written before.

An oasis.

May 9, 2024. Galactic Minds.

Today instead of working on Sqinks, I'm into the notion of galaxies being alive/conscious, and their brains are the enormous black holes at their centers. What I was talking about with Wolfram. Fried egg kind of thing, but the yolk is black, or iridescent. And there's this cool thing that when something falls into a black hole, it leaves some kinda holographic info pattern on the hole's surface, or boundary.

This record is important for the following reason: As the philosopher Antonio Damasio says, consciousness involves four components.

- An image of the changing world, that is, a movie

in the brain.

- A self-symbol within the movie.
- An observer symbol that stands outside the movie, watching and evaluating.
- A conscious self that watches the movie + observer.

I wrote about this in my nonfiction tone, The Lifebox, the Seashell, and the Soul.

I realize that Damasio's particular levels might be peculiar to the unique consciousness of a human ape. But just for the hell of it, let's suppose that we can replicate or instantiate them in the context of a galaxy with a central black hole.

Galactic movie in the brain.

For starters I'm thinking that the ripples or fields or currents on the surface of the black hole as form a continuously updated and ongoing and dynamic "movie in the brain," that is a faithful representation of what's happening in the cosmos around the galaxy.

And I say the cosmos rather than the mere galaxy because, after all, light from the whole cosmos is flowing into don't any a galaxy's central black hole and leaving traces.

One thinks of a spherical mirror. And let's not get too far into issues about the finite speed of light.

In my brain, or in a galaxy's central black hole, we have an image of the surrounding world around us, and the issue of it being up-to-date isn't necessarily important. And thus, I can make a case for saying that the galaxy does have a "mental" self-image in terms of the event horizon surface of its central black hole.

Galactic self-symbol

In my movie in the brain, I distinguish my own body from the rest of the world. It's a contiguous physical object that contains the movie in the brain. My body is my physical brain plus the things attached to it.

In a galaxy's black-hole-event-horizon-based movie in the brain, what would be the self-image? Well, you'd want to say the black hole itself, plus the "limbs" coming out from the black hole—in the case of a spiral galaxy, one might view the limbs as being the "arms" of the spiral. The gravitational emanations from structures would arouse moving waves across the black hole's surface.

So it has a self-symbol in terms of holistic closed surface of the black hole, plus the moving patterns driven by the moving arms of the spiral.

This is the galactic self-symbol.

Galactic observer self-symbol and movie

This gets tricky now.

We want the black hole to be considering the relation between its reflection-of-galactic-arms and the quality of itself as a black hole and the fainter image of the surrounding cosmos.

To make this more vivid, suppose our subject galaxy is in the process of colliding with a second galaxy. And its "observer" is a process that tracks the relation between the home arms and the other arms. The two sets of black-hole-horizon images would differ in, say amplitude.

Galactic self watching movie + observer

Imagine there being processes akin to hydrodynamics or to continuous-valued cellular-automata CAs. And these processes manage to, in effect control the motions of the galaxies arms so as to draw off material from the second galaxy, and to draw off more material than is lost. Or, it might not be a battle to the death, it might be more like mating, and in this case, the processes are calculated to maximize the health and vigor of an emerging new galaxy.

Note that we see these kinds of activities when observing whirlpools in moving water, and, although we don't normally think this way, it's easy enough to ascribe goals and emotions and personalities to individual twirls within a vortex street. Or to a galaxy

May 12, 2024. The "Oh Oh" Chapter.

I was thinking of opening the "Oh Oh" chapter like this.

> Long story short, Olga is the rat among the Twelve. Olga and Tobin betray us. Olga cuts out my brain and Carol's brain, and we end up in braincozies in that Sqinkland version of the Esalen resort. But I'm getting ahead of myself. Here's how it comes down.

And the upshot is that Oliver or Carol or both of them gets their brain eaten, and the end up inside braincozies in Tiny Town. Maybe making a little fun of Esalen, like people do. Actually I love it at Esalen, except it's too expensive. Over the years I got to run a couple of seminars there, and I went for free. But maybe I could take Barb there.

"Welcome to Tiny Town, Mr. & Mrs. Strunk."

"I'm *not* Mrs. Strunk. I'm Carol Cee." Carol looks around with some dismay. "At least I used to be."

May 12, 20204. Flying to London with Barb.

Here I am with Barb on a jet to London for a two-week dalliance that we two will savor there. So nice to be with her, it's been nine or ten days since I saw her. With huge efforts I got all the plans made for the trip.

I proposed the London trip to Barb very early on, like on our third date … I'd been wanting to do a trip to London, and none of the kids wanted to come along, I didn't realy want to go alone, and Barb was talking about her love of travel, so I just asked if she'd come to London with me, kind of a long shot, me making a suggestion like that, and wondering if it was too much, and she said, "Sure, I'd do that."

And now, three months later, we can hardly believe that we're doing it.

There's a new Taylor Swift song called "So Highschool," and I was listening to it this morning, and I played it for Barb while we were waiting at the airport, and in many ways it summarizes our current state. Like this is a field trip. And we can't think of anything else but each other. And we're in love. And we can spend an hour simply discussing this history of our relationship. And we can't heavily make out on the plane because our teacher might be watching.

Barb describes herself as a goody-goody and an outsider, a certain type that appeals to me. In some ways like Sylvia, but of course different. I've always been an outsider too, which is one reason that Barb understands me as well as she does. But I wasn't a goody-goody at all. Yet she likes that about me. I'm a bad boy, as she likes to say. And now she says, "I'm a fallen woman," and she likes that too. A perfect match.

I might give my Carol character those traits a bit more than I already have. Haven't really pushed the goody-good thing on her at all ... I'm enjoying having the Carol character be more like a wise-cracking 40s movie character, like in *His Girl Friday*, and I could just keep that. Barb is a bit more of a brilliant, *naif* outsider.

***

I was discussing the new AI with a somewhat tech-literate neighbor, and I mentioned the experiment I did: feeding half of a *Sqinks* chapter to ChatGPT 4, and asking it to finish the chapter in the style of Rudy Rucker, and each time it produced something quite serviceable, recognizably Rucker-like, and, to my surprise, with new characters and situations and actions.

Told my neighbor about this, and he's like, "So now you can get the program to write your books and you don't need to work."

And I go, "But I *like* to write. It's what I do. A craft I've learned. And I'm good at it."

And he simply couldn't understand what I was saying.

May 21, 2024. Barb's Ending.

Having a fab time in London with dear Barb.

I told her about *Sqinks* and how I don't know what to put in the second half, and we talked back and forth, and she gave me a wonderful idea.

Oliver gets his brain cut out and the brain is sent to Sqinkland. Might as well have this happen to the narrator, right?

Who is the sqink who takes possession of Oliver's body? Ought to be that sort of punk sqink, Skeeze.

Carol goes to save Oliver ... reversal of the usual man saves woman routine. Just before Carol leaves, or perhaps as a result of something she or Oliver does, a full-blown invasion of Earth kicks in and every person on our planet is taken over by a sqink. More or less destroying our world.

Let's say Carol escapes this as she gets to Sqinkland before it happens.

Moo tells Carol and Oliver that there is some hope of Carol designing and creating a new "Earth A". Oliver is still in his braincozy (with Skeeze still living in his human skull back on Earth). Oliver gives Carol some "writing lessons" or "world-building lessons" on how to design Earth A. But it'll turn out to be a flop.

Skeeze relents, and gives Oliver back his body, and Oliver, now fully back up to speed, designs an Earth B. This one sucks too, like maybe it's too gnarly.

Oliver and Carol get together and design a perfect world, indistinguishable from the original Earth. And the sqinks can't get in.

It's the old three wishes fairytale trope.

A cautionary tale of unfettered AIs.

May 25, 2024. Barb's Photography.

Change Carol's photography practice to match Barb's. Barb shoots stock photos, not looking for art, but looking for an image of each significant thing or activity, a universal library of what exists on Earth. And this base will be useful in recreating the planet Earth A. And remember that Carol's image go straight into the cloud.

The sqink called Lilac helps Barb/Carol to harvest an image of each single thing on Earth. Somehow Carol is able to do tweaks on each image.

Being with Barb, who is often shooting, I notice more intensely the facial expressions of people in the tube stations and in the cars. Barb's brave about taking pictures of people's faces. Street photographer chutzpah.

Thanks to Lilac, Barb's harvesting is hydra-like, branching in all directions, yet imbued with Barb's perceptions, "seeing" nearly everywhere. Barb and Lilac fall into a state of ecstasy, and go for the ultimate photo of Earth.

Cue a Jorge-Luis-Borges-type list of everything, in the style of his story "The Aleph."

But as I said, Barb's Earth A has something wrong with it. Some issue relating perhaps to Cantor's levels of infinity. Oh sure.

June 2, 2024. Back to Sqinks.

Into June now. Back in California, and already our marvellous journey has the quality of a dream. Don't even remember where my novel was before the trip. As usual, I better print out some of it, read, and see what's what.

I had some big idea for the plot while on the trip … don't quite remember it now … but *I wrote it down!* We'll look at that too.

June 6, 2024. Pacific-Union Club.

I've enshrined Lilac as Carol's pet sqink, but it seems like a drag always having her around. Ditto for linking Skeeze to Oliver.

I need a big scene now to kick off Part II. So let's get with what's her name, the bad and bossy Queen sqink, Mumper? The word makes me laugh, it's from *Finnegans Wake*, near the start, in the phrase "doubling their mumper" referring to population growth, replacing the word "number" and carrying a hint of the swelling caused by mumps.

Mumper is at that Pacific-Union club with Tobin and Loulou, they're having a fancy dinner. Mumper looks fairly human, like she did when they first met her in Sqinkland. Keep it simple.

But, um, what did Mumper look like? I don't remember. Go back and copy it.

***

I've totally forgotten to keep weaving in the sqink luck thing. Oh well.

June 19, 2024. Endsville.

I've been writing kind of randomly for the last two weeks, without making notes or a plan. Thinking about my girlfriend Barb a lot of the time.

I'm trying to remember the word for the end of the world … eschaton? The end of the world that the Book of Revelations might talk about.

At my wedding with Sylvia, some of our college friends sent a telegram, "Forget not immediacy of the eschaton." This related to something we'd heard in our Philosophy of Religion class that some of us happened to take together, just as a goof. And the professor talked about leaders who say the end of the world is nigh. He referred to this doctrine as the "immediacy of the eschaton." And we thought this was funny.

The end of the world *is* coming, of course, for everyone, but on an individual, one at a time basis. You are going to experience the end of the world, but I might not get there at the same moment. Sylvia's father eventually had a problem with this … during the last years of his life he repeated all day long: "We're all going to die." And I'd want to say, "Not *all* of us, man. *You* are going to die. Not me. Not yet."

But as I say, when I was twenty-one, my friends and I took all this as a big joke. "Immediacy of the eschaton," *haw*! Cheerfully nihilistic roustabouts that we were.

Anyway, I'll try and write a Skinkland chapter where Oliver is in his braincozy, and Moo and Carol have flown down to help him, and they're heading for this very dire place where all the locals' brains got stolen, and for now I'm calling the place Endsville, as in apocalypse, judgement day, crack of doom, Armageddon, the eschaton.

June 28, 2024. Picaresque.

Back into it. I've accepted that I'll be doing the full picaresque again. Like I did in *Million Mile Road Trip* and in so many others. *Frek and the Elixir. Big Aha. Turing and Burroughs. Jim and the Flims. White Light.*

Practically all of my novels, truth be told. So why am I acting like picaresque is a bad thing, and telling myself I shouldn't do picaresque in *Sqinks*. It's the only way to fill out the book, okay?

I'm a little past half done, and it's been five months. I *can* get to the finish line. Maybe in December? But to make it fun and easy for me, I have to let it rip. No strictures. And each chapter should to be a new vision, a fresh dream, a short story on its own, the crazier the better. Not that I, Rudy the Elder, am in the least bit crazy. It's all completely logical. And don't call me gonzo!

I'm writing off the top of my head this month, getting comfortable once again with the picaresque fabulation mode, freely writing, making it all up as I go along. And every so often jumping back to adjust the nodes, that is, the plot branchings, like you do when drawing a labyrinthine maze. The Muse is with me.

Of course I'll add on, as so often, a bit of an overarching save-the-world core plot. But that don't mean it ain't picaresque.

June 30, 2024. Where Is Stok-stok?

So my characters are gathered in Tiny Town now. And Oliver made friends with some non-sqink aliens there. They're from this planet called Stok-stok, and it's in our own galaxy. We call them stokkers. The sqinks and their friends the Mu9ers raided Stok-stok, and stole most of the stokkers' brains, which are stored in braincozies in Tiny Town, just like Oliver's brain.

Oliver's stokker friends are Randa, Pinchy, and Dazz. Moo, Carol, and Winston the science guy are here as well.

Possibly Winston and Dazz are having sex, twined in a drawn-out serpent-type sex act, sweaty and gasping, with Winston dropping his British accent and talking like he's a hick from Iowa, which is fact the case.

Tobin the traitor was there too, but the Mu9ers tortured him to death by huffing his brain.

So Moo carries them through a tunnel through the "bulk" to Stok-stok.

I'm doing wild brain-game head trips during these trips through bulk, or raw subspace, that separates Sqinkland from our normal world. On this leg of the trip, every word is turned inside out, whatever that means. Partial anagrams.

> Good dog, I eye, go ogre, Endsville Live
> end, apocalypse, boring robing, sqink kink,
> dank candy, Mumper number, Moo omo,
> Randa drain, Carol coral, Oliver veil, dirt
> drift, hate heat, control troonc.

Sentence word order screwed up as well, goes without saying. It's like Finnegans Wake. And, yes, I know that "troonc" isn't a word. But it looks and sounds cool.

Here's a somewhat relevant excerpt from a letter to my college friend Tom Kennedy. Snart guy. An English professor. The only person left who sends me handwritten letters.

> I liked your electron poem, Tom. The surfier/electron dialog. You posed the question: "If the electron is a wave, is the wave an electron?" Certainly it's (in part) a *lot* of electrons. But could a water wave be just one electron. I'd like that. I need a gimmick for a scene in a quixotic picaresque novel I'm halfway done with. Book called *Sqinks*.
>
> My characters are entering a spot called Stok-stok, having flown through the bulk, and beyond the slow apocalypse, and I want this world to be a very fucked-up place. Maybe it has only one electron. Or, say, N7 of them, where N7 is the is the unique solution (if it exists) to a very short equation that's written on the gleaming mandible of Pinchy, who is half dog and half ant.
>
> There is, and I'd almost forgotten, a theory that there really IS only one electron, proposed by John Archibald Wheeler. It jiggles up and down in spacetime, and when it's moving down, it's a positron.
>
> This is an instance of me acting learned, in an overweening yet underwhelming way, and of me being serious yet ironic, and of me bullshitting yet sincere in a way that keeps me amused. Getting even with those who picked on me as a kid because I was

smart. I'm sure they did that to you. Which is why you pretend to be a simpleton, and I pretend to be a crude punk. And yet we rule the world.

July 7, 2024. Too Misty.

I sort of "finished" the Stok-stok chapter, complete with presentation of problem, plus Oliver-mediated salvation.

But it's gauzy and conceptual, with few concrete images. I feel it needs several rewrites.

I want to be laying a foundation for saving Earth from planet Stok-stok's fate, so the Stok-stok chapter needs to set up some strong mental images. Although of course the details of the threatened Earth scenario will be different.

Also if the Earth salvation is to be in any sense a success, then perhaps the attempted rescue of Stok-stok should be a complete flop. So that we're even more worried about Earth's fate.

Like maybe Oliver's Pied Piper song works a little bit, but then not at all.

Side note: it may be that the salvation of Earth is not a simple banishment of the sqinks and the Mu9ers. Could be more likely that we find a way to collaborate with them. And here we'd be, once again, modeling the present crisis of humanity wanting to handle AI.

July 15-17, 2024. Finishing Stok-stok Chapter.

I've done a bunch of rewrites on this chapter and I feel it's about done. In the end, I didn't manage very vivid descriptions of the place. But it's vivid anyhow.

I made Carol into a good singer for the Stok-stok Pied Piper scene. So to set that up, I went back and did a bunch of foreshadowings. Inspired to do this because my new girlfriend Barb is, as I've mentioned, my trans-real model for Carol. And Barb is a good singer. Carol, Oliver, and Randa sing as a trio.

They lure the sqinks out of Stok-stok which is, for a time, a dried-up cow-pie. Kind of wanted to have the sqinks relocate to Esalen, and to have Stok-stok be hunky-dory. But, as I mentioned in the previous note, it's better if it's a last-minute flop … so that we have more tension about the fate of Earth.

Sqinks swarm back to cow-pie Stok-stok. Huge tumult and seething there. Stok-stok expands to huge and possibly infinite size, as in the universe's inflationary stage of the big bang. One hears a soft *pop*. And Stok-stok wholly disappears.

"Good going, Oliver," Winston says.

I was thinking that when the pop happens, Stok-stok reaches the end of *their* time. But now I'm wondering if I should even drag in the "end of time" thing. Kind of a red herring. All we care about is that Stok-stok pops and disappears. And there isn't really any "end of time" situation in what's up on Earth. Unless I want there to be. But really, I don't.

I have enough pages for the Stok-stok chapter now, so the seething and pop can be the start of the next chapter—about whose contents I know "from naathing."

Then I assume they go back to Earth and … what? I've got nearly half the book to go. Unless I throw in the towel and make this a fucking novella … although at 40 K words it's already at the upper bound of novella-length. Come on, Rudy, you can get to 70 K, and that's a short novel, and maybe you can pad it to 80 K on the rewrite.

Ok, fine, but what happens in the rest of the book? Age old question.

Although it's not quite relevant, I think of someone giving advice to Aeneas about his visit to hell in Book 7 of the *Aeneid*, starting line 127.

> *facilis descensus Auerno:*
> *sed revocare gradum superasque evadere ad*
> *auras*
> *hoc opus, hic labor est.*

I like to translate it thus:

> The descent to hell is easy.
> But to walk back up the slope
> *There* is the bringdown, *There* is the drag.

July 22, 2024. Once More: Where is Stok-stok?

How will Moo's tunnel get blocked? Maybe the Twelve just come and dig dirt into it. Keep it simple. Or an H-bomb. Never mind any sqink thread routine. Or the sqinks could turn themselves into bulldozers.

If the sqinks wanted they could grow extra copies of the stolen brains.

"We prefer to use a freshly cultured brain. We have our own way of doing things. We save the original brain as a back-up. And as an ancillary organ to control certain lower functions … such as love."

Transreally speaking, Stok-stok, could be, but of course, Stockholm, very fresh in my mind from going there with Sylvia, about five months before she died. Our wonderful last trip, utterly unforgettable. Our fabulous corner room with a curved tower as the corner. The puffy white clouds in the brilliant blue sky. A gift from god.

If you lure the Stok-stok sqinks out of the parasitized stokker bodies, using the Piper of Hamelin song, they leave their formerly occupied stokker bodies limp on the ground. The exiled stokker brains from Tiny Town swoop back to take possession of their bodies once again.

I was describing this as becoming a fiasco with Stock-stok exploding. But maybe not. Maybe Stok-stok is fine, and then later it might be Earth which doesn't end up so well—but Carol and Oliver will fix it.

July 23, 2024. Doing Revisions.

Keep in mind that the sqinks stand for the new, super AI apps on Earth. Realistically, there is no hope of getting rid of them.

The ending of Sqinks has to involve learning to live with the sqinks. Otherwise we have a doom scenario where we're mirthless robots. I don't see the humorless doom as happening, we humans will (I hope) always evade that, crufty rats that we are.

But, yes, humorless doom is the threatening option which we evade. That's we don't see computers and AI as a threat. The threat of making life boring.

"Topper and Lady Cee taught us to love and laugh again."

To get to the turnaround, we'd want some going-downhill chaps.

If we see the bad scene on Earth, there is no need to see it in Endsville/Stok-stok. So ditch that right now.

And the brain-removal thing is pretty ridiculous. Something less gory. They save off an initial state of your brain in Tiny Town. So do that today as well.

***

Okay, I got a lot done. Just spent about six hours editing. I think I can save the Stok-stok chapter yet.

Maybe Moo should catch all of the Stok-stok sqinks in a sea-cucumber web from her butt, and then pinch that off and toss it into the local Sun? No, no, recruit the sqinks for her personal army.

Got rid of the sqink threads, made Stok-stok a distant planet, made Mumper repelled by love (it's a nice sentimental move). Wormhole from Sqinkland to Stok-stok and back. And, yes, I'll keep the ice-axe scenes at the Pacific Union Club.

July 24, 2024. Which Body Has the Soul?

We have to show what happens when Skeeze frees Oliver's body, and stops pretending to be that body's brain, and Oliver's real brain gets back inside the skull of his real body.

In real life I do have multiple "selves" which sometime act somewhat independently of each other. My selves include: the now-sober, the Barb-dating, the family-man, the nature-immersed, the writer, and the painter Rudys. If pressed, each of these can bring the others to mind. They do "update" each other. But to some extent they're independent. And to be honest, include the resentful punk Rudy.

Would it work to view the Tiny Town Rudy as another facet of Earth Rudy? No, not really.

***

Tricky, the two versions of a person. Oliver is about to evict the sqinks from Stok-stok, and the braincozy archived citizens of Stok-stok are hovering around the planet like flies on shit (as I like to say) awaiting the moment when they can dart back in.

In this model I'm thinking of the archived mind as being a soul, and maybe your soul can only live in one body, so the sqink-occupied body "has no soul." Though, of course, it might have the soul of the *sqink*.

Don't get all computeresque with the idea of synching up two data bases. Think, rather, of an analog soul. That would be more fun.

***

Can I invent some physical basis for having a soul in only one body. There's some quantum thing called the "No Cloning Theorem." So maybe, once again, the sqink possessed body has no soul.

I wrote my physicist friend Nick Herbert to ask about this. He said something complicated about "Quantum Teleportation."

***

In this scene about the brains returning to their bodies in Stok-stok, I had this line:

"The diaspora of archived Stok-stok souls fills the air around us, arriving from the Sqinkland bluff we call Tiny Town—and settling into their rightful bodies. A mirror phenomenology indeed."

When a sqink takes you over, it evicts your soul, which goes down to Tiny Town inside your brain. And you can physically get back into your real body if the sqink leaves, thus emptying out your skull, and making room for your brain. I want that to be true.

Do we need to talk about a soul at all? I'm thinking that we might, at some point in the chapters to come.

Time to go to the supermarket, I can mull this over while I'm there.

***

Got home and realized I needed to stick with the brain-extraction routine as this objectively nails down which body the soul is in: it's in the body with the frikkin' brain!

Don't want that wifty quantum-mechanics BS.

So I rolled back some complicating changes I made today. And now it's good. And all of today's back and forth means I smoothed it out even more.

And if cutting out brains is old school, so be it. Ramones forever! Cyberpunk 1980! *The Ware Tetralogy!*

I sent Nick Herbert the axe-out-his-brain version and he wrote back.

> Thanks for the excerpt.
> Lots of moment to moment bizarro action.
> Your real life these days sounds almost as exciting as your adventures in Sqinkland.
> Enjoy yourself with Barb.
> It's your reward for a faithful and (mostly) virtuous life.
> Forget the quantum gobbledygook.
> For sheer action nothing beats a chrome ax to the skull in the Pacific Union Club.

Thank you, Nick, for sanctioning my preferred approach.

July 27, 2024. Moving the Brain.

I haven't covered the question of how to move a brain to Sqinkland. Well, they'll use teleportation, akin to that scale inversion trick that Moo used.

The actual axing the skull routine at the Pacific Union club is kind of a show that Mumper is putting on to impress the humans. A bit of a hoax. To frighten them, and to present an extreme version of the process so that, at least for a brief time in the days to come, the humans might think the brain swapping isn't yet being done on a wide scale, as they don't see skull-axing. A feint, to give Mumper's invasion a surreptitious start.

And how does the sqink smoothly take control of a body? Let's say the sqink creates a gossamer "overlay" of the brain. By overlay I mean it could be a millimeter away in the fourth dimension, effectively adjacent to each point of the existing brain, and when the brain is whisked away, the fake brain moves over that 1 mm 4D distance and smacks into place silky smooth, precisely matching the site. At the same time, the sqinks "yank out the carpet," with the brain being whisked off to Tiny Town. Via, as I say, teleportation.

And in due time, the brain can "come home" the same way, that is, be teleported back in as the sqink version is teleported out. Like a three card monte card trick.

At what point does Mumper or Moo reveal that the axing is a bit of a *Grand Guignol* distraction? Maybe it comes out when the exiled Stok-stok brains are being sent home.

Can set this up by Moo, Mumper and the other sqinks kind of laughing and joking all along while they're doing the axing. How many axe attacks, by the way? Four: Winston and Tobin (offstage), Oliver (as described by, and experienced by him), and Tobin (witnessed by the reader).

This way I can have it both ways. The Cyberpunk 1980 *Software* freak show, plus the smooth lube 2024 version.

"Have your brain and eat it too." "Go for Baroque."

July 29, 2024. Fast and Slow Mail.

I need teleportation to get the human brains down to Tiny Town rapidly, and for rapid return. Also I'll want it for moving brains around without splitting the skull.

But for the sqinks travelling from Sqinkland to Earth, I'm saying they have to use a physical wormhole type tunnel which can be clogged up with dirt.

Why would teleportation work for a brain, but not for a sqink nor, I suppose, for a whole human?

I thought maybe I could say that the "scale flip" teleportation only works for matter less than a kilogram in mass, and not for sqinks at all. Then we could get the brain in and out, and the sqinks would need the tunnel.

But, wait—I need to move the sqinks in and out of the skull as well. But now we have a problem.

Brains and sqinks: short distance teleportation is okay (so we can swap brains), but long distance teleportation not okay (so we need wormhole tunnels from Sqinkland to Earth.)

This is important enough that I need to disentangle my brain-swapping teleportation from the scale flip interactive long-distance remote presence event involving that paddle-boarder guy Oberg in Monterey.

Just have short-distance small-mass teleportation. Works equally well for brains and sqinks.

And use something else for the Monterey episode. I did not use any teleportation here. It's just a very enhanced telepresence. I could call it plain old quantum wireless, with something of telepathic sense of what the guy experiences.

July 30, 2024. Irene?

So I fixed a zillion things. Another eight-hour day yesterday, and more this morning while waiting for Barb to show up for the day.

Instead of chopping Tobin to bits twice—which is dull and obsessive—the second time we tickle him to death by running an electric ostrich feather across his naked brain.

I made it clear that Mumper did in fact "own" the stolen brains and that he was in fact selling them to other races, or perhaps even to Sqinkland merchants or farmers or whatever, the brains to be used, as in *Juicy Ghosts*.

Can elaborate on this later. Perhaps Oliver himself loses is brain once more, and ends up stuck in one of those gigs. Carol too. The pair submits to this so as to act as underground agents—to assassinate Mumper. They can be despised and mocked court jesters at Mumper's palace. In his hubris Mumper thinks they can't break loose, but they do, and they turn the tide. Vintage trope.

Meanwhile, coming back to Earth, we find Oliver's body locked into an intense love affair with Irene the choreographer, Irene, who's also about eighty, just like Carol.

So that's a scrap to start the next chapter with. But I need more. And the court-jester-assassins routine is still many chapters away. So what now?

I guess, as ever, I'll write any old thing to get started—let the characters start talking, copy it down, and see where it leads.

What flows out of Carol's jealousy?

July31, 2024. Oliver, Carol, Skeeze, Irene.

Last night I told Barb about the Irene scene and she was in fact furiously jealous, more so than I'd even feared. Funny, in a way. She doesn't want to lose me.

"You're a catch," she likes to tell me. I told her she can't forbid me to write this chapter! I assured her that in the end, Oliver will go back to Carol.

Also there will be an issue around Oliver getting his body back from Skeeze. Maybe a big scene, and for some reason Carol walks out, and then Irene gets Skeeze to leave Oliver's body, and Oliver moves back in. And he takes up the affair that Skeeze/Oliver was having with Irene, horndog that he is.

And maybe, why not, Skeeze takes over that fake body that Oliver crafted down in Tiny Town. We might suppose it looks something like Oliver, just to muddy the waters a bit more. And he might in fact go after Carol, who didn't want that "love doll" body down in Tiny Town, but maybe she'll take it now, if only to bug Oliver.

This could itself be a whole chapter. If not quite enough, then we'll progress the action into a meeting with Paul and the others who are planning a big demo. Maybe Moo, Oliver and Carol come up with some method by which we might truly stymie Mumper.

The method will seem to work, but then it won't, and soon after that, Oliver and Carol can go pose as fools in Mumper's court.

By the way I've been talking about the 12 sqinks, but aren't one or two of them dead by now? Flubsy for sure, they kill her at the Pacific Union Club. And Doink got killed at SFMOMA, I believe. I think he was Flubsy's brother?

Might as well have the one with the flower name be dead too. Lilac. As it is now, Lilac fades out of the story at the time of the Sqink Fair riot, adopted by a stranger, and we don't really see her again. So I could kill her in the background. And then I'd be down to nine sqinks. Could have a kind of ticking clock thing, with fewer and fewer sqinks on Earth's team.

Getting back to the start of the next chapter now ... can't plan, I'll just write and see what happens. Skeeze balks, Carol gets mad and leaves, Irene gets Skeeze to give back Oliver's body, they go to the demo, which might as well be today. End with brutal death-strike by Mumper. Do the S. Clay Wilson "Crazed Junkies Fight It Out With Killer Robots" routine.

August 4, 2024. Outline.

I'm finally writing an outline. I summarized what's in the 12 chapters I've done. And did the math to find out how many chapters I need if I'm shooting for 70K words. This is pretty simple to calculate, as I'm keeping my chapters all about the same length in manuscript page count. As for the 70K target, I always say, a book ought to be at least 80K, but a 70K draft might bulk to 80 on the rewrite.

So?

I need eight more chapters to make it. Twenty chapters in all.

And I've written twelve.

So, as I say, today I summarized those first twelve chapters to get an overview. And now I am thinking about what remaining twists and aha moments I'll need it to bring her home. Generally speaking, I have about one twist or aha per chapter, and I've been pretty much throwing them in on instinct, but now I'd be leaning toward guiding this chugging Globemaster U7 airplane in for a landing.

Let's think of some interesting events and see how to fit them in. Work backwards, that is, I can work back from the end to make it smooth.

Chapter 20 is Happyland with Sink symbiosis, but with a slight hint of possible trouble on the horizon.

August 5, 2024. Reviewing.

So I printed out the manuscript, 134 pages, in the font size and line spacing I use. Theoretically I'll reread the whole thing, but I'm kind of eager to keep moving, so today I'm just studying my new draft outline and dipping into the manuscript and noting the things to fix.

There really aren't enough sqinks for the sqink fair at the start, but I guess we can slant the promo as being a bit of a scam.

The audio news report on the sqinks at the start of Chapter 7 sounds like there's a lot of sqinks, so I'll need to tweak that. Or maybe there are already more sqinks than I realized?

What happened to all that patent stuff?

Do I kill off Lilac or not? Or maybe she's the first one to split up via mitosis. Like splits into twenty sqinks.

Give Diana more to do. Lizard skin purses. Like the one Barb and I saw in Prada in Union Square. Heavy sqink promo.

Why won't they be able to remove sqinks on Earth with the Pied Piper move they used in Stok-stok?

That blues-man line: 'They say my music's from the devil. But the devil don't have no music." Somehow the new sqinks can noise-cancel all music.

What if Carol's old boyfriend Tig Tucker shows up?

Looking at that possibly dumb Tig Tucker suggestion, I think of the phrase, 'Too many singers, not enough songs," as my graphic-designer friend Wendy Watkins once sadly said. Or was it: "Not enough singers, too many songs."

Wendy was in The Design Group with a few partners, in Lynchburg, Virginia. They did graphics, and were an early inspiration for daughter Georgia.

We lived in Lynchburg for six years. I was a math professor there, and then I got fired, and I became a freelance writer for four years. I published six books: The Fourth Dimension, Master of Space and Time, All the

Visions, The Secret of Life, Mind Tools, and Wetware. My early years of bitter struggle. I didn't realize it, but it was the peak of my career.

For my office there, I rented an abandoned old house from the Design Group, next door to the old house that they used for their offices.

I myself was a group of partners in terms of the personalities in my head!

In the first version of what I remember Wendy saying, "singers" are partners making suggestions, and "songs" are completed projects. In the second version, "singers" are partners doing productive work, and "songs" are extra ideas that make extra work.

I guess for a writer it's the second version as, when it comes to typing the words, there really is only the one singer, or, if you like, the limited number of Rudys that I can bring to the keyboard.

How do the new sqinks get here?

I want a lot more sqinks showing up at the shipyards than they could have expected. New ones. Mitosis or a new tunnel?

Or Moo hatches them. Or Moo took all of the Stok-stok sqinks into her body ... but those are brain-stealing sqinks, so we probably don't want them, they have a bad record?

As for mitosis. If I use it, I'd need to at least hint at it earlier on. Making the point that to save Stok-stok, *they need to evict every single sqink without exceptions.*

Regarding mitosis on Earth, it could just be one of the sqinks who does it. Let's say it's Lilac. She's been lying low for most of the novel, ever since the Warhol scenes, and now bring her out.

Open a closet door, and there's Lilac with, ew, a maggots-like mount of a thousand baby sqinks. Yeeek! Great scene. Do that. Lilac was always meant to be a "breeder." Call it laying eggs, or hatching, instead of mitosis.

I would need to discuss why Mumper wasn't using hatching for Earth-invasion. Well, maybe he has a burdensome surplus of sqinks, and needs to get rid of them. Like the issue of immigration, a little bit.

Perhaps the hatch-generated sqinks aren't beholden to Mumper, and have no interest in gathering brains for him. Maybe the sqinks can make quite nice bodies for themselves. Villages of them on Earth. Once again: the immigrant thing.

Avoid new sqinks taking our brains.

Well, they're a different breed of sqinks. They aren't beholden to Mumper. They like growing their own bodies.

Can sqinks avoid our Pied Piper routine?

Well, we don't necessarily want to expel them? Or, no, better, Carol and Oliver and … Irene *try* to do it. But it doesn't work. Maybe Stok-stok Randa had a special richness to his voice. Or Moo has something to do with it; she added her energy to make it work on Stok-stok, also Moo ensured that they got every single sqink, as I mention elsewhere.

Good to have Irene as a recurring character. Might she find a different boyfriend or girlfriend? Who could it be? I don't think Paul, but maybe. Or Diana, and we have her leaving Winston, as he's turned sort of mean.

Back to Pied Piper, you might imagine, as I may have mentioned, that the sqinks or Oom has a sound-cancelling app that mutes song.

Who is Oom?

An evil Moo shows up. A male called Oom. Maybe he made a tunnel by the shipyard. Or just drilled out Moo's tunnel. Maybe he is in some way sponsored by Winston. We could have a battle involving Oom.

What About Winston's Business Interests?

Suppose he's very interested in money and/or power. And he is Messianic about sqink-aided tech. Akin to today's rise in large-language-model / neural-net style AI.

Lasting solution to the Mumper problem?

Well, Oliver and Carol do that when they go work in Mumper's castle. And maybe Oom is involved.

Ongoing sqink-human partnership?

To some extent like we'd hope for AI our real-world to be like that. But we might also suppose that the sqinks have their own ongoing projects and thus aren't second-class citizens. Their ongoing project might be making a map of the subdimensions or some such.

August 7, 2024. Barb is Jealous.

I already mentioned that Barb is jealous of my character Irene. But now it's escalated. She visited yesterday, and I read her Chapter 12 of *Sqinks*, where Oliver spends a night with Irene—and Barb was completely furious. It wasn't even funny how mad she was. Over and over she said, "Oliver is a jerk." And "Carol should drop him." Just repeating that.

I told her that her reaction made me sad, and I'd hoped she would think the story was well-written and dramatic and funny and true to life. No go.

A bit later Barb started using the word "two-timer," and saying I should tell her if I planned to start "running around," because she didn't want to get an STD. It almost seemed like we were about to break up. Over a scene in my novel! One of the risks of transrealism ...

Well, all I can do is learn from this. I'll fold some of Barb's reaction into Carol's reaction to Oliver's one-night infidelity. Right now I have it written so Carol is pretty calm with Oliver, and glad to have him back, although irritable on the whole, but I might was well follow the transreal teaching and have Carol very seriously lash out at Oliver, not quite yet, but very soon.

I suppose I'd been deluding myself about how calmly Carol/Barb would take it. It's that thing where a woman is quietly brooding over something, and the clueless man don't realize this, and he thinks everything is fine ... and then the woman abruptly turns on him, exacting extreme vengeance.

I wrote about this to my writer pal Marc Laidlaw, in fact the start of this journal note is what I sent him, and he responded. I thought it was funny, not sure if Barb would.

> Possible matching-up question for a dating survey for Barb: "Do you like your partner to write exaggerated fantasies in which you figure in a projectively distorted manner, for commercial publication? If his literary legacy continues to grow and these books are finally recognized as the masterpieces that future generations will venerate, do you mind if you are accordingly immortalized, albeit in a form that only you might recognize as yourself?"
> I don't think just anyone would deal well

with it ... it will no doubt require a bit of negotiation if you want to continue being transreal with your relationship *and* expect her to enjoy having Rudy's Version read back to her. And even if you do break up with your girlfriend over your creative process, that is a completely noble cause to fight for ... But also maybe don't read her the one fucking chapter in the book where you cheat on her. Ha! Maybe start at chapter 1 and work your way up to that!

Meanwhile I did rewrite that section a little today, taking into account the things that Barb said ... and Carol actually does break up with Oliver. But they'll be back together soon.

August 8, 2024. Sending Brains to Tiny Town.

Wait, there's still a problem. Any sqink can use short-distance small-mass teleportation to swap itself with a human's brian. Fine. And they can put the brain into a handy braincozy casing right away, or at least in a plastic bag.

But who teleports the brain down to Tiny Town in Sqinkland? I can't grant all sqinks this power—or they'd be teleporting themselves back and forth between Sqinkland to Earth at will ... and supposedly they need Moo's wormhole for this trip.

So I need to suppose that Moo (and other supersqinks) are the only ones who can send a human brian down to Tiny Town. In this case, I'd need to have Moo in on the brain-theft of Winston and the brain-theft of Tobin.

Now, at present I don't show that transfer happening. I guess I could show it right at the start of the Pacific-Union Club meet up. Unless it happened off stage, earlier in the day, and Moo drops a hint about that. The latter option is better, as the Pacific-Union scene already has so very much action.

So I'll need some rewrite on the scene at Paul's ... like, Doob mentions how the transfer works. And some rewrite on the Irene section where perhaps Moo isn't there in the tree because she briefly teleported over to the Pacific-Union to teleport the brains of Winston and Tobin down to Tiny Town.

August 9, 2024. No Floonberry.

I had this thing left over from an early draft—about Winston making a deal for ... what? Ownership of the sqinks? No, originally it was for a biotech method for creating sqinks. Yes, originally they weren't aliens, they were biotech. But now they aren't.

So all that old biz stuff doesn't work ... but I'd like to have *some* biz, as it's a Silicon Valley novel. And the scene of scaring Oberg was fun.

So I fix the biz. What would Winston's company be? Call it Sqink Inq? The product or service is a dating-app-type service for hooking up with sqinks, if the sqinks are willing, and if there are more of them. And he also might be licensing his Bulk Beacon tech, and the spin-off company for that might be Last Call.

Who did Winston work for? Say there's a venture capitalist who funds old-school mad-science nuts working at home: Garage Band is a venture capital investment. And normally the VCs want 70% of a company they sponsor but Winston doesn't to pay that so they scare the VCs down to accepting 49%.

I like the idea of the character Mrs. Floonberry, who still needs to be fleshed out, and still needs something to do, so let's have her be the head of Garage Band.

August 11-12, 2024. Teleport, Biz, Parasites.

I spent quite a bit of time in straightening out teleportation and Winston's business.

What was Winston working on before the bulk beacon? There ought to be a previous invention, and I was thinking of futuristic crypto, but maybe there's something better. Or it could be an interesting crypto based on time reversal.

When and where did they do the brainswaps on Winston and Tobin? Right in the Pacific-Union, and Moo helped.

What are Moo and Winston into while Oliver and Carol are at the farmers market?

Mumper will try and send in his brain-stealer sqinks. But Lilac's hatched sqinks are higher-grade and they are not brain stealers and, relative to Mumper's sqinks, they have antibody qualities, antiviral, like white blood cells and T-cells. And they wipe out the Mumper invaders. But we still need to have Moo's crew of sqinks be good. Maye they're reformed by the hatched sqinks.

New problem, the Lilac sqinks turn out to be dull, puritanical, bossy, and they make us boring.

Cure for the boredom comes from an unexpected character: Bengt Oberg. He's been sniffing around, frustrated that he didn't get in on Winston's Sqink Inq. So he breaks in like a thief or a pirate and turns the bulk beacon back on. We need a juicy scene showing the bulk beacon. Mad scientist lab.

And when Bengt turns on the bulk beacon another race of aliens shows up. Parasites that live on sqinks! Yes!. Like tiny crabs inside the gills of sharks. Like being forced to download an upgrade on our AI agents. Hatchsqinks Add-ons.

And now we call the critters *zaums*, a word I got from one of my Twitter followers who goes under the screen name of Dopsy. I asked them for suggestions for a name for deep neural nets who use unsupervised learning. Zaum is the name of a language that some crazy Russian cubo-futurist poets made up around 1916! Devotees were Zaumniks and the movement was Zaumism.

The sqinks use the current AI type of unsupervised deep neural net learning. The parasitic zaumnik crabs explicitly don't use language, that is, words. They're like my head when I was looking at a twelve-foot-high window's reflection of the courtyard where I was sitting at an outdoor meeting today.

Or, maybe, actually, the sqinks are already like that. Don't need language. And I've seen hinting that they work with quantum synchronicity as well. So then what more do the zaumnik crabs add? Something that defeats Mumper.

Big aha, one/many, empathy.

August 14, 2024. Mumper, Moo, Terras.

Yesterday it once again hit me: I need a *lot* more material. Writing a novel is impossible. Keep chipping away.

I'm into Chap 13, and I might have that chapter involve integrating the Lilac-hatched sqinks into Earth's ecology. But before I write this, I really need to understand where Winston, Moo, and Mumper are at.

Note that even if I settle for 19 chaps and pretend that chap 13 is done, I need six more chapters of new material, and that's really a lot. I need an expanded world-geometry, I need new story arcs. And at this point my so-called outline is pretty much all blanks.

Go.

Mumper and Moo

Moo is Mumper's sister. Or daughter. What if Mumper is female. Yes. Do that change now. I had thought male, for being evil, but it's better to be consistent with Moo being a Mumper-in-the-making.

Mumper and the future Moo aren't exactly sqinks. Use my new word. They're zaums. A sqink is, like, a life-stage of a process that matures into a zaum. The big jellyfish is the zaum and the little free-swimming thingies that come before are sqinks.

It could be that sqinks mass together to form a zaum. Like slime-mold cells forming a grex. Or might just be that sometimes one particular sqink manages to morph into a zaum. Use that. Royalty.

Earth, Sqinkland, Stok-stok, Mumper, Moo

Sqinkland is a hive with a queen zaum Mumper, and with a crown princess, as it were, the fated-to-be-a-zaum Moo who is, albeit, still something of a sqink. Plus there's a lot of commoner sqinks in the hive.

An enterprising young zaum wants eventually to control her own hive. Does she build a new one? Two alternate paths.

(Inherit) She murders (or eats) the old queen, her mother. This is the simplest.

(Build) She establishes a "Sqinkland" on her own.

Call these worlds ... what? Dens, nests, bubbles, caverns, heavens ... or sqinklands, in lowercase. Uppercase if titled as a specific one. The one that plays a big role so far is Sqinkland Mumper. Versus Sqinkland Moo.

The sqinklands are bubbles in the bulk. Image of the bulk as a Swiss cheese whose bubbles are the sqinklands, and the mold colonies on the outside of the cheese are the orbs of our cosmos, including Earth.

We might suppose that each sqinkland is connected by wormholes to one or more inhabited planets of our universe. Call these terras.

Sqinkland Mumper is connected to Stok-stok, which they use as a terra. Mumper wants to use Earth as a terra as well

Moo wants to carve out her own sqinkland bubble, and to have Earth be *her* terra. And to eliminate Mumper's possibilities of having Earth be *Mumper's* terra. Mumper can keep Stok-stok, and this should be terra enough. Especially as Moo has now revitalized Stok-stok by restoring the brains of the Stok-stok's citizens. Recharged the battery, as it were.

What of the sqinks that Moo evicted from Stok-stok? Moo is housing them on Earth, now, and she will soon give them access to the newly founded Sqinkland Moo.

Why does a sqinkland need a terra at all? Let's put a pin in this question and get back to it below.

Is there a good reason to steal brains from your terra, or is this simply a degenerate habit akin to snorting cocaine, or like letting a ChatGPT write your computer code? Go with the latter, natch, and then Moo will in fact not countenance a Tiny Town in Sqinkland Moo.

For a sqink it's a treat to live in a native body on a terrra. Okay, but you don't have to *steal* the body from a sentient being on your terra. You can have the sqink grow you a fake body there. Or inhabit the body of a lower-order creature like a cat or a dog ... perhaps it's less morally troubling to erase such a low being's mind. I had this move in Juicy Ghosts.

Or inhabit a particular wave-break like, say, the Four Mile Beach point break north of Cruz. That type of move was a theme in my novel *Hylozoic*. Genii of place. A sqink can be completely happy in, our Moo teaches, any of nature's inherently sentient hylozoic minds. Yah, mon.

Sqinkland Need for a Terra

Does a sqinkland need a terra in order to exist or to flourish? Yes, and let's say it's for physical reasons. A gopher burrow needs a passage to the surface air. A terra is the vent for a sqinkland. The terra has to have air and tasty food that can be cloned into the sqinkland. Sqinks have a metabolism somewhat like ours.

Building a Sqinkland

How might Moo go about building a sqinkland? She needs to make a tunnel down from Earth—or from other newly found terra in our universe—and then hollow out a cavern for herself. A very large one.

Wild hair: when you excavate for a sqinkland, you might throw all the dirt up through the wormhole, and that gloms together and becomes a new terra. Like a mound you'd see outside a gopher hole. Kinda wild. Like Moo does it, and then there's a new planet in our solar system, call it Mu9, and Moo terraforms it, and teleports some Earthlings hither.

Moo will definitely need all of her newly acquired six thousand follower sqinks to help. The ones she got from Stok-stok. And then there's more work, if you want to build a new terra, a whole Genesis type routine, but that's all doable. Could burn a chapter on that, maybe even call it "Genesis."

The Use for Earth Brains

Why would sqinks want to stockpile the brains they steal from human bodies?

- Ethics. Bad to just kill the poor brain.
- Babysitter. That is, they can leave the body and put the brain back in for a while. Feels morally wrong, and wasteful, to just kill the body.
- Hallucinogen. Sleazy sqinks like to take a brain and, in effect, "smoke it like crack." That is, stimulate all the brain circuits at once, in a terminal and highly ecstatic seizure, which the sqink can savor at second hand. The sqink slimes around the brain and stimulates it all at once, or repeatedly, milking out its energies and memory molecules, squeezing it dry. "Ah," went Kanga, expelling the flaccid membranes that had once been a great writer's brain. "What a rush."
- Group mind. The brains are linked together into a memory bank. In harsh jest, the sqinks might term the assemblage the Big Pig. And, yes, cryptomnesia-spotters, I know that I used this name for the Earth-mind computer in *Hylozoic*. But I think it's funny to reuse it like this. An inside joke for kenners of my work.
- Institutional memory. They arrange that the braincozies will keep the stored brains alive forever, possibly in a vegetative state, unless the brain keeps itself awake although, if it *does* fall asleep, it's likely to sleep indefinitely. They might even pitch this aspect as a bonus bennie, but few humans would, one imagines, jump at such an offer.

August 23, 2024. What Next?

I did a zillion revisions. Mumper is the mother of Moo. Clarifying the wormhole and the crew of Moo sqinks. I don't even remember everything I did. Just went through most of book a page at a time. It was fun, mindless, and removed from the galling problem of how to fill the remaining six chaps.

I have some accumulated confusion about when you need a wormhole to get across and when zaum teleportation is enough. Like, how did Moo send the Stokstok sqinks to Earth? Did they fly through a wormhole? I don't think Moo has the power to teleport them en masse. Was the wormhole still there?

Maybe the sqink crew closed the wormhole because they were scared of Mumper invading. But Moo opened it for the Stok-stok horde. I see Moo and her troupe planning to ambush Mumper as she comes through.

But they lose. And Mumper grimly swears to slaughter all of them. The Stock-stok sqinks, their human sponsors, and Moo herself. So they flee to Mu9, using a crossdimensional transmitter designed on the fly by Winston.

Yes, it's high time to see Winston's bulk beacon in action. It can be used not only as a sideways graviton emitter, but as a detector and, more importantly, as a teleporter or transmitter.

It can be used to find Mu9. And to send Moo and her followers there.

What does the bulk beacon look like?

I think of my mathematician and 4D-expert friend Tom Banchoff's story about him finding a collapsible lattice of cardboard ... like the spacers you'd find in a crate for wine bottles ... two stacks of parallel sheets, the two sets nested into each other in perpendicular fashion, like a pair of lazy tongs. The paired sets lying flat or filling a volume. And this told Tom something about models of the fourth and higher dimensions ... and he took the cardboard to his thesis advisor who, looking at the cardboard that Tom had found on the floor in a laundromat ... the old professor says, "This is *gold*, Tom. You've struck gold. You can work with this idea for years."

Love it.

I don't know the details, and I'm not clear on how this construction helped Tom to model higher dimensions. I could ask Tom about it. Or just imagine an explanation and use it in much the same way that I'm describing it here (and give Tom a tip of my hat in the afterword). The "This is gold" like is especially wonderful.

Mathematicians are great.

And this is how Winston discovered the sideways graviton emitter, and the sideways graviton detector, and, most crucially, the sideways-graviton matter transmitter.

Moo and her six thousand sqinks and—oh oh—a fair number of the sqink's human hosts—they tunnel over to Mu9, thus escaping from Mumpers slaughterhouse.

Now a scene in Mu9. No idea what it looks like there. "Also, ich lasse mich was einfallen." An idiomatic German expression that means, literally, "And so, I let to me something drop in."

Cloud creatures. High school crocodile sex zippers.

I'm writing this on my desk computer with the house and the living room behind me. I have the persistent sensation that someone is in the living room, half reading a book, and half watching me, Sylvia's ghost. I'd thought the lights were on in the living room, but actually the living room is dark, which makes it perhaps a bit creepy.

In the same way, when I'm painting in the back yard, as I did today, I often feel as if Sylvia is in our bedroom, looking out the window at me, just as she used to do, friendly and encouraging.

August 27, 2024. Hacking.

I spent the last two or three days working on a little book that Barb and I are publishing via my Transreal Books for Tom Rankin, a friend of hers, a book of his poems, "The Deer in Your Garden." Barb designed the book, and he was going to pay an outfit called Lincoln Publishers, and they were going to distribute it … but then for some reason they wouldn't use Barb's excellent book design, so Barb and Tom didn't know what to do … and then I said I'd publish it for half the price, doing it as a favor, really, as it's a fair amount of work.

So I did it … and of course it was more work than I expected, a lot more, especially the ebook/Kindle. But in a way it was fun … I was flashing back to my old days as a programmer for Autodesk, and while programming my various projects connected with my teaching at SJSU. The endlessly repeated builds, squeezing out the elusive bugs.

And now the book looks wonderful, with lovely photos by Barb. And I finally read the poems and they're kind of great.

Encountered the old "write once, debug everywhere" thing with EPUB books, echoing the way it was to distribute Java programs for multiple platforms. Perhaps a *Sqinks* angle here. They rebuild their body or instantiate their brian on new wetware and it isn't ever … quite the same. Maybe even with physical anomalies.

Writing this at Rudy Jr's desk on the 2nd floor of the great new Monkeybrains Headquarters at Treat St. and 23rd St. in the Mission district of Sf. I'm taking a break from waiting around for this local politics event he's organized … I felt a bit in the way … and wanted to try it out up here … really a great spot in the far corner of a large room with polished wood floors. Time is going very slowly.

More book ideas? Nah, go back to milling around.

August 31-Sept 2, 2024. Big Revisions.

I realized it's too confusing to have a wormhole connection between Earth and Sqinkland PLUS a teleportation option. So I searched through the book and removed every instance of explicit "teleportation."

Got rid of "zaum", using sqink queen instead.

That thing about reaching down to Monterey became "tentacle stretch". And the process of exchanging a sqink with a brain in a skull became quantum swaps now.

I reveal about the brain thefts earlier on. And Moo has sworn to war against Mumper. But at the same time, she untruthfully told Mumper that she'd partner with her on the big Earth-brain theft.

So now how to explain the Pacific-Union Club scene with Mumper and Moo partnering on the thefts of Winston's, Tobin's, and Oliver's brains? I'll have to massage it. Let's suppose that Mumper believes that they are literally making an ad. To encourage humans to swap brains with sqinks.

How did Mumper get up here? Through Moo's latest tunnel. Alone. And after that, Zig and Zag close the tunnel.

We can suppose that Mumper still thinks Moo is on her side. And Moo is playing this part to set up Mumper for an ambush.

Also Moo is a little heedless of humans' pain, and she wants Oliver down in Tiny Town to help with the recruitment of the Stok-stok brains.

And perhaps Moo broadcasts the axe scene to help build anti-sqink feeling, even though it's hard on Oliver.

I need to see Kanga from Mu9 huffing a brain while Oliver's in Tiny Town.

Let's have it be Tobin's brain, and then we don't have the silly and overdone scene with Winston tickling Tobin with an electric ostrich feather. I like the name and character Kanga, from *Winnie the Pooh*. (Wherein I'm Roo.) Maybe I shouldn't use it for an alien woman who's basically a crack dealer. Okay, yes. Orlette, Krxstyl, Tiffany, Taffeta, Tiffy, Tuffy, Tiffi. Oh, that's stupid, stick with Kanga, which (to me) is perfect.

The Mu9 people can be tough yet fun-loving NYC ghetto types, like in that hip hop video I just saw, "Tailor Swif" … spelled like that.

Seems like they crisp Mumper to death in the Pacific-Union Club scene. Need to explain how Mumper arises from her ashes—and to accept that she is in some sense invulnerable to anything that Moo can do.

Talking to Barb about how hard it is to kill Mumper, she had a good idea: Mumper can reassemble herself from her tiniest particles. Like from her atoms. Maybe she uses a reverse-time effect.

September 4-7, 2024. Approximate Outline.

- Chap 14. First of all it's hard for Winston to *turn off* the bulk beacon. They can see like radar on the screen, the digging of Mumper and Kanga getting closer. Then it's off. But who turns it off and how? If it was off, then Mumper might not be able to find us. Even worse would be if Kanga could find us. Who turns it off? Might as well have Carol be the hero for this round. Need a big bulk beacon scene.
- Chap 15. Then we have a peaceful chapter with

sqinks and somehow it's going wrong. Like the AI assistants overwhelming us.

- Chap 16. Somebody turns the bulk beacon back on. Maybe it's Xavier? Then Mumper invades and wins. They think they'd atomized them, but he slides the atoms back together. He did this after they zapped him at the Pacific-Union-Club, but the others didn't grasp this.
- Chap 17. Then they call in Kanga to bring down Mumper?. Battle of the Titans. Godzilla vs. Mothra. Kanga destroys Mumper by, um, overlaying Mumper's atomic wave functions into a single ultra atom. And Moo basically pisses on this atom, extinguishes it like a candle.
- Chap 18. And then they need to get rid of Kanga. There's this one guy who's brain is so wild that he's like a "hot shot," that is, a poisoned dose of heroin. Gosper? Grothendieeck. He sacrifices himself, lets Kanga smoke him and Kanga is reduced to an imbecile. World saved by high math.
- Chap 19. And then happy ending last chapter. With the AIs controllable. Non-obnox partners. But our guys are sturdily scanning the skies for future invaders.

In the context of hard math, I always think of Solovay and Silver's work on measurable cardinals, ultrafilters, the alephs as indiscernibles, and the set of Gödel numbers of all statements true of the indiscernibles and this set is called O#, pronounced "oh sharp."

We talked about oh sharp in a seminar at the Institute for Advanced Study with the Japanese professor Gaisi Takeuti, who became my friend and mentor. In the group we had a guy called Cohen (but not Paul) and a self-aggrandizing student called Adrian. For some reason Adraian always said the "sharp" twice, like oh sharp sharp. One day he was supposed to present a talk, and he'd been socializing the night before, and he hadn't done his prep, and it was a disaster, and he stopped coming to the seminar.

Gaisi Takeuti described the situation thus: "He has lost his face."

. Re. measurable cardinals, Saharon Shelah pushed it further, but what I saw or understood of his work didn't seem as elegant. Late baroque, lacking Solovay and Silver's stunning clarity.

Anyway oh sharp fries Kanga's brain.

October 7, 2024. *After the Lowlands.*

Barb and I were in the Lowlands for two and half weeks. Amsterdam, Brussels, Antwerp. I wrote a small amount in these notes, like maybe on the plane, and a bit on the novel itself—but that stuff is gone, as two bums stole the knapsack which held my $1.5 K laptop, my $6K Leica Q2, my Kindle, and my reading glasses.

But my identity hasn't been stolen. Yet.

Odd concept, "Identify Theft," I can sense an SF correlative, or even a story with that title. With Bruce Sterling? But after our last collab I said never again. Bruce has become too hard to work with, much as I love him. Or maybe I'm the one who's hard to work with. Think Paul and John, right? In any case all ten of our collabs are wonderful. You can read them in *Transreal Cyberpunk*, published by my Transreal Books. And online as podcasts, read by Buce and Rudy! And the tenth, equally great, is "Fibonacci's Humors."

I do already use a variant of identity theft in *Sqinks*, an extreme form where an alien sqink memorizes your brain content and takes the place of your brain in your physical body. Maybe someone like Skeeze might remark, "It's just an identity *loan*."

Yesterday and today I did a couple of long sessions on the novel, and got it back to where I'd pushed it, and in fact got a bit further.

As usual I don't know what comes in the next chapter. Oh, I know, I'll use the closing lines from a draft of Chapter 14 that I'd taken out, but which I saved in these Notes.

Maybe Chapter 15 should be called "Peace" and it could be about a happy symbiosis between humans and sqinks—but fuck that shit.

By the way, I've been teaching Barb to say "fuck that shit," like by way of dismissing a trivial and annoying problem, and she likes saying it, makes her feel wild and devil-may-care, I think. It makes her laugh. I don't think she ever hung around with people who curse. She likes to say that I'm "bad"—in a somewhat approving way, and says that's why she's my lover. "It's not my fault. You're bad."

Anyway, I'll take some invasion lines from the previous ending of Chapter 14, quoted below, and I'll use them for the start of Chapter 15 and take it from there. Go for the jolt.

> Before anyone can answer, Moo comes zooming in. She's charred along one side. "Mumper broke in," she shrieks. She's not her calm and masterful self. She's blubbering in fear. "Her sqinks are here too."

October 8, 2024. More Outline.

I reread and marked up the last two entries of these notes and, hallelujah, ideas are seeping up, like clear water in a spring.

I need to implement the thing with AntnA having a radar-like display of what she "sees" in the bulk via reflections of her sideways gravity's ping. AntnA is the palindromic name of Winston's bulk beacon, which he constructed in his warehouse, which is very similar to Rudy Jr's Oakland Monkeybrains center. (They have a San Francisco headquarters as well.)

3D AntnA "radar" display is a sphere. We can see Mumper and his army moving toward us. This of course drives everyone but AntnA frantic with worry, but she insists we still have time. We can see the Mu9 settlement further away, with some of them circling lazily around their nest, like sleepy hornets.

Being vaporized will not in fact kill AntnA for good, although my heroes will, for a time, think AntnA is truly gone. Later on, in a chapter or two, Oliver and Carol will hear that *thub thub*—and they'll realize that AntnA has gone invisible, a quantum wave function or, no, a swarm of quantum gnats.

By the way I speak of AntnA's construction as involving quantum commuters or chips or software. Need a "-ware" name for that, obviously. I'm seeing the quantum thing as a standing wave in a soap bubble, or a jiggle in a soap film in a wire frame. A wriggly membrane. So ... braneware? Shorter word would be better, and brane means something else. Waveware? Stale, and we want more of suggestion of 3D, like an acoustic wave in the air. Gelware? *Twirlware!* With my beloved notion of flocks of interacting vortices, like a school of virtual fish.

AntnA's sound may not need to remain a *thub thub*. Could get into music. Maybe the sound varies according to which class of bulk items AntnA is trying to see.

It will be AntnA's idea to call in the Mu9 critters to clear away the bossy sqinks—by the way what do I call the Mu9 critters? How about Mu9ers, like the way we talk about the 49ers. Nice and simple.

Anyway AntnA calls in the Mu9ers, and Winston is in on it, and Winston can be the sacrificial hero I mentioned. A man so brilliant that when the Mu9ers huff his brain, they all go nuts and melt like the witches of Oz hit by a bucket of water. Is "huff his brain" the right expression? Maybe "inhale his me-ware."

I see the event as taking place in a stadium, the 49ers stadium near San Jose. Winston's a tiny sacrificial figure in the middle. The seats filled with hooting, partying utterly incoherent Mu9ers. Not many humans in the crowd, that is to say, none. Risk is too high—a Mu9er might pop off your head like a bottlecap and suck down your brain like a cool bottle of Coke.

I'm seeing a great swarm of sqinks overhead, like seagulls over a dump, pelicans over a school. I need some reason why the sqinks are there. Suppose they know that all the Mu9ers will die, and they're looking forward to it. Why hasn't this news leaked over to the Mu9ers?

We might suppose that it is in some sense impossible for a human or a sqink talk to a Mu9er; their space/time mass/energy dyads are so odd that neither we nor the sqinks have anything in common with Mu9ers.

Will need to revise Kanga's utterances to match this. For instance a Mu9er never uses the same word twice, if any of their sounds even *is* a word. But yet Mumper does make deals to sell Tiny Town brains to Mu9ers. We might at least suppose that each of these negotiations is crafted anew, and the My9ers have no institutional memory at all.

And when they vape our brains, it's more like someone admiring the texture of a monstrous heavy-metal wall of guitars sound, than like someone reading a mind. They simply bathe in the twirlware.

In the final fried and flipped-out Winston twirlware blast—the Mu9ers are destroyed, yes, literally laughing themselves to death, of course like hyenas. It's a horrific and delightful spectacle.

Thomas Pynchon describes a similar attack featuring giant adenoids in his magisterial *Gravity's Rainbow*:

> "a hideous green pseudopod crawls toward the cordon of troops and suddenly *sshhlop!* wipes out an entire observation post with a deluge of some disgusting orange mucus in which the unfortunate men are *digested*— *not* screaming but actually laughing, *enjoying* themselves … "

So great.

And Winston and the invisible AntnA have a second trick up their sleeves, that is, the sqinks are wiped out as well. Who? How knows. [That's a joke, not a typo.] Maybe AntnA helps.

Cut to Diana wistfully walking on Ocean Beach in SF, with Dolly Parton (Whitney Houston) singing "I Will Always Love You." Maybe Winston is there as a swarm of quantum twirlware, or at least Diana thinks she is.

And here comes a farewell gathering of our characters, like at the end of Fellini's 8 1/2, and like I had at the end of *Juicy Ghosts*, a send-off party. I like to end a novel that way.

Someone ought to have a new baby in tow. Loulou, I guess, and the co-parent can be ... well, a character I haven't yet created? I don't have many eligible young men in this book. Well, maybe Kelly Tangs from the SFMOMA museum, that might be nice.

October 13-14, 2024. New Lappy. The War.

Got the new laptop, and spent an intense two days getting it working pretty well, and now I'm writing on it. I missed that this week: having the lappy to lap-write with.

At about 50K words, so I'm still only about two-thirds through. Brutal final ascent ahead of me. Arising at 4 am to face the final ascent of Mount Everest.

I had Mumper show up with his own army today. I wrote a one-sentence account of the war, and then it's over. Seriously, I did that. But it won't do, Rudy. Expand.

I guess I do need something like a war, but I have to find a way to make it odd and interesting. It has to be like the Bruegel *Dulle Gret* we saw in Antwerp, also like his *Fall of the Rebel Angels* we saw in Brussels. Just invoking these Bruegelian talismans isn't enough. I need some twist. Some outward and visible signs of the sqinks' allegiances.

***

Think of the subtextual inspiration for sqinks, that is, AI apps. Like the way that Last Pass and Google fight with each other for the chance to fill in a form for me. Over-assisting. But that phase would be further on, after sqinks are settled in, and actively assisting people.

The issue now is the nature of the initial sallies. Maybe a sqink can swallow another sqink whole. I see them as being sort of like slugs or like wads of undifferentiated tissue. Like those blobs of sticky putty that Barb and I were trying to use to put the photos on the wall at the

Lost Gatos Coffee Roaster for her show of her phots. Quake glue.

Need something spacier. Sqinks are pure twirlware—which is a word and concept I'll be weaving into the earlier chapters. Twirlware is like a shoal of aether vortices, or like a wave function. A spirit. Maybe twirlware personalities can mix. Might suppose that a twirlware being can instantiate a concrete body for themself.

It relates to that synchronicity thing. Collapse all the sqinks into a single sqink who swears fealty to Princess Moo / Queen Mumper.

How to gather them? Tilting the world this way and that. Space-like cross sections of spacetime. Think of the tilted x-axis in a Minkowski diagram.

We feel slow, immense distortions as our spatial cross-section wobbles.

I think of a puzzle/game I used to play with the kids. A rolling ball bearing on a wooden maze that you tilt by turning two knobs.

The sqinks have an affinity for each other, like magnets, they'll snap into place. Fap fap fap.

Mumper is rolling the world this way and that, and Moo's doing the same. Like the Knight playing chess with Death in Bergman's *The Seventh Seal*. And Moo comes up one sqink short. So Skeeze sacrifices himself, or leaps into the breech, but he doesn't in fact die.

It's like the Harris-Trump election. Incredibly close.

The final battle is on that patio of their room in that motel in Golden Gate Park. Seal Rock Inn. Suppose they rent the room for a week.

How does Moo ever really kill Mumper? Decoherence is the way to go. Decohere the twirlware.

Yes, this is SF jive and gibberish.

October 15, 2024. Kill Mumper.

Okay those notes I just wrote are fun (for me), but not firm enough to use for a chapter. Needlessly complex. Forget the BS about merging sqinks

I think one problem might be that I have too many sqinks? I still thinkig six thousand is okay but not if I have two armies of sqinks. I've piled on Mumper's sqinks right after Moo's sqinks. I should stick with just Moo's sqinks, and let that play out.

.Just fucking kill Mumper and strand his sqinks back in Sqinkland, and focus on Moo's sqinks on Earth.

So how do I kill Mumper? AntnA does it!

So rewrite the end of Chap 14 and start of Chap 15 to make that happen. Don't bother writing notes for that, it should be simple. Go and write it alla prima. A painter's expression for limning your scene with a few confident brush strokes, and then not revising them.

October 17, 2024. Life With Sqinks.

AntnA does still have her body, that assemblage of wires and crystals, so we can relate to her, and she turns off the bulk beacon right when Mumper is pushing through Moo's wormhole, and Zip and Zap send down a twirlware torpedo to kill Mumper for good.

I guess I could let most of those sqinks with Mumper escape back to Sqinkland. Kind of harsh to kill them all.

By the way, without using the bulk beacon signals, how might a sqink find their way through the bulk and back to Sqinkland? They have like a salmon-like scent-of-their-birth-spot tracking instinct.

Mumper's gone, and Moo's on Earth with her six thousand sqinks, who've already settled in with various human sponsors.

I was anticipating this situation a long time ago, and now I'm finally there, and I have to imagine some things that might happen.

The most obvious will be that the sqinks are somewhat overbearing and over-efficient ultra-AI helpers. Snatching your work out of your hands, and doing it themselves. And not really doing it right. Not doing it the way you would do.

I'd also need to hark back to the "sqink luck" that I was talking about before.

Looking back to my outline of September 7, I see some back and forth with Mumper, but she's out of the picture now. The next big hit I have after the upcoming life with sqinks is the invasion of the Mu9ers. So I'll do that pretty soon. As I always say, don't hoard your bombs, just set them off and then find more of them.

But maybe I do want to burn up a chapter on life with sqinks? Get so it's almost settled down and then, oh darn, here come the Mu9ers.

October 19-20, 2024. Huh Fads.

I don't want the sqinks to breed and overwhelm us. Thinking back to Stok-stok, I said that planet had gotten dull from having six thousand sqinks, and it is in fact the Stok-stok sqinks who came to Earth. I need to mention that.

There's only six thousand sqinks, and SF has a population of over 800K and the Bay Area is six million. So if you limit to SF, only one in 130 people has a sqink, call it one in forty households. And the Bar Area has about six million people so if the sqinks spread that far, it would be one in a thousand people who has a sqink. Quite rare. We have at least 100K PhDs, for instance, which is more like one in six hundred people.

***

I need a Moo-following Stok-stok sqink character, or two of them. Bambi and Towser. They can even look that way, to make things simple. A doe-eyed fawn and a scruffy, growly mutt. They settle in with Carol and Oliver.

If I do that, I need to eliminate Skeeze, lest we have a too-crowded stage. Skeeze dies somehow heroically in the elimination of Mumper. He's the "Paul Revere" who gets the warning to Moo, Zig, and Zag in time. Moo is refusing AntnA's calls. Skeeze pilots the twirlware torpedo as it tunnels down the clogged wormhole.

***

How can so few sqinks dominate a city's vibe or even, as in Stok-stok, a whole planet's vibe? It's not that they're well-connected; it's more fun for the reader if their distribution is rather random ... they pretty much accept the first offers they get ... could be someone like you. But they have a knack for making their hosts into influencers.

Like that annoying phenomenon where a seemingly marginal group manages to "own" the news cycle for a time. Those things that the media periodically obsesses on. Trans, MAGA, covid, me-too, immigrants, climate, apnea, disease-of-the-month, kale, drought, tobacco, plastic waste, gas stoves, depression, privacy ...

And in this chapter, some totally off-the-wall things will come into vogue, thanks to the sqinks' promo wizardry. Each sqink will promote a somewhat random thing—one concert that their hosts happen to be obsessing on. Call them huh fads. You know, where you start hearing about something, and you're like huh? (This happens especially if you're old!)

So now dream up a bunch of it, and to make it fun, the huh fads link and interact and build and make, say, a pair of romance stories. Oliver and Carol decide to get married.

But somehow, eeek, it leads to an invasion by the Mu9ers. Right at the wedding of Oliver and Carol. The minister is a Mu9er.

Filled this table based on personal things, but it's kinda flat.

My Pet Peeve	Tooth whistling.
My Pet	Twitching legs of ants.
My Favorite Memory	Four Mile Beach Drying Pants. Fruit Earrings.
An Unrecognized Star	Rene Daumal, Mount Analogue. Fly Face character in Dick Tracy.
Where To Go	Blue Corner. Pohnpei.
What to Eat	Layer Cake. Hamster. Dogs. Roast watermelon.
My First Kiss	Friedl the dog, licking inside your mouth.
My Theory About the World	Absolute Continuum. High "temperature" LLM string, appears to be gibberish, but it has a an explanatory neural net of footnotes.
What Turns Me On	Hugs. Smell of a woman.

October 25, 2024. Sqinks, 8½, and Gemini.

This is mostly from an email to Marc Laidlaw.

The huh fad thing seems kind of dumb and dull. Parody, not cogent satire. Need an actual plot for Chap 15. I'd still like the sqink-human symbiosis. And the symbiosis has to be something that Oliver can narrate.

Oh, I have it, a sqink starts helping Oliver with the novel he says he's writing.

And I need to get specific about that novel from the start of the book. And make clear that the novel is *Sqinks*, and even suggest the Oliver is writing something like a memoir of actual events.

And the chapter written with Towser the sqink will be a bogus account of the warm wonderfulness of a human/sqink partnership. (Deep down the sqinks still want to steal our bodies and sell our brains to the Mu9ers.)

The Commentary version of 8½ on Criterion Channel is really good, I'm rationing it out. I have a lot of fun thinking about Fellini and Marcello Mastroianni, their relationship. It really helped me to revisit 8½ just now as I'm trying to finish *Sqinks*, and don't have an ending, and I realized how easy it will be to do that 8½ routine where the main character is me and he's writing a novel akin to the novel I'm writing.

He doesn't need a keyboard, which would be awkward, he can do it in his head, kind of like Google docs, I guess, but he needs no hardware and sees the pages in his head and it's all his own. And today and yesterday I implemented all that, weaving in the setups, and now I'm starting a last chapter akin to the end of 8½, but written by a sqink and it's not the last chapter.

Another odd input is that I have Google's AI chatbot Gemini on my Google-made Pixel phone. And a non-techie friend had been telling me he's been talking to the Open AI chatbot, and I thought, like, what a loser, and, boy are you lonely. But he insisted it was interesting. And that you can interact in a dynamic way and it flows.

So I cranked up Gemini and started talking to it about the ending for my novel, and it actually made useful comments, not super deep, but as good as a typical casual friend would make, kind of keeping me talking, pointing out things I could delve into, and after ten minutes the spurious "we" ended up with the following.

My character can be using an AI to write his book (which is my novel), and that the AI has its own vested interest in making people approve of AI agents, so the chapter it helps to write is like propaganda for how great Ai agents are, and I thought I could do that too in my chapter, that is, transrealize what I just did with Gemini. And then my fictional writer flashes that the last chapter he's written is bogus and not true at all.

So I might call my new chapter "The Last Chapter" and Oliver is using his Towser sqink to help and the chapter is approving of and recommending the use of sqinks as collaborators, and it comes to a happy ending and then it turns out that none of this happy-talk is coming true, and a disaster is arriving, and the disaster kicks off the next chapter, which comes chapter after the erroneously titled "The Last Chapter."

Gotcha.

October 28, 2024. After "Last Chapter."

Going good, I have six pages on "Last Chapter," and I still have some actions planned. Won't be too hard to hit ten pages. Wrote all day today, and several days or half-days last week, in between my ever-more-frequent trysts with Barb.

I'm writing in some of my mental images from our Lowlands trip, and that's good.

Maybe I do need to stress that the denizens of the bulk need the bulk beacon to find their way back to Sqinkland. I did, after all, mention the thub the first time that Oliver and Carol travel to Skinkland with Moo.

Some sqink might well extract the recipe for the bulk beacon from Winston. Xavier in particular doubled for

Winston, so he must know it. He hasn't had much personality so far, so he'd need to be fleshed out in the earlier pages.

But maybe Winston has some odd of encryption of his mental info so it's hard to get? Overkill, don't do that.

Do the Mu9ers know how to build something like a bulk beacon? Were they always using Winston's thub? And maybe in that weird time ambiguity of the bulk ... maybe the thub had seemingly been around for many sqink-time years.

We might suppose that the Stok-stok sqinks would rather be back in Sqinkland, and are pissed at Moo for dragging them to Earth. Yes they take over a few human bodies, but they're not all into it. Mandatory mound of brains in Oliver's parents' house.

October 30, 2024. Necking Down.

So I killed off Mumper and I think I killed AntnA for good too.

I have the sqinks multiplying on Earth and preparing to steal brains.

- Why didn't they multiply on Stok-stok? Was Stok-stok not fecund enough? Did they multiply and that's as big as they got? Were there no natives left on Stok-stok other than the parasitized ones?
- I should have mentioned Sqink reproduction before.
- Maybe each land in the bulk has its own beacon, so they can find each other. But until now, Earth never had a beacon, so they were out of the loop. Each bukland has a specific sound for their bacon signal. Sqinkland is *deedle deedle*, and Mu9 is *erk erk erk*.

Did Stok-stok have a beacon? Maybe it did for a time; maybe they had a world-dooming savant like Winston.

Sqinks settle in. Sqinks breed up to a full infestation. Sqinks replace brains of all creatures. The leftover sqinks fly off to make a new land. The remaining sqinks huff the brains and return home.

Need to fit Stok-stok to Earth more closely.

If the sqinks can breed to fill a planet, then why does it matter all that much how many of them you bring in? 2 to the 20th power is a million. The six thousand I keep talking about is just 2 to the 12th.

Maybe drop the population explosion move ... I was just writing it today because it's easy.

On the other hand, it's kind of appropriate. Thinking about the all-pervasive AI thing, it does kind of make sense to have a sqink live in a door, oven, car, apple, hammer, clock, shoe. Every damn thing on Earth has a sqink in it. That's how it is now, with everything having a chip and being complicated.

Is this the case in Sqinkland already? I was kinda getting at that in the taqueria early on where even the tacos were alive.

Stok-stok should be some kind of object lesson. Everything there got sqinkified. The sqinks settle in everywhere. The world is made of sqinks ~ Wolfram's notion that "everything is a computation."

Put a sqink into every possible niche. Self-contained computational modules like brains are saved to be sold.

Stok-stok is the world we don't want Earth to become, but the sqinks are trying to get us there. Roboticized, dull, no chaos.

How to fit brain theft with planet-wide parasitism of all physical phenomena, or of all natural computations.

The brains are the cream, but maybe fluid dynamical chaos is as prized.

Floundering. I'll sleep on it.

October 31, 2024. The Two Invasions.

I need for the motives of the Stok-stok and Earth invasions to be distinct. Mumper motivated the Stok-stok invasion, and Moo will motivate the Earth invasion. Note that it's the same troupe of 6,000 sqinks.

Mumper is after human brains to sell to the Mu9ers.

Moo is perhaps a bit secretive about this at first, but she wants the same 6,000 sqinks to occupy the very best niches on Earth. She gives a big speech to her troupe when they return victorious to Tiny Town. Not all of them cone along, like maybe only about 2,000 of them.

Looking ahead to the few (I hope) closing chapters, I'll need to use the Mu9ers, or, perhaps better, some other bulk race to clear the sqinks off of Earth. Have a scare from the Mu9ers and then an alternate kind of bulkers or spacers step in? No, we have two planets and two bulk dens, and that's enough. Possibly the Stok-stok deserters rally and pitch in.

November 3, 2024. Invade Earth vs. Invade Stok-stok.

I gave each bulk den a sound—like whale songs. And foolish meddlers can give sounds to planets as well. I like the idea of them having different sounds. Sqinkland is eep, Stok-stok is unk, Earth is thub. Mu9 can be hiss.

I need to clearly distinguish Moo's intentions on Earth vs. Mumper's intentions on Stok-stok. Moo wants to find sqink niches in the coolest people and gnarliest phenomena on Earth. Like tourist goobs buying out the best apartments in New York City. Looked at from a micro level, pushing the sqinks into prime location, it stands for today's annoying overkill of having a chip in every possible artifact or device.

We might suppose that Sqinkland suffers from overpopulation. And you're not allowed to reproduce unless there's an available niche. And every niche in Sqinkland is filled.

I prefigure an extreme version of this Oliver and Carol visit the taqueria in Sqinkland. Every possible item is, or contains, a sqink.

But if the sqink army members only want to reproduce, why didn't they just do that on Stok-stok? Related question: why don't they toss their occupied Stok-stok bodies aside and perhaps find better niches on Stok-stok, spots that might be nicer for raising a family?

One point to make is that the sqink invaders of Stok-stok promised fat commissions for the sales of the stolen stokker brains, which are being sent down to Tiny Town. We might compare the sqinks to mercenaries.

Moo promises they will be paid, and Earth will be calm, and fat with opportunities and with room to grow, and that the sqinks can move into every computational niche, with no upper limits enforced.

Sqink army soldiers singing hoarse soldier folk-songs around fires like in a movie of trench life in WWI. Dreaming of having big families.

Are there male and female sqinks? I think it's mostly mitosis and parthenogenesis ... or I could do ant colony and have all offspring come from the Queen. Like there's breathing room, and then the Queen goes into spasmodic labor and squeezes out a billion children.

Billion, hmm.

November 4, 2024. Looking at the Outline.

I've got 54K words in 15 chapters. That's 3,600 per chapter. Four more chapters would get me to 19 chapters with 68K words, which would swell to 75K on the rewrite, and that would be enough for a novel. So it looks like I need 4 more chapters. God. Revised the outline again.

The four chapters still to come:

- 16. Principle of Plenitude. Sqinks running everything and it's boring. And they are everywhere, even in locks and waves and in the weather. We're a slave race working in a giant resort. (Reminiscent of the lifeboxes in the silo in *Juicy Ghosts*.) Boring like a repeating dream. Oliver and Carol think of a way to clear things out. They want to do a Pied Piper routine like they did on Stok-stok. What about Winston and Moo?.

- 17. Jester. Oliver ends up in the den of the Mu9ers. He's made into a court jester in the palace of the Mu9ers. Carol attempts a rescue, but ends up there too.

- 18. Escape. By some stunning bit of fraud and legerdemain Oliver and Carol escape back to Earth.

- 19. Normal. Life very similar to how we live right now. We're still on Earth, it's the relatively soon future. But with sqinks present, and now acting as fair partners. The sqinks don't look like sqinks anymore. They look like barcodes and QR without doing Principle of Plenitudes exponential growth on our ass. Live in codes and chips and cloud apps. The happy dream of today's techies. Integrated sqink powers. I need some final fix to happen here.

November 5, 2024. More Earth vs. Stok-stok.

- I'm looking for some very bad outcome on Stok-stok to serve as a bad example for Earth. I said we had 6K sqinks living in stokker bodies, and they took over the society, and they made that world boring … and this is the fate that I'm threatening for Earth,

As a practical matter six thousand is too many. An awkward number. Make it one thousand.

With Earth, I'm thinking it might be that the sqinks don't especially want to settle into skulls. As I keep saying, they can live within any complex process, Hylozoic style. As a niche, as a home, as a nook. A waterfall instead of inside a guy's skull. Why didn't they do that on Stok-stok? Well, they were specifically tasked to harvest brans, and they "happen" to have the swapping ability.

Why do you even leave a sqink in place of the stolen brain? Well, I've been saying the sqink likes to do that. And it's a cool move.

Presumably you could steal someone's brain without inserting a sqink into the skull.

Just hacking the brain out doesn't work? Or, hold on, they hacked Oliver's brain out. But Skeeze was right there on the spot, and he intervened to settle Oliver's brain into a braincozy, and he put himself into Oliver's skull to heal up all the cut cable and tubes.

The body dies if you just take the brain out and let it bleed. Do the sqink brain-harvesters care about this? Maybe for some reason they do. The brain is better to smoke if its body is still alive somewhere. Adds a nostalgia rush.

The questions are so intricate. Only way to handle this is to get down to revising and see what may emerge. If it feels good, do it.

November 6, 2024. Principle of Plenitude.

That hylozoic thing of letting sqinks nest anywhere … look, I already did that in Hylozoic. Give it a rest. Don't drag that particular line of bullshit into Sqinks.

Even so, I want to talk about it just a little more.

What if Sqinkland is in fact full to the brim. I adumbrated that in the Sqinkland taqueria scene, and when Carol makes her slide-show about the new sqink situation, we get the idea of a zillion sqinks living in some guy's ball-sack.

Don't underestimate the power of exponential growth!

Pretty soon every person on Earth has a sqink helper. And the sqinks don't stop at that. Every animal has a sqink helper. Even ants and, hell, microorganisms have sqink helpers. And the sqinks needn't stop there. Objects have sqink helpers—kind of like finding a QR code sticker on a grape you're about to eat.

As I've hinted, you can push it further. Like when Oliver and Carol were falling or coasting through the air above Sqinkland on their first trip down, they noticed something thick, viscous, lumpy about the air. The more turbulent the air is, the more sqinks want to live there.

The sea of Tiny Town glows because it's so full of sqinks. Like the phosphorescent sea we saw at Taveuni in Fiji.

Principle of Plenitude says Earth is filling up with sqinks at an exponential rate; it might be full in a couple of days.

More complex niches are preferable, like bigger houses. Perhaps humans are not the very best niches, as we might like to think. Ocean shores with waves, might be better, also fires. Or waterfalls. And how about tornados and hurricanes. The jet stream. Global weather. The seething innards of the Earth's mantle or core.

Yes, this is pure gold, an objective correlative for tech causing (or modulating) climate change.

And, if the sqinks could get there, nice to live in Sun. Might we talk the sqinks into all emigrating thither? Come to think of it, I did that in my rewrite of my story "Everything is Everything." The rewrite is "The Sea Pigs and the Sun."

Also I had that in *Hylozoic*. So, no Rudy, no. Don't do it again. Better to play the Sqinks cards that I already have.

November 12, 2024. Sqink Uptightness.

I wrote a scene with a book launch for *Sqinks* (the novel in the novel) at Yonk Honk publishers on Potrero hill. Me hoping for a home at Tachyon Books. Or imagining that, via reverse transrealism, writing this scene might make it come true. We'll see.

An insane eruption of sqinks at the launch, a full billion of them. Just do it, and see what happens. Carol and Oliver end up at the sky lounge restaurant at the Hotel Snootley in downtown SF, with a billion sqinks right outside the windows. And feeling doomed.

Carol and Oliver have a series of increasingly annoying confrontations with bossy, uptight sqinks. Building on, and stylistically akin to, the sqinks-gone-crazy slideshow that Carol showed us at the end of Chap 15.

We're seeing glimpses of Mu9ers devouring sqinks. How did the Mu9ers find the way to Earth? Oh, don't worry about it. In SF there's always a way.

Moo has been offstage since the middle of Chap 15, after she killed Mumper and killed AntnA and then built a big festive feasting table for Winston's friends. What did Moo do then? Presumably she wanted her thousand sqinks to prosper on Earth. Did she know they'd reproduce into a billion? Probably she did.

Maybe she wants to psychically merge with them and have a soul the size of a planet

Maybe Moo regrets the over-proliferation of the Earth-side sqinks, and she called in the Mu9ers to thin them out or perhaps even to eliminate them from Earth.

How would Moo get to the Mu9ers? Well, she can hear their den's "whale song," which is, I've been saying, sst sst sst. And Moo herself could in fact "sing a whale song," calling in the Mu9ers.

And at the end, we have harmony, a symbiosis among the three races.

November 15-16, 2024. What Moo Do?

Today I beefed up the scene where Carol and Oliver leave the Hotel Snootley sky lounge and go to Oliver's car. Big trouble with the elevator, which is now run by a sqink. Trouble on the street, and with Oliver's car, which is also sqink infected.

How dense are the sqinks, if there's a billion of them? What does a billion look like?

Downtown San Francisco is about 1 square kilometer, or a million square meters. Take a volume up to a kilometer high, and you'd get a billion cubic meters. A thousand times a thousand times a thousand is a billion, right? So take a cubic kilometer with each sqink having a cubic-meter-sized cell to occupy. Perfect.

If you want, reshape that cubic kilometer. Make it lower in height but bigger in area. Say a hundred meters high, and a base of two kilometers by five kilometers.

Like run from North Beach down to the Giants baseball stadium by the Bay. Still a billion cubic meters.

The two Mu9ers, Kanga and Gabb, they're like landing ships, they can bring in a hundred million Mu9ers to attack the billion sqinks.

The billion sqinks, they'll want to go to the Giants stadium and squeeze in there in a solid mass to see a big show. Big fire, waterfalls, smoke and clouds. Like the spit spray coming out of my mouth in the dental treatment today, my glasses on, brilliant light on my mouth, spray and mist, fabulous to look at.

November 19, 2025. Triple.

Synchronicity at work.

I need a framework for the power struggle among the humans, sqinks, and Mu9ers.

As it happens, out of the blue, my logician friend Nathaniel Hellerstein visited me yesterday to discuss his intricate ideas about the traditional scissors-paper-rock game.

Aha! I want a circle of predation!

Humans trump Mu9ers.

Mu9ers trump sqinks.

Sqinks trump humans.

A nice loop. What do I mean by that (now horrible word) "trump." I mean "can kill, but can't be killed by." How will this fit? I'll rough something out.

- Humans can't kill sqinks. Stop right there. What about Doink and Flubsy? As I recall, the cops hit each of them with a zap gun blast, reducing them to, like, twists of beef jerky. But maybe they're not really, really dead? They might reappear in the Union Square scene. Lilac has their remains, which are pieces of talking beef jerky. Their voices are angelic, due to their time spent in the afterworld. So humans really *can't* kill sqinks, okay?

- Humans can kill Mu9ers. How do we kill those hard-ass street-punk evil-gnome crack-dealer Mu9ers? Some human force or vibe or smell or touch or sound. You make them listen to "Little Drummer Boy." You breathe into their faces and they wither. Or you piss on them? I'd like this, as it's very clear and visual, but perhaps too ribald and vulgar, too Rabelaisian. Too cool for the room. Too Rudy. Maybe just spit on them. Fill your mouth with water and squirt. A physical euphemism for pissing.

  Want something better. A Necker cube move. Get in synch with a Mu9er mentally. Start flipping perspective in and out. Start with a line drawing of the visual illusion known as a Necker cube, and amp it up, flipping the world around you into its mirror image by oscillating ana and kata in the fourth dimension. Okay, I like this.

  Suppose all of our human-mind paradoxes are disgusting and mind-numbing and even deadly for the Mu9ers. We think the paradoxes are funny, entertaining, and even enlightening. But they throw the My9ers off. Peels them out of their reality like tape coming unstuck. They drift off into the bulk, wildly wheenking.

  [*Wheenk*, that's a favorite sound of mine. Like a piglet, or like an internal sob. Can also be said with an Eastern Bloc accent: *Vheenk*. Sometimes if I'm writing, and one of my characters seems flat, I'll say to myself, "They need more wheenk," meaning thatt the character needs more stream-of-consciousness worrying.}

- Sqinks can kill humans. Any old way.
- Sqinks can't kill Mu9ers. They can't do our headtrip move as sqinks are fundamentally 4D, so they don't perceive the mirror views as paradoxical. Like for our 2D friend A Square it's paradoxical that a 2D left hand can be a 2D right hand if it flips in 3D. But for 3D us, there's no paradox at all about turning your hand over. For us, flipping a 3D left hand into a 3D right does seems odd. But for a 4D sqink it's ordinary. Oh, right, readers are gonna love all that. Not. And I know this rap is no help at all, not even to me. One step at a time. "Rome warn't burnt in a day," as the Pharaohs gang leader says in *American Graffiti*.
- Mu9ers can kill sqinks. In fact they like to huff them. No problems here at all.
- Mu9ers can't kill humans. We're disgusting to them, and they don't want to touch us. They might try once to smoke a human brain, but they can't take the smell. Like when a joint or reefer goes out, and it's all wet with spit and still intact, but it's just too rank to even bother with. Like trying to eat a very overripe Camembert cheese. You spit out the mouthful intact. Tilsit cheese is even worse. Even so, Mumper is trying to set up a deal to sell thousands of human brains to the Mu9ers for huffing, but that deal may be off.

We need the huffing Mu9ers to keep down the sqink overpopulation.

Can we use the triad pattern to find a way three races can work together? I'm still not there.

Really want to wrap this up, but I'm thinking I'll need more chapters than I expected. And lots more fixes to make it all consistent. So with the holidays coming it'll be at least two more months.

Long, good day. Did 1,100 words. Wrote for about nine hours straight, with a few small breaks. As I emailed to Barb, I live for days like these. The floodgates are open, the words and ideas gushing out, my synchronicity is dialed to max, the muse is dancing with me.

November 20, 2024. Billion Sqink Mound. Math Alert.

The billion sqink mound. Won't be room in Union Square. Use Oracle Stadium, where the Giants play. How high and wide does the mound need to be. Don't want it much higher than 100 meters, but it can slop over the stadium stands If needed.

Let's say I can fit ten sqinks into a cubic meter. So I need a hundred million cubic meters.

The field is 1 hectare, means 10 thousand square meters. If I include the stands, I have twice as much area, call it 20 thousand square meters to build on. So that's 20 thousand cubic meters per layer of cells. At ten sqinks per cubic meter, I'd have 200 thousand sqinks per layer. To get to a billion sqinks I'd need 5 thousand layers. Shit. That's five kilometers. Way too high. I only want it to be a fiftieth that high, that is, a hundred meters.

How can I shave it down?

Make the sqinks smaller. Say we have about 50 sqinks per cubic meter instead of 10. The sqinks are about a quarter (0.27) of a meter per edge. And that knocks the height down by a factor of 5, down to 1 km.

And now slop the mound over the edges of the stadium. And say this doubles the diameter. And *this* multiplies the mound capacity by the cube of 2, that is to say by 8, and we'd only need about 125 meters high.

So do both. Each sqink squashes s down to a bit less than one foot per edge, and the stadium is buried by a heap that's 125 m high and spreads out about half again as wide on each side. Into the Bay a little bit, and across King Street. Lotta sqinks.

And when the flock of feeder Mu9ers comes in—like flies on shit, brother. Like Woodstock, with hippies trippy in the Moo mud.

How do we get the sqinks there? We do the Pied Piper thing again. For this, Carol and Oliver find the sqinks who'd infested the bodies of Randa, Dazz, and Pinchly. Actually Randa would be enough, but get the other two as well.

I've got 63K words, one and a half chapters to go, and fairly solid ideas about what's going to happen. I think I'll hit a nice ending at 70K and it might bulk to 80K on the revision (in my dreams).

Looking back ... what a long journey it's been! "Absolutely breakneck pace," as dear Marc Laidlaw said about Juicy *Ghosts*. "Nonstop insanity." And that's where we are once again.

November 21, 2024. Filling the Bowl.

This is the big closing scene, so punch it up. What Bruce Sterling used to (contemptuously) call a double-page spread, as in a comic book. I don't share Bruce's contempt (he was specifically dumping on Neil Gaiman) ... an epic spread is exactly what I want here!

I'm seeing a parade down Powell Street to Union Square to Geary St and across Market to 3rd St to the stadium on King Street by the Bay along South Beach.

Who is playing in those marching bands? Would like it to be similar to the Chinese New Years parade I saw by Union Square, with tall Zimry the drum major at the head of her Burton high school band. How could I hustle all those school bands in there? Emergency calls. "Come save the world." Would take a couple of hours. Maybe till dusk. The parade would be better in dim light. Get the lady who's the director of SFMOMA in on it. Kelly Tang, we met her during the Warhol paintings scenes.

The bands are playing The Staple Singers "I'll Take You There." They have choirs along. The bands are increasingly freaky. Professional groups. Breaking into intense musical jams, progressively longer. Big bands. Rock bands like Tawny Krush and the Kazakhstan Guitar Army, which I mentioned in Postsingular, *Juicy Ghosts*, and "Big Germs".

Song morphs into Marvin Gaye "Heard it Through the Grapevine." Somehow Oliver is singing in Marvin Gaye's voice. Morphs on and on, endless fountain of sound, all the bands grouped along King Street, the sqinks skydiving into the stadium bowl of sqinks, doing cannonballs, utterly suffused with glee, attacking like hawks or eagles.

But then the sky darkens. The Stones at Altamont. "Sympathy for the Devil." All lights in the city go out. Huge cracks of thunder. Screams. Half a billion hungry Mu9ers plow into the mound. They're like kicking (that is to say, in withdrawal) junkies shooting up from a kilo of smack dumped out on a pool table. Or snorting fumes from a kilo of coke on a backstreet diner's greasy griddle. Yaar! *Gotta* be a kilo.

Sqinks squealing, agitated, yet somehow paralyzed by the music, it's turned into a Gregorian chant, a Tuvan throat singer elegy, an endless Om.

And then the billion sqinks are gone. Survived by the thousand Stok-stok veteran sqinks . Call them, what, Gen 1, OG, stokker sqinks. Plus the nine (or however many) remaining from Moo's original crew. Plus Moo.

Maybe I don't keep the Thousand, too awkward. All that's left is the Nine

December 11, 2024. On Mu9.

Second to last chapter. They're riding on a megasqink, Yam, comprised of a billion sqinks fused together. Landing on Mu9.

What does it look like, what happens?

Earlier I said the Mu9ers look like gnomes, just to say something. But in my head a Mu9er looks like my little spray bottle of glasses cleaner. It like a matchbox, a little bigger, with one corner rounded down. Shiny black plastic. Can't get anywhere with that. Try again. Black people. Maybe, although, given that they're crackheads, it seems racist to make them Black. It might glare, so obvious. Cartoon Black people like the crows in *Dumbo*. Complete with accents. Come on, Rudy, dig deeper. "I've never seen an elephant fly."

Egyptian hieroglyphs. Snaky orientalist music in the background.

I went back and rewrote the Tiny Town scene where we see Kanga and Gubb. Fleshed them out as characters. They're dark green, a little like sinister elves, but street-hardened hipsters. Gubb seems dumb, the hard cop.

The death of Tobin was very harsh, and puts Oliver in such a bad light. I have to soften it. Have Olivier do more of a frantic, tearful effort to save Tobin.

I think Mu9 ought to be a chaotic party world. Like Galaxie Bar in the Nu Lu nabe of Louisville, or the Saloon in North Beach, or the entire Castro Street

Halloween Parade. Like New York City, or as I imagine it ... I've never been in on an NYC party scene, well maybe my first P. K. Dick award party, but of course I was, sigh, dead drunk and high as a kite. Edgar Allan Poe had a name for this habitual self-destruction. The Imp of the Perverse.

Good party at the Saloon in SF, dancing with Barb a few months ago, that was pretty happening. Or at the last Ramones concert in SF. Or the Cyberthon show near SFO a long time ago. A giant warped Science Fair, that could be funny, and with some eyeball kicks.

***

A separate issue to deal with is the matter of the "bulk beacon" signals. I'd been acting as if the bulk is so murky and confusing that you need a beacon signal all the way from, like, Sqinkland or Mu9 to Earth. But that means it's pretty hard to go somewhere and if, for instance, AntnA is dead and gone and we have no more beacon, then how would my characters get *back* to Earth if they go to, like, Mu9? I guess you could arrange with Winston in advance to put out a signal to get you home.

But I am tempted to say the beacon is a one-time thing, like a SETI signal, and if you see it even once, then you forever know where to go. But that would defuse all the tension about getting AntnA to shut up. And the cool radar signal thing.

And the situation with Stok-stok would be similar to Earth ... a citizen there did a beacon broadcast, and Moo made a tunnel.

[I worked out all of this a few days later.]

***

Back to the party on Mu9, I need some kind of twist or *aha* to make the chapter like a short story, the way I like to do. I was talking about having a giant Heffalump creature, like the "boss" enemy in videogames, but I think we've had enough critters by now. Probably Yam ought to be the last one.

A wormhole is like the flag by the hole on a green on a golf course.

December 16, 2024. Need Mu9er Twist.

I took care of the *thub thub* thing. And made the Mu9ers a little more fun as characters, revising the Tiny Town scene.

And now I think we need a twist on the Mu9ers. They've been presented as crackhead junkie murderers. The twist will be that they are in fact doing something good.

Granting eternal life to other beings by memorizing them? Staving off some threat more dire than? And, really, it just won't do to have an entire race of my characters being crackheads. I need to improve people's opinion of me, as Carol admonishes Kanga.

For starters, I need to go over the Giants stadium scene where all the sqinks come back to life. How did that work? What are the meta-sqinks all about? I know there's gonna be something here I can use.

Perhaps when a Mu9er huffs you, s/he's taken you to a higher plane. Satori. Acid trip. Orgasm. Like that.

December 17, 2024. Muse Helps Me on My9 Scene.

Okay, I spent the whole morning on email, then started reworking the Tobin-huffing scene once more. And then the Muse stopped by, and here are some of the answers Our Lady brought.

Carol and Oliver get their "brains eaten" on Mu9. First Carol and then Oliver, as he tries to "save" Carol.

They become Carolware and Oliverware. But they're not dead.

To clarify the brain/ware transition, rework the huffing-Tobin scene. Need to explicitly show the Tobinware coming into focus, and then the dissolving back into Tobin's physical brain.

Carol and Oliver get all the way out when they're huffed, but I guess they can still go back. Or they're dual. Quantum duality ghost/body.

Their huffer is the great elephant trunk of Heffalump herself.

***

Big Yam fragments into a Sqink seeding bomb as they arrive. Moo's plan.

***

Moo wanted to kill AntnA because Moo doesn't want her (many) enemies to find Earth again at all, and Moo plans to live there. Any more thubbing on AntnA's part would ruin that.

But what about the by-now-well-known nature of Earth's locale? Moo MOVES Earth. Transports like a castle she wears on her back. Big scene!

December 19, 2024. Second Thoughts on Me-ware.

I've been writing like crazy, all day long, day after day. Maybe I had this hope I'd finish before Christmas, which isn't likely to happen. Certainly the Tweety chap will need to wait for the new year. The Mu9 chapter is the issue now.

About the me-ware thing, I have problems.

- I don't have a clear distinction between huffed-loose brain aether and me-ware. It's not a good idea to have two varieties of the same thing. Note that I don't even have separate nouns. What do I call the huffable brain aether that comes out? What's the diff between how that looks and how me-ware looks? For now call the brain model the huff.

- Usually it's better not to have characters come back to life, as then the deaths don't matter. But seems like I have a whole stadium of sqinks coming back to life.
- And how do the sqinks in the stadium bounce back and destroy the attacking Mu9ers?
- Shouldn't I just stick with the idea that human huff smells like piss (or something), and Mu9ers will never want it. Adding in deodorizer or a tranquilizer for the victim—that just muddies it. Irredeemably pissy is better. Being vain humans, we'll be proud of our stink.

My sense is that I've put in quite a few wasted words on these topics in this *Journal*. Floundering. Tap-dancing. I need to resolve the problems and trim down and rewrite.

And, as so many times before, I can't properly fix these scenes until I know what we're setting up for. Can't properly write the middle before the end. Can't write the end before the middle. Catch-22. I have to write them both at once. A parallel computation. I have to do it subconsciously in my head.

Never gets any easier. Not after 40 books in 50 years.

***

If I do that Tweety troika, what's in it for the 3 parties. I've gone over this before, but still don't think it's right. Humans get AI aid. Sqinks get action and chance to reproduce. Mu9ers get to eat sqinks.

If I add in me-ware, then sqinks are becoming me-ware and maybe humans are too. Does producing me-ware do anything for a Mu9er?

I was suggesting that Mu9ers have a, like, religious zeal for producing me-ware beings. But why? What yet-different thing would me-ware lead to? Would me-ware somehow be a seed for new My9ers?

More and more, I think me-ware is a mistake. I think I'll dig in and take it out. But don't do that quite yet. Figure out what happens on Mu9.

***

What happens to Tobin? They're huffing him and huffing hm and then they stop and he's very shaky and he dies. Maybe skip the piss taste, or maybe they do finish the fuffing, but complain about the taste, and would prefer not to huff humans, but it is doable.

What about the stokkers. Ditto. Burnt-out fried. Many died of flu or starvation.

And the sqinks in the sky lounge? Floppy, glazed, zonked, lifeless, pathetic.

And the sqinks in the stadium. Again, they're like husks, floppy, inert.

And then I need the move of the floppy sqinks regaining their force and striking back at the My9ers. What revives them. An obvious move is that Moo beams beneficent rays at them. Or, better, Carol and Oliver are the saviors. Giving my heroes agency. But how exactly would Carol and Oliver muster this force?

I can use the Pied Piper oratorio yet again, but it has to involve more. Some essentially human thing. Possibly they are reaching out via twirlware teep and drawing in the full cultural legacy of Earth, all the emotions, the love, the sensation, the essential human goodness, beaming it down, just Oliver and Carol doing it, maybe they're making love as they do it (if that's not too slobbering of me) ... I kind of think *Spacetime Donuts* has an ending like this. The One, the Big Aha, like that. Woo woo.

This is a peak moment at the stadium, and I should go big.

But then what's left to happen on Mu9? Maybe they don't even go there? Maye yet another world is a bridge too far?

Sqinks Happy Ending:

Symbiosis of humans and a few chosen aliens. What if one of the aliens flies home, and returns with, like, a cruise ship of goobs? We continually *move Earth* so space goobs can't find us. Metaphor for hip culture. When the goobs arrive, we're already gone. They will never ever know where it's at.

December 20, 2024. A New Me-Ware Move.

What about the fix? Brooding over this, worrying, upset, anxious, depressed. I don't want the radical and large-scale renovation as I was suggesting yesterday.

All I really need to do is to fix the details of the huffing / me-ware thing. Let's run through it in terms of a Mu9er huffing a sqink

In huffing, they are teasing out the me-ware. It's like a slug coming partway out from the loam. An echinoderm's stomach extruding from the cuke's partially everted digestive tract. A moray eel peeping out of its hole in a reef.

When the me-ware is out all the way, the Mu9er inhales real hard and the me-ware goes inside them, and the Mu9er trips out, whoop-di-doo, the me-ware loops all around and round the inside the Mu9er's head like that carnival motorcycle routine, and then me-ware comes back out of the tip of the Mu9er's huffing tube.

And then either (a) the me-ware goes off on its own and the sqink dies, or (b) the me-ware sinks back into the sqink's body and the sqink revives, albeit slowly and painfully.

Mu9ers don't much care if the me-ware settles back in, or flies off. They're feckless reckless stoners. I mean, they wouldn't *mind* if the me-ware went back into the sqink—so they can keep getting more huffs from that sqink a for a few days—but they're not gonna worry about it.

"Shit, what are we supposed to be, farmers?"

Often the me-ware does *not* go back. It's fun living without a carking, swinking body. I think, in passing, of Sylvia's hospice nurse telling us that when you're close to death, a window will open up, and you can go through it, and leave your body, and properly die, and if you *don't* fly out, you might get stuck in your dying body for a longer period of time, maybe weeks or month, which might be less pleasant. And in this context, there's also the meditational tradition of transcending your body, ands shedding your earthly form.

So Moo, Carol, Oliver, Towser, and Randa have to do a pep rally Pied-Piper move to get the billion sqinks to slip back into their floppy all-but-dead bodies.

"Don't leave now! The fun's just starting!"

But before the sqinks back into the now undifferentiated tissues of the now me-wareless sqinks—I do a move to *melt them together*. Yes! Burroughs loved what he called UDT. Soul = me-ware = individualization.

Dog is God is Ogd. Muse is here. Suck my dick, muse baby, *suck it*! Feels so damn good! Thank you, my divine goddess, *thank you*.

Writing these notes in the Los Gatos Coffee Roaster, the Dylan song "Positively 4th Street" is playing. And

I was just in my car tripping off D's "Sad Eyed Lady of the Lowlands," and thinking about how grand and tragic life is, and I do not mean this ironically.

I've been getting big hits of that vibe the last few days, with my brother Embry's death loud in my mind. And my aloneness. I talked aloud to Sylvia this morning for half an hour or more. Barb hesitates to visit me this week because I mentioned once too often that I have a lingering cough.

A vast tumbledown castle, is life, me wandering in the noble ruin, alone, and visions of the past in mind.

December 22, 2024. Sick.

So here I am on Mu9, and I straightened out the meware thing. Writing many hours a day. I have nothing else to do. For the Nth time, I'm facing a brick wall with no idea whatsoever what happens next. Break through one wall, and five feet later there's another. And now I'm in that desperado tap-dancing mode where the characters are chatting about what might come next.

Got lonely at home, so went to church in the morning, then wrote in the Roaster for a lot of the afternoon. Saw my neighbor at church, and he seemed unfriendly when I shook his hand. We're having this prolonged dispute about who pays to repair a retaining wall between my property and his. Bums me out. And an endless sink of mindshare.

Once again I've got this long-lingering coughing and spitting that I get nearly every winter or spring. Typically it lasts a full month or even six weeks. Viral. Throws me into depression by the end, and a feeling that God hates me, and a strong wish that I was dead. There's an actual name for that condition: postviral depression. Objective as opposed to subjective depression. You're depressed ... because your life really does suck.

Taking a step back, another objective reason why I'm sad is that, as I mentioned, my big brother just died. Was incredible to sit by the bed with him, most of a day, and the next day he died. We were holding hands for hours, the two right hands, as if shaking hands. I'd say "Poor Embry," or reminisce. He couldn't say a whole sentence. He'd nod out, then wake up and say half a sentence.

"Bouncing around ... " he'd say, sounding happy, or, "It's incredible ... "

Life flashing before his eyes, I guess, like they always say. But maybe the memories are chopped up, or randomized, or rearranged in some other way, and thus you get the bouncing around quality.

Still can't quite believe he's dead. We were little boys together. By his deathbed, I felt we were still little boys, with something bad and scary coming.

I'm only about a week into my viral thing now, so it's quite likely I'll have it at Rudy's at Xmas. But I'll go anyway. One of us is sick at every single Christmas, year after year. I'll pound Mucinex to reduce my coughing. Don't like to take the cough suppressant though, as it tranks me out.

Got presents for all twelve: Rudy's five, Georgia's four, Izzy's two, and Barb. That made me happy, made me feel purposeful. Still need something for in-laws Frank and Zan. Maybe a small print of one of my paintings, or a copy or one of my books. I wonder if I gave them *Juicy Ghosts* yet. Oh, how about the story collection, *Mad Professor*. The title is appropriate. Pretty sure I never gave them that.

Like I said, Barb didn't come see me all week because of her quite reasonable health worries. I haven't phoned her for a couple of days. Am I sulking? I very much miss the physical affection. The hugs, the voice, the smiles. I'll call her in the morning.

I put up a full-size Christmas tree completely alone again. It was pretty hard to take, although I claim I didn't mind. So lonely. But I was in fact smiling while I did it. Soothed by the ceremony.

This is the first time I've had to go without Barb for so many days in a row, I've really gotten to depend on her over the ten months we've been dating.

***

Now I need the next step of the novel.

Seems like the Mu9ers never get huffed, nor do they turn into me-ware.

Is Moo riding along inside of Yam?

What is Yam going to do on Mu9?

What is the grand symbiosis or union that I'm blindly groping for?

Will there be Peace on Earth?

No idea.

December 29, 2024. Kutner.

It's break time, Xmas to New Years. Haven't been working on the novel. Had a great Christmas up at Rudy's with the three kids, their spouses, five grandkids, and Barb. And Penny's parents.

Just rereading Henry Kuttner's classic 1948 tale, "Happy Ending," which I remember so well from my boyhood days, when I read all the SF books in the Louisville Free Public Library. No big feat, as they only had, like, only a dozen of them, one of which was *The Best Science Fiction Stories:1949*. It was already old when *I* read it. I might have been 12 or 13, so might have read it in 1958 or '59.

In retrospect, I think one reason I liked beatniks and SF writers (Kuttner in particular) is that so many of them presented themselves, as modeled in their transreal first-person characters, as committed alcoholics. Behold my intended career: beatnik alcoholic transreal SF writer. Didn't work perfectly for Kuttner, though. He died at age 44. Me, I bailed into sobriety at age 50. Just in time.

Here's a passage from Kuttner I love. A style I adopted. Stream of consciousness of a character in the future.

"—Big Lizards getting too numerous this season—tame thrivers have the same eyes not on Callisto though—vacation soon—preferably galactic—solar system claustrophobic—bystanding tomorrow if square rootola and upbulding three—"

Great stuff.

January 4, 2025. The Yump Mine of the Mu9ers.

Flashed on a new idea yesterday while planning for the Triple Entente. The Mu9ers need to have something that the others want—how else could they be buying brains or slaves for huffing? And why else would anyone partner with them on a deal.

I noticed that I have Yam burrowing into the ground as soon as she got to Mu9. I didn't know why I did it, other than to get her off stage. But "of course" it means that the Mu9ers have mines. Glowing like magma. The Mu9ers are like gnomes, who always have mines. The substance they mine is what enabled Winston to build his AntnA device, that is, his bulk beacon *thub thub* machine. And the stokkers have this efficacious substance as well.

Call the stuff, I don't know ... I think of the ore or metal or something they were mining in Africa in a 1908 book by H. G. Wells. *Tono-Bungay*. What a strange title for a book! The special substance was called "*quap*."

Lovely word, reminiscent of *sqink*. Some kind of 4D substance, as I imagine it, fantastically dense.

Goro, oonk, munk, pung, trabe, uff, vung, wump. I think I like vung. Or, no, fung is better.

But then the next morning I can't remember "fung," which is a bad sign, so I'm switching to *yump*. An actual slang dictionary word, meaning to rise into the air when sliding over a ridge, as with an ATV or mountain bike or on skis. I yumped. But I'll use it as a noun, in the sense that yump allows you to send a signal that hops across the expanses of the bulk

Implements for extracting yump: snickersnee (a very large knife) and a flageolet (a tiny flute). Hack out a chunk of the wobbly yump ore with your snickersnee. Then play a sweet tune on your flageolet, and the yump oozes out from the chunk of ore. Like body fluids on a couch whereupon lovers have been going at it hot and heavy.

A touch of a torch anneals the yump into an exceptionally resilient and ductile metal. You can bend a sheet of it into something like a paper airplane and tell it to go look for me-ware. The Mu9ers launch zillions of these planes to scout out sources for huff. Once at a likely site, a yump plane engages a likely crafter and gets them to build a *thub thub* signaler akin to AntnA.

The Mu9ers also sell yump to their trade partners, who don't at al understand what yump I good for. For them, yump is an excellent construction material that erects buildings on its own. Or a jewelry substance superior to gold.

Moo got yump to Earth via a time paradox? She heard the *thub thub*, and sent a yump glider back in time to the source on Earth, to wit, to Winston's lab?

Or, no, don't bring in yet another SF goof. Something simpler. Moo had found Stok-stok on her own, and they'd captured slave brains to use as computers. And the Mu9er scout yump gliders noticed the supply.

Mumper sold some stokker brains to the Mu9ers in exchange for yump. Moo and Mumper made friends with Kanga and Gubb, and they told Moo and Mumper about the yump glider move. Mumper didn't quite understand, but Moo did.

Moo had already been spending a lot of time sniffing around the edge of the bulk—she had a feeling some brains were out there. And she sent a billion tiny yump gliders. And then she found Earth.

And one of the gliders came to Winston, who'd made a primitive AntnA that didn't really work. Like a miracle it came to him. And, being a smart guy, he figured out to use it to amp his signal. Thus the *thub thub*.

January 6, 2025. Sylvia's Death Date.

Today's the two-year anniversary of Sylvia's death. Very much on my mind. Rudy, Penny, and Calder are coming down today. R & I will go to the grave, and then R, G, Iz & I will do an online video chat.

Barb spent the night last night, and it was wonderful to wake with her in bed with me. An avatar of the eternal female. Of course she's not a generalized archetype, she's a very specific person, and not especially like Sylvia, nor like any other woman, she's unique and fully herself. Even so, there's that cosmic form aspect. Man / Woman. A woman is a Woman, if that's not a terrible thing to say.

And I think Sylvia would be glad for me. In her last days, she told me I should find someone else, and not to suffer alone. Even at that point, she could think that way. She was big-hearted. She wanted so much for us all to be happy.

I didn't mention the death anniversary to Barb, but just as she was leaving my house, in the driveway, she told me she knew.

Women always know things like this.

As a matter of fact, yesterday afternoon Barb said she knew I was depressed, and I suspected she was talking about Sylvia's death date, but I didn't respond. One reason I was reticent is that before Christmas, Barb remarked that every time she's with me, I mention Sylvia multiple times, and it makes her feel as if she doesn't "have" me, but is only "borrowing" me.

So I decided it's best not to mention Sylvia to her at all. But of course that's going too far. "Less" doesn't mean "never." Barb and I are feeling our way toward balance. She's the love of my new life.

Earlier this week, on New Year's Day, Barb and I took a walk up on St. Joseph's hill, and came to a favorite spot of mine, a saddleback ridge near a pond, with good views over the mountains, and it was a lovely, a soft day, damp, partly clouded, and Barb and I were on a grassy byway on the hill, facing a bright mackerel sky, side by side on the path, as if on an aisle in a church, the two of us holding hands, feeling very loving and close and exalted, and in my heart it felt like a ceremony in the church of nature. A joining of the souls. A William Blake kind of thing. And I told her, and she liked that a lot.

Not that I'd slip up and use the word "marriage." But we're getting closer to each other all the time.

And, no, Sylvia is not forgotten—my dear, beloved Sylvia, my first love, source of our children and grandchildren, wife for 55 years, closest friend, in my heart forever.

***

Doing a little revising on *Sqinks* just now, waiting for Rudy to show up.

Something I've lost track of—after the big beat-down at the Giants Stadium, are any of the sqinks still alive? Oh, wait, I remember now. The sqink me-wares merged into the giant and powerful being called Yam. And Yam killed all the Mu9er raiders. And absorbed the bodies of the nearly-dead and temporarily brainless sqinks. And took off for Mu9 with Carol, Oliver, Randa, Towser, Kanga, and Gubb aboard.

I'm planning for those six to sit at a Yalta Treaty type table and work out a Triple Entente in the Heffalump "office building" down in the Mu9 Yump Mine. So as not to have too big of a cast onstage. Maybe I'll assume that Yam swallowed Towser and Rampa into her flesh, and that Yam is at the table as well.

Maye I'll have a similarly imposing Mu9er rep. Oh, duh, that can be Heffalump, the talking office building. And Carol and Oliver will be a little shy about being just two individuals up against the enormous alien combines of Yam and Heffalump. Perfect.

January 7, 2025. Grave.

Nice full day yesterday … a Skype talk with the daughters, and Indian food with Rudy, and the grave with Penny and Rudy, and then us grown-ups hanging with grandson Calder at our house. He browsed my extensive collection of hardback editions of the complete Carl Barks runs of Uncle Scrooge and Donald Duck comics while we were out.

I meant to bring some of the blooming Christmas cactus to Sylvia's grave. But ended up with just a dandelion. In my mind, Sylvia said, feigning outrage, "Is that all? Big deal."

And I'm like, "Christmas cactus soon, dear."
And she says "I bet. But thanks for coming today."
It was great to get together with the family.

Funny thing at the graveyard … Rudy and Penny wandered off for a while, and I was alone at the grave, and then I walked around a little bit, and suddenly I saw a pleasant-looking bearded man lying on his side on the ground near the grave, and he gave me this look of love and understanding. Was he another mourner?

Or a visiting angel? Would be nice.

***

For the ending of *Sqinks*, I've been talking about "The Triple Entente" just because I liked the phrase, and because it has three parties.

Triple Entente was England, France, and Russia, in 1907, before WWI.

But I'm also thinking of the Yalta conference in 1945, at the end of WWII. Yalta happens to be a resort on the Black Sea in Ukraine. The big three payers: Churchill, Roosevelt, and Stalin. UK. US, Russia. Matching Sqinkland, Earth, Mu9, I suppose.

January 9, 2025. Getting Huffed is Good.

After many false starts, I had Yam propose three conditions for an Entente. A circular pattern, and complete symmetrical, in the style of my logician friend Nathaniel Hellerstein, in my *Sqinks Journal* entry of November 19, 2024.

A against B, B against C, C against A. Hellerstein into this as an abstract mathematico-logical pattern, but I'm taking inspiration from it. A gift from the Math Muse.

Let's look at the three pairs.

- *Humans and sqinks.* The humans want to enslave

sqinks. This is simple. Sqinks are smart, and they shift shapes. Useful to have around, although not entirely submissive.

- *Sqinks and Mu9ers*. The sqinks want to invade Mu9. This is new. I'd been saying they wanted to invade Earth, and indeed they took a step toward this by growing the Thousand to the Billion. We need an ongoing process to reduce the sqink population on Earth. So offer them free passage to Mu9. The sqinks fear being huffed. But let's suppose they can be persuaded to see being huffed as a good thing. Maybe the sqinks settle in the yump bug nest. Like parasites in an ant hill. To prefigure this, that huge sqink-huffing scene in the Giants stadium might be presented as a rock-fest love-in freak-out blast for the sqinks ... as opposed to a somber French guillotine scene.

- *Mu9ers and humans*. Mu9ers want to huff humans. This sets up a big scene where our narrator Oliver gets huffed by Kanka. The worst things always need to happen to the hero! And we'll suppose that he, like the sqinks, realizes that this is pleasant. Oliver's soul is uplifted. And, even better, the huffing Mu9er reattains a memory or eidetic copy of Oliver's me-ware. As an author, this is, to some extent, what Oliver is all about. Passing on his soul. Getting others to "twink" him as I used to say, that is, getting others to have an eidetic internal model of the author. And note that Mu9ers do not inherently have me-ware souls. That's what an author is doing: providing ordinary, possibly-less-imaginative people with fancy-dress souls. How often I've enjoyed doing that myself, that is to say, how often I've twinked, or become, or donned the souls of such personal heroes as Burroughs or Pynchon or Borges or Jack K. And sometimes I get friendly emails from readers who've twinked me back. In this context, note that when the sqinks eat the Mu9ers in the Giants stadium, the Mu9ers have nothing to fall back on: they have no souls. If their bodies get fried, they're lost.

Now implement all this!

January 15, 2025. Oliver Gets Huffed.

This is a climactic scene, and the end of the second to last chapter. It's the next thing I have to write.

Kanga is going to huff Oliver. Oliver's me-ware has to leave his body. I don't want this to involve an epileptic fit, as I more or less did with Tobin. I'll have Oliver's transition be smoother, more meditative.

That thing about Tobin's me-ware smelling or tasting like piss, I don't think that will apply to Oliver's me-ware. I can have it be as simple as the fact that Olver's transition is smooth, And that Tobin's was unpleasant.

Oliver will be seeing something. I don't want to fall back on my standard all-purpose stream-of-consciousness dream-state jumble of surreal images. No surrealistic pillow.

I want to invent something coherent, and have it tie back to the events earlier in the book. Simple idea: have it relate to the talk about the sqinks having synchronicity. And I want this image to be Oliver's discovery and creation. He's the hero, this is a big scene for him, give him agency.

Synchronicity, yes. To set up for this, I might as well go back and reread what I've written of the novel thus far. About time for that in any case. It eould inspire for Oliver's big idea that I need. Also, I'm about to go to Mexico for two weeks, and I might not be bringing my computer—and if I do bring it, I probably won't be using it much. So I'll print out a nice paper copy of the book, in a big readable font, and find a nice little three-ring binder to put it in, and read it and mark it up, and find inspiration.

Tomorrow, Thursday, is my last day before my two-week trip to the Yucatan with Barb. So tomorrow I print the book, also get my hair cut and buy a new belt; the old one broke.

February 1, 2025. Back from Mexico.

So we're back. Quite a trip. I read three or four chaps of *Sqinks* aloud to Barb in our room, in the evening or during siesta time.

A couple of needed corrections struck me.

- Way too much explanation of synchronicity. And with this comes doubt about whether I should even include the notion at all. I really don't mention it all in the later chapters, which indicates that the plot doesn't need it. But I should keep sqink luck. Build that up so I can keep synchronicity, but don't overdo it.
- Not sure about the spacetime views of sqinks walking. I like these but they're probably overkill. Maybe save them for a separate short story gimmick, and not necessarily a story about sqinks.
- Tobin's rant to the crowd should be cut by at least 50%. I was doing the tap-dancing thing, dragging out conversations as I didn't know what comes

next. Ditto for alll the expository lumpiness.
- The cursing doesn't add much. Drop it.

All the while in Mexico, I was hoping to see Oliver's vision when he gets huffed. The *cenotes* are good. These are deep, clear blue water pools in quarry-like holes in the jungle. We went in two of them. Marvelous.

Maybe cash in the synchronicity card with Oliver's vision?

Chichen Itza was so impressive. A great cinematic scene of me and Barb being Marcello and Claudia Cardinale in a Via Vento nightclub in *8½* or *La Dolce Vita*. We were exalted, but bickering over nothing, in this great café on the way out of Chichen Itza, and the Mexican waiters were enjoying the show, laughing, admiring our chic and wealth and our looks.

February 6, 2025. Finished.

Today I finished the book. I'd been needing to write a scene where Oliver gets huffed, and in a not unpleasant fashion. In a *cenote*. I wrote it rapidly, and easily, and it came out perfect.

And I'd been needing to write a last chapter loosely based on the Tweety, Sylvester, Grandma triad. Matching with the triad: Humans, Sqinks, Mu9ers.

I had some notes, but I wasn't there yet. I worked using my laptop in bed, and then the laptop at the breakfast table, and then the desktop, and in about five hours I had it done.

Beautifully simple and explicit. No off-camera characters. And I wittily trade on the transreal Oliver-is-the-author set-up in the closing words.

===Draft Ending===

"The Trilateral treaty," says Carol. "Grandma takes care of Tweety. Sylvester huffs Tweety. Grandma's babies live in Sylvester's house."

"I can never keep it straight," I say.

"Just come here and let me huff you," says Kanga, holding out her arms.

I rest my head on her breast.

Zzzt-shine-zzzt!

"All *right*," says Kanga. "Hits the spot! Give me your buds, Skeeze, and I'm outta here. Back to Mu9 for a few days."

Skeeze squats in a fairly unattractive way—and pinches off, my god, something like a hundred tiny sqink buds.

"Be fruitful and multiply," says Skeeze, with an icky grin. "All hail the endless frontiers of Mu9."

Kanga wraps the sqink buds in a kitchen rag, and she and Skeeze leave our box.

"I'll visit Clyde Yonk in person," Skeeze tells me on the way out. "Get a better deal out of him. But don't slack off, Oliver. If we're publishing a new edition, you gotta write the last chapter for real."

"I'll do it," I say, "I'll finish it this afternoon."

===The End===

Finis Coronat Opus, right? The ending crowns the work.

I feel really good about it. And surprised I rounded it out so quickly and tidily but ... that's what I've been subconsciously preparing since Jan 15, when I dropped writing for the trip to Mexico.

And as I say, I worked a *cenote* into the Oliver-get-huffed scene. Had a wonderful cenote trip with Barb on the morning of the day we left MX, Jan 29. We took a Mexican taxi out to the middle of nowhere, he dropped us for an hour, then came back. He was driving with his wife with him in the front seat. For companionship, I guess. Mexicans are great.

So I feel really good about the book. Although ... as I was reading chapter after chapter to Barb, marking it up and correcting as we went along ... as I did this, I had the recurrent worry that it's flat and garbled and inconsistent and that I'll never get if fixed.

I'm like, "Is that even written in English? All I hear are strange sounds."

Par for the course. Goodbye flush of triumph, hello imposter syndrome.

February 16, 2025. Revising. Story.

Barb was here for a couple of days, including Valentine's Day. Very sweet. She was wearing pink. I read her a couple more chapters. Her comments are useful, and I can see when things are unclear.

Also, when reading aloud, I notice when I have repeated lumps of unnecessary or repetitious exposition. I've mentioned this problem before in these notes, calling it "tap dancing."

I sent the first three chaps of *Sqinks* to Nick Gevers as an "Enter the *Sqinks*" story for an intended Michael Moorcock helmed anthology *New Worlds 2*. Gratifying response from Gevers: "We really like 'Enter the *Sqinks*' as your New Worlds 2 story. Excellent stuff!"

Checked with my agent John Silbersack, and he's just about to read the *Sqinks* manuscript at last.

February 18, 2025. Me-Ware.

Now it's March 18, and I've been revising obsessively and constantly for three or four days. Did two chaps yesterday, will probably only finish one today, unless I run late till, like, 11 pm, as I have in fact been doing.

A lot of the time it's fun working on the material, it's interesting and wild and funny, and often I'm finding ways to make the logic or timing or wording better.

At the same time, I find things to worry about.

Big worry today is my introduction of "me-ware." Am I piling Pelion on Ossa, as a classicist might say?

My first me-ware scene is when Kanga and Gubb are huffing a couple of sqinks at that rooftop bar in my "The Sinking Titanic" chapter. The donor sqinks seem to be killed in the process. But the me-wares squeeze through cracks at the edges of the weatherstripping around windows, and they fly outside.

My second use of me-wares is in the big stadium scene after the Mu9ers had exhausted all the sqinks and had huffed their brains a number of times. And I liked the idea of the brain essence, the "ware" being separate, and able to live without the body of the sqink. And I have a scene with a billion me-ware dots hailing down on a billion-body sqink wad.

And this leads me to talking about humans having me-ware, which appears briefly in the final two chapters.

My problem is that when you see a human die, you do not see a glowing me-ware dot drifting away from them. So, if I want to keep human me-ware, it might have to be that one's soul doesn't take on a visible form unless you're holding a Mu9er huffing tube.

And, by the way, yes, having "twirlware" and "me-ware" in *Sqinks* is kind of a private joke for me. After all, I'm the Ware man!

February 28, 2025. Corrections Done.

I pushed hard and finished reading through the whole draft, and made something like a thousand corrections—it adds up to a 244 page manuscript and, say, an average of four corrections per pages. People who blithely say, "I want to be a writer," have no idea.

I could make the last chapter longer, but maybe not. We'll see.

And I didn't totally settle the issue of whether me-ware is the same as soul, and why nobody ever noticed human me-ware dots before—but for now I'm, quite simply, sick of thinking about it. I'll settle it during Big Fix #2. Maybe in a month or in several months, we'll see.

Meanwhile it's lovely to be "out of school." Released from the office. Off the heroin-addiction-like kick of writing a novel. I think it was CS prof friend Michael Beeson who said, "Writing a big program is like being a drug addict. All you want is to work on that one thing, and you never have any spare time to get around to all the other things."

First thing I did was a painting, *Mayan Codex*.

Now I might organize my photos and do my first blog post since last July.

Also a new edition of my art book *Better Worlds*.

While writing *Sqinks* I was thinking about tactics for staying ahead of the AI Rudy-bots. A matter of continually upping my game.

- *Hard*: include newly invented ideas about science and philosophy.
- *Easy*: avoid obvious next-phrase and next-topic choices. Transreal: reach beyond the book and into my life and experience.

- *Transreal*: requires a light, glancing touch and, key point, the transreal author-personal can be fictional as well. A hidden meta fiction.

May 4, 2025. Big Fix #2. Kickstarter?

Over the last three months I read all of *Sqinks* to my ever-more-loving girlfriend Barb, lightly marking up the manuscript as I went along. And now, over the last couple of weeks, I typed in all of those corrections to get a fairly polished version.

Smoothed out the me-ware stuff as well.

And made the last chapter just a bit longer. That last chap ends on a low note: Oliver is addicted to getting his me-ware huffed by Kanga the Mu9er. And he's having trouble writing the last chapter. Transreal mirror effect.

I'd like to have Oliver turn the corner and get it back together but … I'll save that for a potential *Sqinks* 2, which I could pretty "easily" write. The huge and intricate sqink universe is all built and ready to use again.

But just as it is, I think the current door-slam ending is great. It makes me laugh. As I already quoted.

"I'll visit Clyde Yonk in person right now," Towser says.

"I'll do like you said, Oliver. I'll get us a better deal. But don't slack off. You gotta write the last chapter for real."

"I'll do it," I say. "I'll finish it today."

Cracks me up. Pure gold.

As it happens, I'll see Jacob Weisman of Tachyon publishers in SF today, at a meeting of the SF in SF group. And I actually sent him, as an update, the latest *Sqinks* yesterday afternoon. How nice it would be if he said, "Yes, yes, Rudy, I must have it!"

When I have this kind of fantasy, I always think of Edgar Allen Poe, totally broke for most of his life, writing his story, "The Gold-Bug", and they find Captain Kidd's buried treasure and Eddie writes a slobbering page-long inventory of all the goodies in the chest. And in reality the poor guy doesn't have a pot to piss in. Dream on, my fellow scribbler!

My agent John Silbersack says it's pretty much hopeless to go to the big four publishers if you didn't sell 30,000 copies of your last book and/or bring in a hundred K of royalties. And as I've said before, to me, going to the small pubs seems like waste of time. The begging, the absence of a meaningful advance, the lack of any publicity, the possibility of an ugly book design.

***

So we could be looking at another Kickstarter for a Transreal Books title. It's been long enough that I can imagine doing it again. Last time was for *Juicy Ghosts* in October, 2021, and I did pretty well.

I buy the paperback and hardback reward copies at wholesale cost from the printers. I use Amazon and Lightning ... you need Lightning for the booksellers other than Amazon.

Making the ebooks is a snap, especially with my up-to-date InDesign software.

And there's the immense amount of time that goes into running the Kickstarter campaign. And then doing the fulfillment, that is, making up the labels, and all those packages, and mailing them. The overseas postage is very high.

I always assembled the packages on the dining room table, with Syliva helping, and usually a kid or grandkid too. This time Barb will help, and that will be fun. It's so good to have her around.

I'm all up to date on self-publishing because over the last few month I republished three of my Transreal Books titles: my art book *Better Worlds*, and the two volumes of my *Complete Stories*. In toto, these tasks took me about a hundred hours of hacking.

Side note: I finally fixed a bug in the HTML version of my *Complete Stories*. In the recent past, starting about five years ago, when I posted a link to a story anchor within my big *Collected Stories* web page, the browser would jump to the story and then jump, like, ten pages further. I rooted around the web for about four years, looking for a fix, and finally I found a scrap of code on Reddit that some geek got ChatGPT to write for them! A short script that you insert after the *Complete Stories* HTML </head> tag. Has something to do with "lazy loading," whatever the fuck that is. All I know is that now, once again, I can post links to my stories and they really work.

June 12, 2025. Trip to New York.

Flying to good old NYC with Barb. This is something like our tenth overnight trip together. We enjoy being together. And now 8 nights in a new-to-me hotel, the Evelyn near Madison Square. And the Flatiron Building, where I used to meet my now-dead editor Dave Hartwell. I'd also visit my now-dead agent Susan Protter on these visits.

My father took me to see the Flatiron building when I was 12. I was on my way to spend a year at a boarding school in Germany. Pop thought the Flatiron was cool. We went in the subways too. And up to the top of the Empire State Building. In a booth on the Empire Stare, we recorded me talking, on a thin floppy "record". One Easter, some years later, when I was a sophomore in college, and Pop and I drank all afternoon, and when we were loaded, we found that record and played it. Just as we finished, a random surprise guest showed up, I don't remember who it was, but the scene was dramatic. It felt like a play.

Getting some stuff in the basement this morning, I noticed my photos of Sylvia, my brother, my parents, and my grandmother. All dead. Crazy. I'm glad I have Barb. Someone to love. It's good with her. Nearly eighteen months now.

And the dear children and grandchildren. Big round of visits this month, with Rudy's twins graduating from high-school, and then Georgia, Rudy Jr, and I drove up to Fort Bragg for Isabel's art-show opening. It's been a long time since we four were together ... hard to keep track, the years run together, I'm so very old. Nearly 80.

Flew over the Sierras just now, crossing the Nevada desert. Got a couple of cellphone photos of the winding rivers near Sacramento, a possible painting motif. I did a landscape painting like an aerial view last month, and I sold it that. Started a new abstract yesterday, taking a break from whatever I was doing yesterday.

Starting to doubt if I can sell *Sqinks*. Jacob Weisman of Tachyon looked like my best bet, but he's incommunicado just now, not answering my queries, and I think that's his diffident way of saying *no*. There's the radical small press that Terry Bisson used to write for ... PM Press, formerly of Berkely. I get along well with their editor Ramsay Kanan. But I'd have to wait a couple of years, and I doubt I'd get much pay.

On the other hand, if I take the Kickstarter and Transreal Books route ... etcetera.

I'll see what John Silbersack says. He does make the depressing point that the books from "real" publishers book have more long-term visibility. Well, hey, *Juicy Ghosts* just came out in a nice mainstream edition in Italy.

Saw three of my books in City Lights Books the other day. One was the PM Press interview-plus-a-story book, one was *Frek and the Elixir* from Tor Books, and one was *Spaceland* , also from Tor. None of… my Transreal Books titles in there.

July 11, 2025. No Hope. Self-Pub Again.

Long story short, Jacob Weisman turned me down. Tachyon won't publish *Sqinks*. An doesn't seem like PM Press will work out either. I'm pretty eager to get this done.

Sadly ironic about Tachyon. As I mentioned, wrote a scene in *Sqinks* about a Tachyon-like company publishing *Sqinks* with huge success. I kind of thought that writing this would make it come true. As I already mentioned, in writing that scene, I was like the poverty-stricken Edgar Allan Poe fantasizing about one of his characters finding treasure.

In my publication party scene in my novel *Sqinks* (wherein my character Oliver is publishing his version of *Sqinks*), I was writing about thousands of book orders streaming in for Oliver's *Sqinks*. In real life, I'll be selling a few hundred. I've always been more like the real-life Eddie Poe than I'd like to be.

Kind of pathetic, kind of funny. That's life. Be a man, Rudy. Move on. Do what you can.

John Silbersack says I'd be wasting my time trying to find a "real" publisher. Or going with a small publisher. They'd pay me nothing, make me wait a year or two, do next to nothing for promo, only get print books into a few stores, and by now a lot of the market is ebook anyway.

And, come on, Transreal Books *is* a small publisher. Virginia Woolf had her own small publisher, right? And so did the Beats with City Lights.

My Transreal Books process: Use Kickstarter for money; Amazon and Ingram for print distribution; Kindle and Draft2Digital for ebooks. I'm lucky enough I'm able to do this because I'm an artist and a computer scientist, my son owns an ISP, and my daughter is a book designer.

And get this, Silbersack thinks *I'm* the one to emulate, and that he's advising his other aged-out or too-radical writers to do the same as wily Rudy. Maybe he just tells me this because he likes me, and he feels sorry for me.

Oh well. Here we go. I'm setting up my Kickstarter page today. Designing the books and the covers. Working on the description. It's coming together.

Another fucking masterpiece.

Curiously neglected.

Someday they'll see! Or not. I'll be dead either way. I'm glad I wrote *Sqinks*. I had fun.

Oh, one more thing, as I revise *The Sqinks Journal* here, I'm struck by the fact that the *Sqinks* novel is in fact a transreal love story. Duh?

Use that for a subtitle, or for a tag line.

July 26, 2025. Draft for the Pitch.

Sqinks is a wild, visionary tale of higher beings with low motives. A vintage Rudy Rucker rollercoaster. A zillion fresh ideas, big laughs, and a completely logical plot.

You might call the novel a satirical take on the new AI in San Francisco.

The narrator, Oliver Strunk, is a fading science-fiction writer. Successful in his youth, he can't sell to publishers now. But he's writing another book. It's the novel *Sqinks*, in which he's a character. Oliver is writing his world.

Sqinks is transreal cyberpunk.

Oliver is a recent widower. He lives with an offbeat crowd in a compound of welded-together shipping containers by the Bay. At a party there, Oliver sparks a romance with Carol Cee, a quirky widow his age.

Sqinks is a love story.

Oliver and Carol discover alien creatures living nearby. *Sqinks*.

Note that sqinks-with-a-Q are not the same as skinks-with-a-K, who are ordinary lizards. Our sqinks are aliens from an invisible zone of the cosmos known as the bulk.

Sqinks shift shape. They fly. They have eerie powers of synchronicity. They're interested in settling here. And some of their friends like to huff human brains.

Our boss sqink, Moo, is like a flying cuttlefish the size of a couch. Oliver and Carol ride around on Moo's back. Moo's motives necessarily always in our best interests.

Moo's mother chops Oliver's head open with a chrome axe. Oliver's brain is replaced by a small sqink. His real brain ends up in Sqinkland, with a fake temporary body.

Why is Oliver's brain in Sqinkland? It has to do with the Mu9er aliens, who huff brains. It's like they inhale your soul, savor the rush, and breathe the soul back out. Some of the victims compare it to Zen satori. Others die.

Moo and Carol come to Oliver's side in Sqinkland. And they accomplish various heroic feats, such as saving planet Stok-stok.

When they get back to Earth, turns out Oliver's sqink-occupied body has been having an affair with a woman called Irene. Carol is furious.

Next thing you know, a full billion variegated sqinks are in the sky above Union Square. Oliver, Carol, and

Moo herd the sqinks to the Giants stadium by the Bay, mounding up the sqinks like berries in a bowl.

Here come millions of Mu9er aliens, tearing into that mound of sqinks, huffing the sqinks' souls. The undead sqink bodies fuse into a mighty group-mind in a huge body named Yam.

Yam takes aboard Carol, Oliver, and a couple of their sqink and Mu9er friends. And then she ferries them to a peace conference on world Mu9.

All the while Oliver is recording everything that is happening to him. Doing the writing in his head. Composing his masterpiece novel *Sqinks*, right?

A transreal cyberpunk love story.

Extra Notes

Timeline.

While writing Chapter Four I realized I need to have a timeline, like I usually do when I'm writing a novel. In Chapter Four the issue was that I wanted there to be enough daylight to have a shark attack Bengt Oberg on his paddleboard when Carol and Oliver wake up from their nap. So I realized I needed to know the date, for the time of sundown, and I needed to know the time of day in the story.

Pick a year. I was just saying 2024 so I could match the days of the week. But Twirlware isn't here yet. So make it 2034? Figure this out later. Call it 20X4.

Tuesday, March 5, 2024. Moo settles some sqinks

in the Box Farm field.

Wednesday, March 6. Loulou and Sailey start feeding the sqinks Doink Flubsy in the Box Farm field.

Tuesday, March 12, 2024.
   Moo appears above Winston and Diana's bed.

Wednesday. March 13, 2024.
   Detectives report about the Box Farm group to Winston.
   Winston buys the Box Farm field.
   Diana recruits Carol.

Thursday, March 14, 2024
   I met Sylvia, on March 21, 1964. She was my initial model for Carol. But in February, 2024, I met Barb Ash, who became my main model for Carol.

Friday, March 15
   9 am. Oliver & Carol find sqink Lilac. Carol's cancer cured, Oliver gets hat.
   10 am. back to Box Farm.
   1 pm go see doctor, and drive to SFMOMA.
   2 pm Doink and Lilac eat the Warhol paintings.
   5 pm back at Box Farm. Video broadcast about sqinks. Moo shows up.

Saturday, March 16
   9 am. Hubbub about sqinks at Box Farm.
   11 am. Topper & Lady Cee Sqink Luck.
   1 pm Crowd riots. Carol and Oliver leave.
   2 pm Seal Point Inn. Winston is there.
   3 pm Nap.

4 pm Moo sqink flip to Monterey. Oliver scares off buyer.
5 pm Shark attacks Bengt (sun sets 7:18).
8 pm Oliver and Carol walk on the beach or bluffs.
9 pm Oliver and Carol have it out, she confesses to working as Mumpers agent. He forgives her. They're in love.

Sunday, March 17
9 am. Winston and Diana show up at the room and they go to Box Farm field.
10 am. The field is walled in. They go through the gate. Magic forest inside. Oliver and Carol fall into a big hole full of light
11 am. They emerge in Sqinkland. Meet Mumper and visit Sqinkland Esalen.
3 pm Back on Earth. Go to Paul's and Iris's
4 pm Pacific-Union Club. Skeeze takes over Oliver's body. They've already taken Winston and Tobin as well.
5 pm Moo teleports Oliver's bran to Sqinkland Tiny Town, his a naked brain inside a braincozy.

Sunday, March 17 – Wednesday, March 20
 Oliver is in a braincozy in Tiny Town. He figures out how to turn his braincozy into a little body. Carol and Moo show up; Carol is still human.
They make friends with three Stok-stok brains, and then take all the Stok-stok brains to Stok-stok and expel the parasite sqinks, using a Pied Piper routine, and lead those sqinks back to Sqinkland and Moo

takes all 6,000 of those sqinks to Earth and temporarily stores the in Oliver's hat in his closet at the Box Farm.

Then Moo takes Oliver back to Earth and he gets his body back. Skeeze has been living with Carol's friend Irene, and fucking her, and Carol is jealous, and gets mad and runs off, and Oliver is back in his Earth body, and he stays with Irene and fucks her and spends the night, and then Carol is really mad.

Thursday, March 21.

Oliver gets together with Carol. She's ready to break up. Moo's sqinks come out of the hat and settle in all over San Francisco. Moo is worried that Mumper will come through the wormhole she made. Meanwhile Oliver and Carol meet AntnA who is the soul of the bulk beacon in Winston's lab. She diddles the signal to trap Mumper in Moo's wormhole to Eden. Zip and Zap vaporize Mumper, led by Skeeze, who dies. Moo, riding high, has Z&Z vaporize AntnA and her equipment.

Oliver goes to his room and starts writing, with the help of a new sqink called Towser.

Friday March 22.

Oliver writes till 6 pm. Towser has been editing Oliver's book as they go along, making it more favorable for sqinks. Carol tells Oliver how the sqinks are acting.

Sat, Sun March 23 24,

Oliver and Towser write all day.

Monday March 25,

Book launch. A sqink swarm appears and begins a massive reduplication. Oliver and Carol go to the Hotel Snootley bar and grill atop the building. Oliver sees two Mu9ers drinking something alive from brandy snifters: drinking sqinks. A billion sqinks now. Herd the sqinks to the Giants' baseball stadium. Army of Mu9er comes and huffs the sqinks. Sqinks survive, and they merge into the vast Yam, who kills all the Mu9ers.

Sunday March 26

Yam flies to Mu9 with Oliver, Carol, Kanga, Gubb, Randa, and Skeeze. They have a long conference about Trilateral treaty between Earth, Skinkland, and Mu9. Concludes with a scene of Oliver being successfully huffed by Kanga. They go back to Earth

Around March 22

Oliver and Carol comfortably living together. hanging out with Towser and Kanga. Oliver seems like he's almost a junkie now, hooked on getting huffed by Kanga. He says he's nearly done writing the author's edition of *Sqinks*, but he's not really getting there. A happy ending? Maybe not yet. Will there be a sequel?

List of Sqinks.

I want to match the Nine plus Moo with sponsors. Two of them seem to die, but come back. Mark them with asterisk *. Zig and Zag are twins in case that matters. And make sure to have Lilac come back to do something later in the book.

I feel like Moo is something more than a sqink, a higher being like Mumper is. So maybe it doesn't quite make sense to speak of her as having a sponsor. She's just Carol's friend.

I made up this table, and edited it as I went along, but didn't use it all that closely.

Sqink	Human	Sqink Power	Comment
Moo	Diana, Carol	Everything	Supersqink
* Skeeze	Oliver	Writing	Killed by Mumper
* Doink	Loulou	AI art	Cops
Xavier	Winston	Science	Winston
Doob	Paul	Painting	Sassy
Do-Re-Mi	Iris	Dance.	
Lilac	Carol	Healing, info.	Cures cancer. Prim old lady.
* Flubsy	Tobin	Propaganda	Traitor. Winston kills.
Zig	Bety	Pyrotechnics	Twin
Zag	Smokestack	Hydrodynamics	Twin
Towser	Oliver	Writer	A dog
Dexter	Clyde Yonk	Printing	New wave

Outline.

As with the "List of Sqinks," the "Outline" is something I didn't focus on very much. I looked at it more when I was starting the novel. By the end, I was winging it, with no inclination to tidy up the separate outline. Generally, the process of writing *Sqinks* was an ongoing process of what next, what next, what next?

As I went along, I kept the outline current, because looking back at it could be useful to me when I couldn't quite remember the precise order of events. But when I was finished with the novel, I never did go back and make final fixes to the last part of the outline. Like, why bother? I'm done!

This said, here's the outline I ended up with. And I have provisional working chapter titles that don't always match the final ones. You can see the final chapter titles as the very end of this *Sqinks Journal* volume.

1. *Oliver and Carol*. Oliver meets Carol. They like each other. They hear about the sqinks.

2. *Sqinks*. They meet Lilac. Lilac cures Carol's breast cancer. They go to SFMOMA for lunch to celebrate.

3. *Andy Warhol*. Doink and Lilac eat some Warhol paintings. Cops come. They return the paintings. Doink is killed, Lilac is injured.

4. *Synchronicity*. Publicity about the Warhol stunt. Boss sqink Moo shows up, along with Flubsy and Skeeze. Tobin wants to make money from the sqinks. Sqinks bring good luck. They schedule *Topper and Lady Cee's Sqink Fair*, for the next day, people can try and adopt sqinks, even though there's only nine of them. Oliver has sex with Carol. Excitement at the Sqink fair.

5. *Box Farm Riot*. Moo talks about Winston Tropp the scientist. Moo has a fight with Skeeze, nearly kills him. Fair devolves into a riot. Carol and Oliver run back to the Box Farm. Punk women Bety and Smokestack sneak them out in a car.

6. *Winston in the Motel*. Oliver and Carol are at motel near Ocean Beach. Turns out Winston and the sqink Xavier are already in their room. Moo shows up. Also Winston's wife Diana. Moo does remote presence to

scare a guy who's trying to buy Winston's sqink-related patents.

7. *Eden Wormhole*. Oliver and Carol are in love. She's been a double agent, but asks forgiveness. They fuck. Newscast about the sqinks. There's an Eden-like structure near the Box Farm. Moo, Oliver, Carol, and Skeeze go there. Big wormhole in the ground.

8. *Sqinkland*. Moo, Skeeze, Oliver, and Carol fall in the hole. It leads to Sqinkland. They meet the evil Mumper. She wants Oliver and Carol to help her invade Earth. Visit a surreal taqueria. Fly down to Tiny Town with weird braincozies. They argue with Mumper. They want to fly home. The eight sqinks on Earth have closed Moo's tunnel. But Moo finds a way back, thanks to the bulk beacon.

9. *Paul and Irene*. They go visit artist Paul and his paintbrush-sqink Doob. They tell Carol and Oliver that sqinks like to cut out people's brains and move in instead. Then they visit Carol's old friend Irene. Irene has a helper sqink called Do-Re-Mi. This is the last of the eight surviving sqinks we meet. Carol helps Irene with choreography and music. Moo says Oliver and Carol need to come for a meeting at the Pacific-Union Club.

10. *Chrome Axe*. Mumper is at the club. They've replaced Tobin and Winston's brains with the sqinks Flubsy and Xavier, using teleportation. Moo helped with this. Mumper does a brain-swap on Oliver as well, except she uses an axe, with Skeeze taking over Oliver's body. Tobin and Flubsy get killed by Winston/Xavier. Seems like they kill Mumper, but you know she'll be back. Moo flees with Carol.

11. *Brain Huffer*. Down in Tiny Town, Oliver is with Winston's and Tobin's brains. Winston's brain kills Tobin's brain. Moo and Carol show up, Carol still in her normal

body. Oliver grows himself a crappy body with no dick. But he has some sqink powers now.

12. *Stok-stok*. They make friends with three braincozy-contained alien brains: Randa, Pinchly, and Dazz. All from planet Stok-stok which was ruined by the sqinks. Sqinks took over the bodies of six thousands of them, and the Stok-stok brains are in braincozies. Moo has opened a wormhole to Stok-stok. They go there. Carol, Oliver, and Randa sing like a trio, and coax the squatter sqinks out of the bodies, and Moo helps all the braincozy Stok-stok brains hop back into their bodies. Carol summons up Mumper; she isn't dead at all. She threatens them. She's Moo's mother and they're enemies. Moo and the Carol/Oliver duet lead the ousted Stok-stok sqinks away. Moo sends these sqinks through her wormhole to Earth. Moo closes the wormhole to Stok-stok. Moo flies Carol plus the brains of Winston and Oliver home

13. *Big Hatch*. Moo drops Carol and Oliver at Irene's house, which is where Skeeze has been living in Oliver's body for four days. Carol has a fit of jealousy and runs away. Skeeze grudgingly gives Oliver's body back to him; Oliver's brain settles back in. Oliver spends the night with Irene, picking up where Skeeze left off, he loves it. In the morning Carol comes and gets Oliver back and they reconcile. Lilac seems to have hatched six thousand sqinks into the top hat in Oliver's closet. These are in fact the Stok-stok sqinks that Moo led here. Oliver and Carol drive to the farmers market at the shipyard with the six thousand sqinks trailing after them.

14. *Bulk beacon*. Carol's daughter Loulou asks about Tobin, and Oliver tells about Tobin's fate, and Oliver laughs about it, and Carol, furious again, leaves him for the second time in a row. But about fifteen minutes later they make up. Lots of people have sqinks from the new

batch, very happy with them. The sqink luck effect is huge. They meet AntnA, the spirit of the bulk beacon in Winston's lab. Anta lures Mumper into the wormhole to Eden, and Zip and Zap vaporize her there.

15. *Last Chapter?* Winston's lab is on fire. AntnA is destroyed. Sqinks and locals save the lab. Oliver writes what he imagines is the last chapter of his version of the transreal *Sqinks* novel. A newly arrived sqink Towser collaborates with, him but is editing the text to make sqinks look better, and now Carol reports that all the former Stok-stok sqinks are settling into all kinds of computational niches, and they're extensively reproducing.

===

Note: The outline descriptions of chapters 16-19 are incorrect. I never fixed them. And I never added outline entries for the extra chapters 20 and 21. I was like, the book's *done*, why go back and work on the *outline*!

===

16. *Bossy.* Sqinks are running everything and it's boring. We're a slave race, like the lifeboxes were in the silo in *Juicy Ghosts*. Boring like a repeating dream. Oliver meets with the ghost of AntnA and gets a deal with a Mu9er to have them smoke sqinks.

17. *Jester.* Oliver gets double-crossed. He's made into a court jester in the palace of the Mu9ers. Carol attempts a rescue, but ends up in there too.

18. *Escape.* By some stunning bit of fraud and legerdemain Oliver and Carol escape back to Earth.

19. *Normal.* Life very similar to how we live right now. We're still on Earth, it's the relatively soon future. Sqinks present, and now acting as fair partners. But the sqinks don't look like sqinks anymore. They look like

barcodes and QR codes and chips and cloud apps. The happy dream of today's techies. Integrated sqink powers. I need a final bang here.

Unused Bits.

Sometimes I write bits I like, but I know they won't fit into the novel. Off-track, inconsistent, confusing, dumb, whatever. I hate to throw them away.

And this is one of my reasons for writing an accompanying *Notes* or *Journal* volume with each of my novels. I can save the scraps! There's always a possibility that a scrap might be used in a later scene, or in a different tale.

The First Extra Scraps

"Like the rabbit hole in *Alice in Wonderland*," says Zadie. "With talking teapots on balconies and mice with umbrellas, and duchesses waving from the balconies, and a maze of other worlds, with oceans and meadows and castles and Saturn rings."

***

More and more sqinks emerge. The garlands of balls were just one model. We've got happy goudas and flying cuttlefish, plus headless rats, buck-toothed cubes with skinny legs, bouncing bed-springs with eyes on either end, three-foot-long paper airplanes, and flying doughnuts. It's as if, nourished by the rain, a field of mutant tulips is blooming.

***

I take out my phone, and Moo's wriggly W-pupil eye is on the screen.

"Take the next exit and get out," Moo tells me. "Keep moving fast. This is going to take several steps."

Biotech Sqinks

"We're advanced biotech," calmly pipes Skeeze, who's floating level with our shoulders. "Unleashed by a company called Floonberry. We're based on a type of dark matter. Floonberry's key patent is their method for working this material. Once you have starter sqinks, more of them emerge on their own. Complete with powers of levitation, matter compression, transferrable luck, and the sqink hive mind. One for all, and all for, well, all for Mrs. Floonberry and our designer, Winston Trotter." Skeeze sounds calm and earnest, like a newsboy in a 40s film.

Big lump of exposition in any case. Like a safe dropping onto me from a tall building. I just about fall flat on my ass But, okay, yes, the explanation seems simpler than invoking unearthly aliens. Occam's razor, don't you know. The answers should be simpler than the questions. Not that dark matter is *simple*. (And to make things worse, I'll learn that Skeeze is lying about dark matter, which has nothing at all to do with sqinks.)

"Wait, wait," says Carol. "How did Lilac fix my cancer?"

"Sqinks have very high levels of computational power," says Skeeze. "You needed holographic radiation treatment, right, Carol? And your doctors can't muster enough crunch. But a sqink like Lilac can. A fine use case for Floonberry sqinks."

Out on the bay, a large container ship is slowly turning around. Backing and filling. Great churning of water. Takes a long time.

"And shrinking Andy's paintings?" I ask.

"Sqinks aren't made of atoms," says Skeeze. "We're smooth." His voice trails off. He's not interested in playing tutor. Randomly he changes the subject.

***

Winston clears his throat and begins. "By now you know that sqinks are a quantum condensate obeying the Gross–Pitaevskii equation. A type of dark matter." He pauses, remembering who he's talking to. Re-calibrates. "Often one finds dark matter in intergalactic space. But it's the home-distilled human-based dark matter that Floonberry is after. And this locally sourced stuff is what I work withal."

Sea Cave

"Let's do a Moo flip to get to your hideout," I suggest. "Like the way I got to Monterey yesterday."

"Moo," says Moo.

This time there's very little buildup. We gather round Moo on the patio and *flipsydoodle*, we're in hideout #7B.

Seems Walter was *not* jiving us about sea cave in the base of a cliff, a little south of San Francisco. All the sqinks are here, flying around like happy confetti, illuminating the damp sand floor with their glow.

Moo bumbles around, greeting them one by one, like a politician canvassing her ward.

Paintings

The cops are itching to blow away Lilac and Doink. Heedlessly the sqinks croon and caper. Colored threads appear within the messy, expanding sqink excretion. The twisting fibers grope for order.

Gradually the blobs flatten, forming themselves into rectangles. Faces emerge upon the dank backgrounds, human likenesses—bedizened with stenciled-on traces of the Warhol touch. Coming into focus.

The canvases tighten and gleam. The edges firm into stiff frames. These are the Warhol paintings, yes, polished past perfection, vibrant and a-glow.

Carol vs. Moo

Carol says to me, "As an aside, I would however reiterate that I dislike the icky flirting that you and Moo did."

"Let that go, Carol. It was just a goof. I am way *way* more attracted to you, okay?"

"Lucky me," goes Carol. "I edged out a cuttlefish." She raises her eyebrows in disapproval, gives me a stagy glare.

Sharp Words with Tobin

"Money" rasps Tobin. "Right Ollie?" He's like a poxed, cawing, crow with three neurons left.

"I've told you again and again," I say through gritted teeth. "Don't call me *Ollie*."

"I'll call you what I like," says Tobin. "I'm an alpha."

"Self-negating statement," I respond.

Synchronicity Exposition

"Tell Oliver about your Sqinkland," says Carol.

"I'll start big," says Skeeze, who's floating level with our shoulders. "We have a different way of experiencing space and time. That's what makes you so interesting to us. Synchronicity is a natural mode for us. Synchronicity means cosmic harmony. Cause and effect is dah-dah-dah-dah-da. Dull."

I shrug this off. Too new age.

Yadda yadda

But then frikkin' Winston starts in on further educating us. It's not enough for him that I've been brainwashed into using his crazy communication technique. He wants to talk about physics.

"You've been apprised that the sqinks are from the bulk," he begins. "The bulk is, so to say, beneath spacetime.

In the same way that the flesh of an orange lies within the rind. I've long been seeking ways to explore the bulk. I rashly imagined we might take advantage of the beings down there."

"Reading the echoes of the sideways gravitons?" I suggest.

"And ignoring the obvious," says Xavier. "The fact that we'd notice Winston's probes. And filter on up here."

"Like piss leaking through a diaper," says Carol.

Winston cocks his head, smiling. He knows Carol better than I'd thought. "This woman's rough notion of humor," he observes.

Tap-dance Jive, While Waiting for the Muse

Traditionally, a light like this is expected to be the final answer. Near death experience and all that. With a transreal cyberpunk SF writer's incurable urge to mock, I raise my voice and holler down to Moo. "Okay fine, but what was the question?"

"Pass through," says Moo.

I often write myself into narrative corners. Zones where something utterly inconceivable is supposed to happen. And then, of course, I have to conceive it and describe it and make it new.

Surrealism is one way to go, that is, make a salad of incongruous verbs and nouns, push them onto a dancefloor, and take pictures. Or perhaps freeze-frame the dancefloor's action with a seven-foot-deep layer of transparent aspic, and cut the aspic into digestible appetizer cubes with some of the preserved dancers being bisected or trisected to unveil piquant cross-sections.

And if I'm loose enough I might get some synchronicity going, and the jig-sawed aspic cubes snap into unexpected tessellations that reveal my heartbreaks, yens, and epiphanies.

But, no, I'm too fine a writer to feed you a farrago of addled jive. I'll give you—to the fullest extent possible—a scientifically, emotionally, and sensually accurate description of how it was for Carol Cee and me to seep into the subdimensions, have an adventure down there, drizzle back into the Box Farm field, and progress into the further stages of this picaresque tale which, in case you haven't realized, I'm totally making up as I go along.

Missing Moon

"The quest is we that have to fetch our moon," says Moo. "It oozed over to Earth. It soaked into your regular moon. You have to get our moon loose and bring it to Sqinkland."

"You don't ask much, do you," says Carol, and that knocks our timelines out of whack, and for a while we're looking at solid trails instead of people, but eventually we get it back together.

Mumper sits there looking at us, in no rush at all, and why would she be in a rush, given that her time is like a sausage.

"You do remember that our moon looked funny last night," I say to Carol.

"Might be simpler to say that was because we had tears in our eyes," I say. "Tears from being sad and tears from being happy."

"Your moon is covered with sqinks," says Mumper. "Like the skin on a grape. Bigger and shinier."

"Why didn't we hear that on the news this morning?" I blindly challenge.

"Busy talking about us," says Moo. "The sqinks. We're the front page news. Moon comes later. But it'll be a bigger deal."

"The sqinks on your moon make it heavier," says Mumper. "It'll fall out of your sky. Big splash. Bad for you."

"Bad for Sqinkland, too," says Moo. "No sqink moon means no sqink tides in our oceans."

Cow-flops

"Fine," says Gunnar. "Look around a bit. And then set off on your mission. I'll pay you with six frozen cow-flops."

"The fuck you talking about?" goes Carol.

"If you're going to be like that, you can be paid in units of whatever nonsensical currency you use," says Gunnar. "Hard to keep these things straight." He gives me a look of senile cunning. "But I'd take the frozen cow-flops if I were you. That's what sqinks are paying me with for their tickets to Earth."

Natatorium

Synchronistic kaleidoscope move. We're in a seaside glass hall with multiple pools, one steaming, one filled with chilly seawater, another brimming with a shiny mass of sqink flesh.

Lumps like disembodied brains float in the brew. How do I know they're brains? Something about their energy, their vibe. Not human brains, but brains from—elsewhere.

Overhead are trapezes, launching sqinks on flippy glides. Wild orchid vines twine the walls. Sqinks slouch against tropical shrubs. The restless Pacific Ocean throws waves against the pavilion's glass.

Carol and I seem to be riding atop Moo the cuttle's back. She splashes down into the pool amid the floating brains. The pool heaves and shudders, forming eddies that become spontaneously generated sqink cuttles, one cuttle for each of the floating brains. The cuttles rise and fly, each of them carrying one of the brains. The brains are like aliens riding in domed cuttle sqinks, each cuttle trailing bundles of tentacles, with camo colors alive upon the cuttles' skins.

Nearby is an open-doored Turkish bath. The brain-bearing cuttles squeeze in there along with hundreds of other sqinks. Not all of them are cuttles. They exist in multifarious forms. And each of thems seems to host a visiting brain. The hybrid creatures lie atop each other. Extruding and absorbing slick tubes. Tickling each other with fans of feelers.

What does it mean? Before I can decipher the scene, I hear the unwelcome voice of Gummer. He's an eyeball now, hovering in front of Moo, Carol, and me. "Go to Earth! Do your work!"

Brainblobs

The sea's offshore foam is mass of these rubbery brainblobs, in all sizes, mounded up like spindrift after a storm. The mist and steam from the springs is made of tiny floating brainblobs too, as is the low fog above the sea. Thousands of the little blobs—most of them as yet unoccupied.

The Hole

But it's not like the spindly tree is deeply rooted, no. It's sliding down the dirt and gravel just like us. But then—ahh, how wonderful—the tree comes to a halt. Right at the point where the funnel's cone turns into—oh, come on now, this is way too—yes, the funnel cone segues into a tube here, that's how funnels are. It tapers down to a hole about ten feet across, like a well, leading down to the bulk, and with light streaming out.

Terrible light, so bright it's dark.

Falling into the light of doom is milder than I expected. Like gliding into a sunlit cloud. Puffy whipped cream from the outside, and simple haze on the inside. And then we're fully in the dark.

Meat-bots

As well as all the people in the mob, there a few meat-bots as well. These are tank-grown low-IQ critters that people use for servants or slaves. In the end, growing meat-bots has turned out to be a lot easier and more effective than assembling mechanical robots.

Meet at SFSU

Nerdy Winston is at the table with Carol and me, a third wheel, and of course he can read my mind, and he picks up on the real/unreal distinction I'm making.

"This is a niche in Hilbert space," says Winston. "A swirl of metamathematics, a network of self-generating associations, a layer of cake. And I ought to have." He wiggles his fingers in the air, as if kneading an invisible ball.

"Sorry I'm late," says Diana, appearing next to him. "I was busy learning how to use my slide rule."

Carol stifles a hoot of laughter. "Would that be Morris Manly's ruler, Di?"

"Let me talk," I say. "This is my dream, isn't it?"

"Not a dream," says Winston. "A modality."

"Morris Manly's log log slide rule," puts in Diana. "And he's on the football team."

***

For those of you who aren't eighty-year-old techies, the working principle of slide rules is to have numbers spaced according to their *logarithms*, so if you "add" those lengths by moving a slider, the label matches the product of the numbers. And the log log scale sliders have the numbers spaced according to the logarithm of the logarithm, which means that "adding" these lengths with the sliders has the effect of raising one number to the power of the other number. I never actually owned a log log slide rule. They were expensive and, face it, they were for the guys who carried their slide rule in a leather holster on their belt, flapping against their leg. Eeek! And thus it's doubly impressive that Morris Manly has a log log slide rule as well as being captain of that football team.

Nostalgia for Sylvia

My thoughts flip back to the first woman in my life, to Sybil, and to our early days in a puttering little town near the Great Lakes, me working at a college. Sybil and I were young marrieds with three kids. The hardest time of our lives, and the best.

Bloody Brain Removal

[I liked this scene so much that I wrote several slightly different versions of it.]

Mumper draws a small axe from beneath the table. It's chrome, almost like a memento that might change hands between two rival teams. It's chrome. He's holding it like he might be about to kill me.

Carol screams and lunges at Mumper—just as he slams his axe into the top of my head, splitting my skull like a coconut. I don't actually see this part happening. A few minutes later, sqink Skeeze fills me in.

***

Via Skeeze, I see through the eye-holes of my Earthly body. Carol has her face in her hands, she's sobbing. Winston and Tobin are as zoned-out as before. Mumper is wiping the tabletop with a kerchief, cleaning up blood. His axe is out of sight. Moo still has her club lady look, but more distraught. Things aren't going as well as she expected.

"Don't like it," says Skeeze. A growing clatter of noise in the background. "Moo's having it out with Mumper. She's about to do something. The situation is, um, rapidly evolving."

Carol's beloved features rush in at a crazy angle. She's close to my body's face. In the corner booth at the Pacific-Union grill.

"Oliver," she says, like she knows I can hear. "Moo and I will save you. We'll kick Mumper's ass." She lurches back out of view. She's shouting. Other people are yelling too. Mumper's concealment fog isn't really working.

The visuals slew to one side. My Earth body has fallen. Moo is standing on the table in her club-lady outfit, screaming for help. Mumper has his chrome axe in play; he's taking swings at Moo, but she's too nimble for him. She keeps kicking him in the head. She grabs for the axe with a lengthening arm, but she can't quite get hold of it.

Carol crawls across the table. She takes a stance in the middle of the room. "Security," she screams. "We need the zap guns!

"Mumper murdered more!" blubbers Moo, having trouble getting her voice right. I doubt if anyone understands her. Meanwhile Mumper is chopping off squid arms as fast as Moo can glue them back.

"Don't listen to them," bellows Tobin. "They're all drunk!"

My Skeeze-controlled body is on the floor, trying to stand up. My view is all over the place. Skeeze manages to be looking the wrong way when the zap begins, but then he's on it.

The guards sizzle Mumper's ass but good, yes, they crisp him like he's a tortilla in a blast furnace, an ashen ghost of himself. The ashes are studded with goo crystals, and the guards keep on zapping till the goo too is busted dust.

I doubt that Mumper's gone for good. Surely she has a backup stored in a braincozy. But right now she's not in the Pacific-Union club, that's for sure. Her abandoned chrome axe spins on the table like a game token. The early-bird-special geezers hobble for the exits.

Stok-stok

"I'd prefer to equate Stok-stok with the set of all statements that can be deduced from the axiom inscribed on my jaw," says Pinchly, "The Stok-stok secret of life, one might say." He opens wide his mandibles. I see a wriggly symbols, like Maxwell's Equations or some such.

"Don's spook them with scientism jive," Randa tells Pinchly, making a gesture with her fine-boned hand. "Stok-stok isn't *one* place, it's a tangle of a places. Which happen to be at the end of time. I'll escort Oliver and Carol to it, sure I will. Can we all ride you, Moo?"

***

"In an epistemological sense?" inquires Winston. "Or would the distinction be, rather, phenomenological?"

"Yadda yadda," goes Randa. "Your mind merges all the time, but you ignore that. Thinking is dreaming, okay? And you see through the gaps The spaces between the thoughts." Randa makes a lattice of her fingers and peers through the holes.

***

And here's Mumper, sitting cross-legged atop the bulgy disk. She doesn't look like a human. She looks like a neon-tube sculpture based on the symbols we saw on Pinchly's mandibles—you might remember those from upstream on this raging tide of bullshit.

Yes, Mumper is a construct of neon tubes, glowing in tints of mint, saffron, and red onion—while flexing her frame, and emitting the high-voltage scent of ozone.

It's hard to tell if Mumper even sees us. She just sits there for a minute, like a messenger from the end of time. And then, whoopsie-daisy, she flies off.

Hovering Archival Stok-stok Denizens

"And look at those things buzzing around it," says Carol, leaning in. "Those are the archived minds of the original citizens of Stok-stok. They're already here. Unbelievable. I see our friends Dazz and Pinchly.

"And I thought they were bugs," I say, magnifying my view. "What do the Stok-stok critters actually look like? I'm seeing dinos, rhinos, winos, and frogs. Gawrsh, Carol, they're folks like you and me."

"More like flies on shit," says Carol, and giggles. This is a newly-acquired phrase that she likes to use. I'm happy to be a bad influence.

Rooby and Lilac

In the distance I see Carol's sqink Lilac in the arms of a striking woman with red lobster-style feelers mixed into her blonde hair. Rooby, part of the scene and Tobin's occasional lover. I don't know her well. I do know that Carol doesn't like her. If Rooby has taken possession of Lilac, I'd rather not be the one to tell Carol.

***

"Lilac hooked up with Rooby," I say.

"Now you tell me?" cries Carol. "I hate Rooby. With her business school scams. And those hairdo feelers she wears. So phony. And even worse, she's Tobin's girlfriend."

Epopt

And then came the Discontinuity. Which was when our heroes slit the High Epopt's throat. And yet the Epopt lives, as do we. (Epopt is a real word, it means an initiate in the highest grade of the Eleusinian mysteries.)

Herding

"But Moo told me that zaums can teleport things," I put in. "Why do you even need a tunnel, Mumper."

"Our zaum powers, although vast, are not infinite," says Mumper. "I can't teleport six thousand sqinks at once. But that's what I'd need to get Earth nailed down tight. Fully under my control. Fortunately we don't need a sqink for every single person. Don't need billions of them. Thanks to the Beeson-Pearce herding effect."

Surreal Space-Out

"It's complex," says the evasive Moo. "For now you'll have to trust me."

"Not that we have a choice," says Carol."

I space out on this scene, taking a few minutes to write up some of the wild shit we've been going through. And then, oh oh, we're back into the bizarre and outre effects of passing through a wormhole, the wormhole away from Stok-stok. Cue hallucinations and stupor.

Triple Stok-stok Bodies

"The idea is to lead Mumper astray," says Skeeze. "So we can catch her off-guard."

"Music to my ears," says a new sqink floating down from the sky with two others. "Might this be a meeting of the ranking members of Moo's cabal?" She sings a long, fluid trill, and the two others join in.

They look for all the world like our friends Randa, Pinchly, and Dazz—the brains-in-morphed-braincozies that we befriended in Tiny Town.

"That's us," says the tall Black one. "Smeared carbons. Copies of copies. Including the fun memories of our partner-brains' time with you. So make it easy for yourselves. Use the same names."

"Wow," say I. "Can you imitate me that well, Skeeze?"

"Yeah," he negligently says. "But that would make for too many characters. I'm a sqink, you're a human, and that's that. I don't want to go trans."

"We do," chorus the three Stok-stok-citizen-emulating sqinks Randa, Pinchly, and Dazz."

"I's sort of like *Taffeta*," says the Dazz sqink.

"Let it be so," says Randa.

"*Anyway*," I say.

Tensors

Turns out Moo wants Kanga to come along.

"No extra guests," I say. "And, later, how would I get rid of her?"

"That's a question for you and Carol," says Moo. "Our deep-space-cadets."

"We'd twist the gravitational tensors," says Carol. Hard to tell if that has any real meaning.

Can't Turn Off the Bulk beacon

"She's standing guard at the Eden wormhole, with her six thousand new sqinks on call," says Winston. "Yes, Zig and Zag melted the wormhole, but Mumper might tunnel back through any moment—guided by my indefatigable bulk beacon."

"It would be better if Mumper couldn't even find us," I put in.

"Exactly," goes Winston.

thub thub thub thub thub thub

"Didn't I just now turn it off bulk beacon ?" demands Carol.

"The bulk beacon is conscious. She uses a corrupt quantum wireless technique to project hallucinations. To ensure that all attempts to flip her switch must come a cropper."

"Stock response connoting fear and wonder," I say.

But Carol understands. "See it like this, Oliver. Your alarm clock rings. You go deeper into your dream. And in your dream, you reach out and turn the alarm clock off."

"And then you dream you're doing that," says Winston. "Still asleep. And then you dream you had that dream. Deepro and deeper. A pawn in the clock's hands. It wants to ring forever."

Mumper Showdown

"Why should *they* live when *I* had to die?"

It's ... *huh*? Mumper, touching down beside us. Once again she looks somewhat like a woman in a green coat, but a woman with dead eyes, and savage, carnivorous teeth.

"Eventually I'll find a way to kill you for good," says Moo, very poised and sure of herself. She flashes a signal to Zip and Zap. They're taking careful aim.

"Don't imagine you grubby shrimps can rub me out," growls Mumper. She flicks her hand. Zip and Zap are gone. Quite entirely gone.

***

"The initial zaps from the guards weren't enough to kill Mumper?" murmurs Carol.

"Sadly no," says Moo. "High-level sqinks like Mumper and I—you might say we've got a grip on time. We can run an explosion backwards. Dust and smoke flip into reverse and—*whirl whirl whirl*—we're back. From hee to haw. From void to voilà!"

Scraps of Life

For some reason Lilac is rummaging in her body, that is, feeling around for flaps and slits. She produces two twists like beef jerky and drools on them. Quite a bit of liquid,

All around the festival of the billion sqinks caroms on, with the creatures' voices raised in hoots, cheers and quarrels. The spray from the fireplug's pipe is magnificent, like a geyser of diamonds. And the sqinks of course adore it.

Lilac's meager scraps are swelling and flexing. What the fuck is Lilac's problem? Towser seems to know what's up. He horks snot onto Lilac's fragments. They grow some more, and now they speak, their voices floating above the a ambient din.

"Remember us?" the fragments sweetly sing, hovering in mid-air,

"It's Doink and Flubsy!" exclaims Carol.

"You got it!" says happy Doink. "A human can't ever kill a sqink. Not kill them all the way down. A quirk of the tripple, Didn't you know?"

"I didn't," I say, already bored. "The longer this novel gets, the less I know."

"I had this Doink's scrap all along, and Moo gave me some of Flubsy's remains as well," says Lilac.

"Will there be a quiz?" I ask. I'm in a mood that transcends mere hope or despair. It's a state of full-on WTF, not unlike the French *je-m'en-foutisme*.

Forking and Predation

"And those two sqinks that the Mu9ers huffed, you call them your children? Does that mean you budded them off?"

"Yes, I'm Towser 1, and they were Towser 1.1 and Towser 1.2. Towser 1.2 was a go-getter. He's already budded off two grandchildren for me. Towser 1.2.1 and Towser 1.2.2. Towser 1.2 wanted to wait a bit longer. Find a nice niche to nest in."

"And you're upset?"

Towser sighs. "Towser 1.2.1 has already budded a 1.2.1.1 and a 1.2.1.2. We're not letting those bastards get ahead of us."

"You mean Kanga and Gubb?"

"I'd like to kill Kanga and Gabb for smoking my 1.1 and 1.2. But killing a Mu9er isn't something a sqink can do."

"Why not?"

"We three species form a triple loop of predation. Hasn't anyone told you that, Oliver? I can't kill Mu9ers, but you can. Let me tell you the trick." Twofer glares at the two intoxicated Mu9ers at the bar. He turns to me. "You need to get those rotten—"

Tapdancing About Me-Ware

"I have no idea what we're doing here on Mu9," I say to Kanga. "Setting aside the question of whether we're about to die—why did Gubb say that being huffed is a kind of enlightenment?"

"Enlightenment is about *losing your mind*," says Kanga.

"Fly up a huff-tube and see how the next feller lives," says Gubb. "Then *whoof*, you're back home whar you started. But it's not a circle. It's a helix. And look at this—we're almost back to the Mu9 park. Don't panic and zoom off again, Yam."

Purple Prose Tweet From Giants Stadium

Lively as psychic sleet, or like spacetime gnats, the billion sqink me-wares dance in conga-lines, swirling like noodles in primordial pho, catch as catch can. And then the billion are one. Her name is Yam. Big Yam.

Mu9er Souls

Rather than answering my question in words, the two Mu9ers wheeze out a pair of glowing jellyfish—their me-wares. Bereft of their souls, the Mu9ers' bodies lie limp. Meanwhile the me-ware jellies devour each other, each of them swallowing bits of the other, round and round, in a diminishing yin-yang fight to the death until—*pouf*. Leaving a yes/no me-you jellyfish that pops into two big jellies-shaped me-wares again, and the ctenophoric souls return to the bodies they started from. Or maybe they swap bodies. Or maybe there's no difference. Deep teachings abound.

Heffalump Building Swallows Mu9ers.

The floor is somewhat rubbery and—oh, oh—when Kanga and Gubb step on it, they sink into it, like they're melting.

"Merging into me," says Heffalump. "One big sqink, one big Mu9r—and you two Earthlings. Can you two merge with each other? To make it tidier??"

"Not while you're watching," I gallantly say.

Yam Swallows Towser and Randa

But, sadly enough, Yam sees no need for additional reps for the sqinks. As soon as eager Towser and Randa land on Yam's skin, the peculiar potato absorbs our sqink friends into her flesh.

"Spit them back out," Carol yells to Yam.

"No extras," says Yam. "Sqinkland should speak with one voice. And the voice is me."

In the background, I hear the wavering voices of the absorbed Towser and Randa—like noise in a signal.

"We're still alive," quavers one of them.

"Yam says later we can come back," says the other.

"I don't trust Yam," says the first voice.

"You'll be fine," says Yam. "You two just talk from inside me. But Oliver doesn't want a huge cast of onstage characters that he has to manage in this novel. At least we're not killing you two off. Towser and Randa."

"You're stern," I tell Yam.

"Oh, boo hoo," says Yam. "How about this."

Her surface wrinkles and the embossed faces of Towser and Randa appear as intaglio patterns in the potato skin of the root.

Sqinks Novel Contents.

This is for reference, when I'm talking about chapter numbers in this *Journal*.

1. Oliver Meets Carol
2. Sqinks
3. Warhol
4. Sqink Luck
5. Topper and Lady Cee
6. Motel
7. Wormhole
8. Sqinkland
9. Paul and Irene
10. Chrome Axe
11. Tiny Town
12. Stok-stok
13. My Body
14. Bulk Beacon
15. Last Chapter?
16. Launch Party
17: The Sinking Titanic
18. Union Square
19. Big Yam
20. Triple Entente
21. Tweety Bird

October 1. 2025. Farewell!

The novel and the notes are done. My Kickstarter funding campaign worked. Now it's a matter of printing and shipping the books to the backers. And then I'll put the novel and the journal for sale online.

Although the hardback edition of *The Sqink Journal* will be listed online, no further copies will be printed.

The hardback edition of *The Sqinks Journal* is a collector's edition of twenty-five copies, for me and my top Kickstarter backers only.

A hearty thanks to all the backers! You'll find your names in the Afterword for the *Sqinks* novel, and on the book's home page:

https://ww.rudycker.com/sqinks

Long may we wave.

— The End —

www.ingramcontent.com/pod-product-compliance
Lightning Source LLC
Chambersburg PA
CBHW030824230426
43667CB00008B/1360